Regulating the Cloud: Poli

MW00478421

Information Policy Series

Edited by Sandra Braman

The Information Policy Series publishes research on and analysis of significant problems in the field of information policy, including decisions and practices that enable or constrain information, communication, and culture irrespective of the legal siloes in which they have traditionally been located as well as state-law-society interactions. Defining information policy as all laws, regulations, and decision-making principles that affect any form of information creation, processing, flows, and use, the series includes attention to the formal decisions, decision-making processes, and entities of government; the formal and informal decisions, decision-making processes, and entities of private and public sector agents capable of constitutive effects on the nature of society; and the cultural habits and predispositions of governmentality that support and sustain government and governance. The parametric functions of information policy at the boundaries of social, informational, and technological systems are of global importance because they provide the context for all communications, interactions, and social processes.

Virtual Economies: Design and Analysis, Vili Lehdonvirta and Edward Castronova

Traversing Digital Babel: Information, e-Government, and Exchange, Alon Peled

Chasing the Tape: Information Law and Policy in Capital Markets, Onnig H. Dombalagian

Regulating the Cloud: Policy for Computing Infrastructure, edited by Christopher S. Yoo and Jean-François Blanchette

Regulating the Cloud: Policy for Computing Infrastructure

Edited by Christopher S. Yoo and Jean-François Blanchette

The MIT Press
Cambridge, Massachusetts
London, England

MIT Press books may be purchased at special quantity discounts for business or sales promotional use. For information, please email special_sales@mitpress.mit.edu.

This book was set in Stone serif and Stone Sans by Toppan Best-set Premedia Limited. Printed and bound in the United States of America.

Library of Congress Cataloging-in-Publication Data

Regulating the cloud: policy for computing infrastructure / edited by Christopher S. Yoo and Jean-François Blanchette.
    pages cm. – (Information policy)
Includes bibliographical references and index.
ISBN 978-0-262-02940-7 (hardcover: alk. paper) –
ISBN 978-0-262-52783-5 (pbk.: alk. paper)
1. Telecommunication policy. 2. Cloud computing–Government policy. 3. Cloud computing–Social aspects. I. Yoo, Christopher S. II. Blanchette, Jean-François.
HE7645.R4184 2015
384.3'3–dc23
        2015001903

10 9 8 7 6 5 4 3 2 1

Contents

Acknowledgments

The initial inspiration for this project began in February 2011, at the conference on "Cloud Computing: Economic and Regulatory Implications," sponsored by the Center for Technology, Innovation, and Competition at the University of Pennsylvania Law School. Even as the conference highlighted the profound effect of the cloud on the computing and policy landscape, it also revealed the absence of a synthetic resource that would take adequate stock of the wide range of policy issues raised by cloud computing. Ideally, it seemed that such a resource would be accessible to scholars and educators alike, while demonstrating the rich interdisciplinary discussions between engineers and policy experts that are today the mainstay of many law and information technology journals and conferences.

As this volume was taking shape, the cloud did not stand still—it continued to integrate ever more tightly with the computing ecosystem and to shape, in both subtle and dramatic ways, a broad range of social practices. Indeed, whether through email, collaborative tools, or shared storage space, the cloud was integral to the development of this manuscript. Since the initial conference that inspired them, the chapters in this book have themselves developed to offer a "long" view of the cloud that can help grasp it as a sociotechnical phenomenon that is at once ancient history and strikingly new. While technical terminology, infrastructural configurations, and social behaviors will inevitably continue to evolve, these chapters will offer durable analytical tools for those interested in the particular ways the cloud weaves together technological practice and policy prescription.

We wish to acknowledge the National Science Foundation (award #CNS-10-40672) for supporting in part the original conference and some of the research in this volume. Our thanks go as well to Marguerite Avery, Katie Persons, and Katie Helke at MIT Press for their skillful help in bringing this project to fruition. Finally, we would like to thank Sandra Braman, Series Editor, for her enthusiasm, support, and contribution at all levels of this project.

Christopher S. Yoo
Jean-François Blanchette

Series Editor's Introduction
Sandra Braman

For one who reads the history of information policy since the revolutions of the late eighteenth century as constantly confronted by the need to reconsider just what is meant by fundamental principles and what we should do with them because of technological change, cloud computing fascinates. Where privacy used to involve drawing the shades and lowering voices, it now can mean specifying the conditions of the route through which digital packets will flow. Where free speech used to mean having the right to stand on a street corner, tell people what you thought, and hand out flyers so they could continue to consider arguments later and elsewhere, it now can mean having effective access to a global information infrastructure and, arguably, the right to store your arguments and the data supporting them anywhere in the world where they might be safe.

In one sense, all is familiar. In a manner that almost seems as if phylogeny recapitulates ontogeny, today's questions about cloud computing include those that have come up across the history of telecommunications and information policy, reasserting themselves all at once. The fact that innovations in communication technologies can provide challenges to nation-states has been evident at least since British control over the global telegraph network spurred network development by other countries, including, influentially, the United States during and following World War I. In the Internet, jurisdictional problems are notably rife, but cloud computing takes these challenges to another level, undermining types of sovereignty and authority that characterized modernity and provided the ground for the Westphalian international system of geopolitical states.

Just as it was said that the Internet incorporated all previous media, so cloud computing may be, as Jean-François Blanchette points out in his introduction, meta-infrastructure—increasingly a type of infrastructure (like electricity) upon which other forms of infrastructure (such as finance and, increasingly, transportation) depend. The complexity of the governance of cloud computing and the range of issues it raises make an edited volume particularly useful at this point in its history. One of the great strengths of this book is that those learning about particular types of policy problems for the first time, whether copyright or reliability, are in most chapters clearly walked through the necessary foundations, so feel free to wade in.

The multiplicity of definitional approaches is another strength. Far from being repetitive, the descriptions of cloud computing across the chapters present faces of the phenomenon that differ greatly from each other deriving from differences in how policy problems manifest themselves when perceived from diverse theoretical perspectives and/or in light of particular primary concerns. The core subject of cloud computing is commonly visible, but the question of when a trace of a software program on a user's drive matters gets quite different answers when provided by an economist, an intellectual property rights attorney, and someone with cybersecurity responsibilities. Similarly, just what takes place when something is stored looks different when viewed through environmental as opposed to archival eyes. That said, chapter 1, "Cloud Strategy and Economics," by Joe Weinman, stands out for also including examples of the cloud model as it works in other industries where it has been long familiar, referring to hotels, taxis, coffee shops, and banks.

A third notable feature of the volume is that in most case the authors bring to their analyses many decades of sophisticated and deeply informed attention to the issues under discussion as they have manifested themselves in round after round of the effort to adapt laws and regulations to the digital environment, a struggle that began in the United States in the 1950s. The combined depth of expertise, breadth of knowledge, and duration of sustained attention and vision in this volume are extremely rare, resulting in a collection that offers insights of particular value. It is for this reason, I believe, that authors such as William Lehr achieve such clarity regarding the transformations of the multiple industries involved in cloud computing over the long haul. And it is for this reason that we should all pay a lot of attention when authors such as Marjory Blumenthal are skeptical regarding the likelihood that a particular proposal could actually be achieved. The problem of achievability appears in almost every, if not every, chapter in the book, whether in discussion of a policy or of the processes that would be required for a particular type of policy to be put in place, let alone implemented.

One could read the combined insights of the authors in this volume as reporting that cloud computing may actually not be governable at all. At the request of former MIT Press Senior Acquisitions Editor Marguerite Avery and of co-editors Christopher Yoo and Jean-François Blanchette, the concluding chapter of this collection is mine. I will leave further discussion of the book's substance for there.

Introduction: Computing's Infrastructural Moment

Jean-François Blanchette

Jay: It went up! It went up to the Cloud!
Annie: And you can't get it down from the Cloud?!?
Jay: Nobody understands the Cloud! It's a fucking mystery!
—From the movie *Sex Tape*, 2014

The interesting thing about cloud computing is that we've redefined cloud computing to include everything that we already do. I can't think of anything that isn't cloud computing with all of these announcements. ... Maybe I'm an idiot, but I have no idea what anyone is talking about. What is it? It's complete gibberish. It's insane. When is this idiocy going to stop?
—Larry Ellison, 2008

Here, there, and everywhere.
— Apple iCloud slogan, 2014

From the perspective of policy analysis, cloud computing presents itself as an object with particularly problematic boundaries. Historically, it appears either radically new or merely a reenactment of a bygone computing era, that of mainframes; spatially, it is present in every mobile device, yet highly concentrated in out-of-sight bit processing plants; and at the design level, it seemingly encompasses, as Larry Ellison has noted, every dimension of modern computing architectures. Indeed, depending on one's mood and perspective, cloud computing can be variously characterized as

- The evolutionary end point of computing and the realization of its promise as *utility*, the freedom to access processing power and storage as instantaneously and flexibly as electricity, water, and gas (Armbrust et al. 2010).
- A new era in the *economics* of computing: together with the virtualization of processing and storage, the economies of scale afforded by data centers

allows providers to price computation at an unprecedented granular level, transforming fixed capital investments into operational expenses and lowering barriers to computing innovation (Weinman 2012).

• After the age of personal computing and its concomitant need to manage the proliferation and synchronization of individual devices, applications, and files, a return to the mainframe era and its model of *centralized control* of resources (Lanier 2010).

• The development of a new industrial form, the *data center*, devoted to the efficient transformation of electrical power into flows of bits: data centers further remove computation from the local experience of users, shifting its material constraints to massive bit factories strategically located in areas with access to cheap power and cool weather (Barroso and Hölzle 2009).

• The computing architecture appropriate to the era of *Big Data/Big Brother*: large-scale data centers make possible real-time statistical processing of the troves of data collected by governments, businesses, and scientists— data that will dramatically increase their capabilities for surveillance, targeted advertising, and research (Mosco 2014; Clarke et al. 2013).

• The computing architecture appropriate to the *Internet of Things*: a new paradigm for designing and assembling distributed systems that fully integrates processing, networking and storage resources, free of the historical divisions of computing and telecommunications (Roscoe 2006)

• The elevation of *access to broadband* as a key economic issue for governments all over the world, as well as the defining material line between the digital haves and have-nots (FCC 2010).

• Another illustration of the power of *modular design*, whereas the enormous processing and storage capacity of data centers is based on the interfacing of thousands and thousands of small-bore individual servers and disk drives, themselves often housed in modular architectural structures—for example, shipping containers (Barroso and Hölzle 2009).

As the chapters in this volume will attest to, cloud computing is all of these things at once and more. Indeed, rather than engaging in the thankless task of unifying the above into a comprehensive functional definition, I propose instead that "the Cloud" is shorthand for the moment where computing has become, both materiality and symbolically, *infrastructure*; that is, a sociotechnical system that has become ubiquitous, essential, and foundational (Edwards 2002, 187).[1] As infrastructure, then, the Cloud necessarily becomes the focus of a series of policy concerns that deal with issues of market regulation, fairness, universal access, reliability, criticality, national security, sharing of limited resources, congestion, inter-network competition, national economic welfare, capacity planning, monopoly, and antitrust, among others.

These issues and debates are familiar: they have, in one form or another, featured in every type of energy, transportation, and communication network deployed in the past.[2] Indeed, like the networks that preceded it, the Cloud develops, operates, and breaks down following specific infra-structural dynamics.[3] It has, for example, developed incrementally, from the progressive laying down of its infrastructural components, including data centers, fiber cables, economic models, and regulatory frameworks. Such incremental development means that early-stage design choices *persist*, often with unforeseen consequences, and become increasingly difficult to correct as the infrastructure becomes ubiquitous, its functionality expands, and the nature of the traffic it serves evolves—for instance, the Suezmax standard for shipping, the maximum number of addresses allowed by the IPv4 Internet Protocol and the best-effort service it provides in the context of the dramatic expansion of streaming video traffic. In addition, like other infrastructures, the Cloud strives toward invisibility. Indeed, as the unlucky protagonists of *Sex Tape* bemoan, by staging the very disappearance of computing resources and whisking them away to far-off data centers, the Cloud introduces yet another level of opacity to information technologies.

Yet the Cloud is also distinctive on several fronts. If energy, transportation, and information infrastructures tend to be tightly intertwined, the Cloud's capacity for real-time measurement and statistical analysis of supply and demand makes it increasingly integral to the functioning of a large number of other infrastructures, including energy (smart grids), financial services, airports, the upcoming driverless cars, and even … the Cloud itself.[4] It has become, in effect, a certain kind of *meta-infrastructure*, while of course remaining entirely dependent on the electrical grid. And while all infrastructures are incremental in nature, developing by the gradual layering and interconnection of similar components, the computing infrastructure has elevated this to a quasi-religious principle, with scholars such as Lessig (2001), Zittrain (2008), and Wu (2010) arguing that the innovative character of the Internet is a direct outcome of its modular design structure and the kind of markets this structure supports.

Perhaps most distinctively, the Cloud is expected to sustain extraordinary growth rates. Internet traffic increased eightfold between 2006 and 2011 and is expected to continue growing at an annual rate of 30 percent, with mobile traffic now accounting for 45 percent of all IP traffic.[5] The amounts of data globally generated by scientific instruments, sensors, systems, humans, digitization of legacy documents, and other sources have likewise exploded.[6] There is no reason to expect such rates of growth will taper off anytime soon: ultra-high-definition television (UHDTV) sets will soon match the resolution level of IMAX, while old and new classes of Cloud-based applications (e.g., massively multiplayer online role-playing games [MMORPGs], file backup services, and video surveillance) will make new and unprecedented demands on processing, storage, and network resources. Indeed, there are few practical limits to the quantity of digital information that can be created—only economic and material limits to how much can be stored, processed, and circulated.

Ironically, these extraordinary rates of growth mean that, just as it strives for invisibility, the computing infrastructure is constantly in our face. From legal battles around net neutrality, to slow-streaming videos, to the constant shuffle of new pricing for data plans, the computing infrastructure refuses to settle down as infrastructure, reminding us that, even as we are becoming inexorably dependent on it, we have yet to work out the conditions under which to accommodate such growth.

The chapters in this volume lay the groundwork for analyzing the Cloud as a familiar infrastructure whose distinctive characteristics require fresh approaches to long-standing policy debates. To distinguish the new from the old, such an analysis must begin by situating the Cloud in historical terms. This is complicated, however, by a persistent mythology that presents computing as a field that, as Matthew Fuller (2008, 7) puts it, needs no history, as it relentlessly moves forward, "permanently in a state of improvement." Yet the Cloud is the outcome of distinct evolutionary processes that hark back to the early beginning of computing, a history that is essential to understanding current policy debates. I begin by providing some of that historical background, so as to set the stage for the following chapters, each of which will address specific policy issues.

The Historical Genesis of the Cloud

The evolution of computing technology is typically portrayed in terms of its extraordinary rates of growth in performance: year after year, processors perform more instructions at ever-increasing speeds, storage devices are able to pack more bits into ever-smaller amounts of space, and network wires transmit more data at ever-faster rates. Indeed, much of our understanding of the extraordinary spread of computing in the past 60 years is based on the idea that the fundamental computing resources of processing power, storage, and bandwidth have and will continue to become simultaneously more powerful and cheaper.[7]

This particular frame of analysis, however, captures only a limited subset of the forces that have driven the evolution of networked computing. Less visible but equally essential dimensions include, on the one hand, the design technique of *modularity*, used to manage the high rate of technological change that characterizes computing technologies; and on the other hand, the *sharing* and *distribution* of limited computing resources. Much of these dynamics take place somewhat out of sight, at the level of the *computing infrastructure* rather than at the level of applications, the more plainly visible space where users extract personal value from computing technologies. Yet, it is only by taking together these three shaping forces—performance increases, modular design, and sharing—that the evolutionary dynamics of the computing ecosystem, including its current manifestation as the Cloud, can be analyzed.[8]

The Computing Infrastructure

In computing, infrastructure can be quite simply defined as the elements of the computing ecosystem that provide *services to applications* (e.g., performing arithmetic functions, storing and retrieving bits, sending packets over networks), in contrast to the applications that provide *services to users* (e.g., processing words, posting a status update). The computing infrastructure is composed of both software and hardware: for example, system abstractions such as file systems and packets, storage media such as flash and hard drives, and communication protocols such as Transmission Control Protocol/Internet Protocol (TCP/IP) and the Hypertext Transfer Protocol (HTTP). It provides the various components from which designers can build computing systems as diverse as the Google search engine, Microsoft Word running on a desktop, and Tivo software running on your TV set. It is what allows computers to be *multipurpose* while simultaneously *managing the high rate of technical change* of computing resources. These two characteristics of computing systems seem largely obvious today, but they required considerable design innovation in their own time.

The first electromechanical computing machines could perform only a limited range of computational tasks. Herman Hollerith's first tabulator, for example, developed for the 1889 US census, was specifically tailored to add up census schedules. Early digital computers, such as the ENIAC, could be reconfigured to perform different types of computation only through a time-consuming rewiring of the various hardware components. The concept of the *stored program*, as formulated by John von Neumann and colleagues, provided one elegant solution to the issue: the activation of the different components of computers in the service of a computational task could be directed by a sequence of instructions called a *program*. A single computer could perform distinct computational tasks merely by executing a different program, and while designing such programs proved to be no simple task, once written, a program could be switched for another one in a matter of seconds.

Modularity

This newfound versatility came with some important trade-offs, however. Even as von Neumann and his co-inventors gave birth to the software/hardware division, the two remained fused: in the early days of computing, there is hardly any distance between programs and hardware. The manual of operations for the first commercially produced stored-program computer, the IBM 701, included such specific timing considerations as "to keep the card reader in continuous motion, it is necessary to give the READ instruction between 20 and 70 milliseconds after the 12-right COPY instruction" (International Business Machines Corporation 1953, 49). That is, programmers had to take into account specific characteristics of the hardware—in this case, the number of operations that the processor would execute before the next card would be available for reading data or instructions from the punched card reader (the dominant input/output technology in the early 1950s). This became rapidly problematic, insofar as each succeeding generation of computers offered new, faster hardware, and programs had to be rewritten from scratch to take advantage of their new characteristics, at great expense of time and money.

By the 1960s, the situation had become a sore spot for the industry as a whole, prompting market leader IBM to seek a remedy. The solution consisted in designing a family of processor lines (initially six), each compatible with one another (including peripherals); that is, any program written for one line would be able to execute on any other of the family, with, of course, different levels of performance. To achieve such compatibility, IBM relied on the design strategy of *modularity*, where each component of the system was conceived as a discrete black box with a standardized *interface* (Baldwin and Clark 2000). In the resulting System/360, for example, all processors responded to the same set of instructions, even though their internal architectures might differ widely. For the first time, programmers could design programs with the confidence that, as long as components retained the same interface, programs would continue to run in spite of technical advances.

Compatibility proved much more than just an engineering feature, however, as it profoundly altered the economics of the computing ecosystem: components with standardized interfaces could just as well be produced by competitors, and many IBM engineers did leave the company to launch their own lines of cheaper compatible processors and peripherals. Modular computing systems rapidly ushered in an era of vertical disintegration of the industry and a new form of market organization. Indeed, innovation scholars such as Lessig (2001), Zittrain (2008), and Wu (2010) have since argued that the extraordinary success of the Internet is a direct outcome of its modular architecture, which effectively lowers barriers to entry for prospective market participants and fosters experimentation at the component level.

Sharing and Virtualization

Another parallel historical development involved the development of *operating systems* and *virtualization*. In the early days of computing, computing speed was hampered by two main bottlenecks: on the one hand, programs were loaded and executed sequentially in a slow and cumbersome process called *batch processing*: at any one time, only one user could access the machine's expensive resources, such as its processor or storage media. On the other hand, increases in processing speed were limited by the extremely slow speed of storage technologies: program execution was often stalled as the processor waited for data to be loaded or written to storage.

A decisive breakthrough came with the invention of *time-sharing*. Instead of executing sequentially, multiple programs were loaded simultaneously and executed under the authority of a new program, the *supervisor*. In a similar fashion to time-sharing in real estate, the supervisor amortizes an important capital expense (the processor) by distributing it among multiple noncompeting users. By allocating to each program a slice of processing time and by circling rapidly in round-robin fashion among them, each user was given the illusion of having full control of the computer's resources, while in actuality having that control for only a small fraction of the time. Because the supervisor could use the time previously spent waiting for storage devices to service other users, individual performance did not suffer overall.

In today's terms, time-sharing *virtualized* the processor: it created an *abstraction* of a computing resource—a whole processor, when only a portion was available—so that it could be more efficiently shared among multiple users. User programs no longer directly interacted with the processor, but with the abstraction provided by the supervisor, which sliced and diced the actual processor among as many users as could be supported.

Just like modularity, time-sharing profoundly changed the economics of computing: by allowing more users to share the most expensive component of a computer (its processor), institutions were able to extract more usage out of their more expensive capital investments. Through the design of appropriate abstractions, enormous gains in computing efficiency could be obtained by the efficient *sharing* of costly and limited computing resources. At the same time, the supervisor ushered in the era of *operating systems*: software that would serve as a *mediating layer* to manage applications' access to computing resources, whether processor, storage, or network.

Distributing Computing

Another strand of the history of computing design can be understood as addressing the problem of the *distribution of computing resources in space*. That is, where should computing resources (i.e., processing, storage, and data) be located in relationship to each other and to users? The criteria for choice includes not only computational efficiency, but also crucial issues of control, cost, maintenance, reliability, security, and access, among others. During the relatively short history of computing, different architectures have successively dominated the landscape.

Early digital computers took the shape of *mainframes*: single-user machines where all computing resources were centrally located, controlled, and maintained, often in the same room. Users accessed the mainframe through computer operators who controlled available software and data, both of which had to be loaded on input/output devices located in the same physical space.

The advent of *time-sharing* dramatically transformed this setup: the virtualized processor of the mainframe was partitioned among multiple users, who could access it through terminals (connected either through local wires or phone lines). The mainframe functioned as a *server* to these multiple *clients*, providing access to software and data, stored either locally or remotely. At this stage, the data traveling over the wires was textual: commands typed by users and the results of their queries, typically textual and numeric information contained in databanks or the output of programs. While access was expanded, control remained local to the machine. Security was a new problem, as multiple users shared access to processors, storage, data, and programs.

Personal computing yet again expanded the reach of computing by providing users with unprecedented control over their own processors, storage devices, software, and data. At the same time, it introduced a host of challenges in the workplace: in contrast to a centralized mainframe, every employee's computer needed to be set up, maintained, upgraded, repaired, and provided with individual copies of software. Also, processing and storage capacity were potentially wasted, as individual machines sat idle at night. Personal computers also integrated with mainframes, insofar as they could be used as terminals to connect to institutional mainframes to access software or commercial services (e.g., databanks).

By allowing personal computers to connect to one another, the Internet yet again broadened the scope of architectural possibilities for the distribution of computing resources. By and large, the dominating relationship has been one of client/server: users' devices download content (e.g., query results or streaming data) from the Cloud to local clients (primarily web browsers), with Netflix as the current paradigmatic example. This is, however, only one of many possible configurations for distributed computing: peer-to-peer computing, in its many flavors, provides a vibrant example of an entirely different model for pooling together distributed resources, one whose applications go well beyond mere illegal file sharing; and grid computing, as exemplified by the SETI@Home project, leverages the idle cycles of thousands of machines to solve computationally intensive problems, such protein folding or climate modeling.

Today's age of *mobile computing* has emerged in symbiotic relationship with the Cloud. Given their limited storage, processing, and energy resources, portable devices such as smartphones, tablets, and netbooks rely on cloud services to provide the required software capabilities for the mobile services users have come to rely on, such as maps and voice recognition. This movement of processing cycles and storage away from users' machines towards data centers depends entirely, however, on the availability of *broadband*. The more data-intensive the service, the more bandwidth required. For many classes of applications (e.g., video editing), bandwidth requirements and availability continue to make cloud-based processing an unattractive option.[9] Indeed, data-intensive services such as Second Life and Google Earth must be accessed through client software (or web plug-ins) that can render three-dimensional virtual environments with the help of a device's local processor. Furthermore, in the cloud model, reliability is entirely a function of service providers, which themselves depend on network service providers—we might say, "live by the Cloud, die by the network."

Moreover, the centralization implied by data centers is already being mitigated by content distribution networks (CDNs) such as Akamai, designed to move resources (processing, storage, and data) closer to the edge of the networks, that is, users' machines. Large content providers like Netflix are developing their own private CDNs (e.g., Open Connect) to bypass the costs and network congestion that results from moving large amounts of data across the Internet. And of course, data centers are themselves being strategically located to minimize not only data movement, but also energy costs. Even in a cloud-based world, then, multiple models remain for the distribution of computing resources, whether by reason of computing efficiency or political conviction, and spatial distribution of these resources continues to matter.

Cloud Shapes

The Cloud thus emerges at the historical confluence of several long-standing technical traditions within computing: *modularity*, which has allowed cloud providers to create unprecedented amounts of computing power by merely pooling together massive numbers of low-cost, off-the-shelf components; *virtualization*, which makes it possible to distribute, meter, and charge for these computing resources in highly granular and flexible ways while allowing continuity with legacy software designs; and *distributed architectures*, which allow for the partitioning of computing resources between mobile devices and data centers.

Within these broad characteristics, several categories of cloud models have emerged, not only in terms of the types of services offered to customers, but also deployment models (e.g., on site or outsourced), as well as different levels of risk, operational characteristics (e.g., performance and reliability), terms of service, and economic considerations. Of primary importance is the *control* that consumers and providers exert over different types of cloud computing resources—application software, operating system, hardware, etc.[10]

The first category deals with that manifestation of the Cloud familiar to most Internet users through the services provided by, for example, Google (i.e., Gmail, Google Docs, Google Maps, and Google Drive). In such an arrangement, usually referred to as *Software as a Service (SaaS)*, users interact with the Cloud in the guise of a software application accessed through a client on the user's computing device (most often a web browser). Other than user preferences, consumers have no control over the software and the underlying computing resources that power it—for example, they must adapt to whatever changes (e.g., new or discontinued features) the software provider chooses to implement.[11]

The second category, typified by providers such as Amazon's Elastic Compute Cloud (EC2) or Rackspace, is primarily directed at system administrators who manage institutional computing resources. In this *Infrastructure as a Service (IaaS)* model, service providers provide access to computing resources in the guise of virtual images of traditional desktops machines or servers. Virtual machines are available in a broad range of capacity and pricing models—from pay-as-you-go micromachines to multi-year commitments on massively parallel systems, and even spot markets for bidding on cheap excess capacity. By allowing customers to reuse their installed software base, such a system allows them to enjoy the economic benefits of the Cloud with minimal disruption.

Beyond these two types of service access (software and virtual machines) lies an expansive *terra incognita*, currently referred to as *Platform as a Service (PaaS)*. Directed at software developers and exemplified by the Google App Engine and Amazon's AWS Elastic Beanstalk, this model offers direct access to the vast computing resources of the Cloud, so long as customers are willing to rewrite their software to take advantage of this new mode of provisioning software, processors, storage, and network resources. In effect, then, PaaS refers to the reinvention, in the context of the Cloud, of the software abstractions (e.g., files and process) that currently live within traditional desktop operating systems. New abstractions [e.g., the Google File System (Ghemawat, Gobioof, and Leung 2003) and MapReduce (Dean and Ghemawat 2008)] have already been developed by cloud providers for their own internal use and are being offered to the larger software community. There is much computational efficiency to be gained in using abstractions directly tailored to the computing resources of the Cloud (e.g., scalability), but, as in the desktop world, lack of standardization between competing platforms will pose significant hurdles for software developers.

In addition to these service delivery models, cloud resources can be deployed in distinct modes: *privately*, for consumption within institutions themselves; *publicly*, as a service to consumers; or as a pool of *community-owned* resources. In each case, resources can be deployed *on site, outsourced*, or various *hybrid* models, such as so-called *cloud-bursting*, where an institution manages its day-to-day workload internally but delegates peak demand to outside providers.

Tackling the Mystery

The Cloud, then, embodies a specific moment in the evolution of computing: the moment where, symbolically and materially, it becomes infrastructure and where a broad range of policy concerns become visible and open to debate. This moment is not static: there exists a wide range of current and possible future incarnations of the Cloud, with different implications for costs, control, reliability, interoperability, and of course, traditional public policy goals of equitable access, economic competitiveness, efficiency, etc. Indeed, focusing on the Cloud as infrastructure allows us to move beyond long-cherished mythologies of computing technologies as immaterial, infinitely expansive, and fundamentally democratic.[12] From such an infrastructural perspective, themes more useful for analytical work emerge.

First, the Cloud, like other transportation, energy, and communication infrastructures, is fundamentally driven by the economics of *capacity* and *demand*. As Joe Weinman makes clear in chapter 1 of this volume, "Cloud Strategy and Economics," the Cloud is first and foremost about a simple move: pay-per-use, the shift from ownership to rental of computing resources and their consumption at a much finer level of granularity than previously possible. Providers enjoy the economies and efficiencies that result from resource pooling and capacity planning, while consumers enjoy the ability to scale computing resources up and down as their needs require. Yet, as Weinman points out, for organizations to effectively capture value from the Cloud will require more than simply dumping their servers at the curb. Many additional factors will demand attention, including the specific shape of the demand, the spatial distribution of data centers and its impact on response time, and even, perhaps less intuitively, psychological factors, such as "flat-rate bias," that actively shape consumers' perception of the pros and cons of switching to the Cloud. While such concepts have long been deployed in the analysis of other infrastructures, they are only beginning to be used in the context of computing.[13]

Questions of capacity and demand immediately raise the complementary issues of *criticality* and *reliability*. In chapter 2, "Finding Security in the Cloud," Marjory S. Blumenthal explores the consequences of our far-reaching dependence on the Cloud and its de facto status as critical infrastructure, while in chapter 3, "Reliability and the Internet Cloud," William Lehr explores the conditions under which the Cloud might provide assurances of its reliability. These are particularly thorny issues: in contrast to the telecommunications industry, the computing industry and the Internet have developed largely outside regulatory purview. Furthermore, as the somewhat unified, vertically integrated market structure of the past has given way to the highly heterogeneous, vertically disintegrated structure of today, the technical and economic structure of the

Cloud has grown correspondingly complex. How can policy makers influence the behavior of a system whose properties depend on the interaction of millions of parts interconnected through modular interfaces? And how can regulation promote the public's interest in a reliable and secure infrastructure while simultaneously preserving the high rate of innovation that has characterized the computing industry to date?

The issue of how to best coordinate the evolution of a largely decentralized, modular infrastructure is also raised by Christopher S. Yoo in chapter 4, "Cloud Computing, Contractibility, and Network Architecture." As more types of computing resources are accessed through networks, new kinds of traffic (e.g., telesurgery) are requiring service guarantees that go beyond the best-effort principle that continues to characterize current terms from service providers—users might need, for example, to ascertain the identity and reliability of the specific paths through which their data circulates. Yet, as Yoo reports, the current layered decomposition of the Internet stack has proved extraordinarily difficult to adapt to its new circumstances. Yoo proposes that the imbrication, within a new layer, of legal primitives drawn from contract theory might provide the means to enforce service guarantees on Internet traffic. While we are only beginning to understand and address the challenges of gracefully evolving modular systems, Yoo's proposal demonstrates how multidisciplinary approaches that bridge the policy/engineering divide can be usefully brought to bear on such issues.

Yet another major concern is that of *privacy* and *liability*. The revelations by Edward Snowden in 2013 about the data collection practices of the US National Security Agency (NSA) have, among many other things, highlighted how the centralized nature of the Cloud has proved particularly convenient to the surveillance efforts of the US government. In chapter 5, "Cloud Privacy in the United States and the European Union," Andrea Renda observes the widely divergent legal and regulatory environment for privacy that obtains in the United States and the European Union in the post-Snowden era. In the first case, a somewhat haphazard patchwork of federal, state, and case law has largely focused on the risks of governmental intrusion; in the second case, the more conceptually coherent and centralized framework of a European directive has focused on the risks of private sector intrusion. In both cases, taxonomies of service providers used to allocate liability map only with difficulty on the rapidly evolving Cloud ecosystem.

Indeed, in chapter 6, "Understanding Regulatory and Consumer Interest in the Cloud," Jonathan Cave, Neil Robinson, Svitlana Kobzar, and

Helen Rebecca Schindler outline a broad range of consumer concerns that arise as part of the restructuring of various markets through the Cloud (e.g., code and data mobility, data breach, and content piracy). The take-it-or-leave-it approach of many providers' service-level agreements (SLAs), as well as the embedded and automated functionality of many Cloud services (Apple's iCloud being a prime example), conspire to produce an environment in which consumers experience many new and unfamiliar risks, often with minimal or confusing control over the parameters of their participation. The situation is likely to get much worse: the marriage of Big Data, Cloud services, and the interoperability made possible by the proliferation of application programming interfaces (APIs) promises to spawn an extraordinarily complex set of commercial relationships among data subjects, service providers, and data processors—making the task of regulators all the more challenging.

Another major theme can be articulated as that of *delocalization*: the Cloud is fundamentally about the movement of computing resources (whether processing, storage, software, or data) away from the desktop and towards geographically dispersed data centers. While this movement can be analyzed purely in terms of technical efficiency, it also has immediate implications in terms of *control*. Yet, as Luciana Duranti argues in chapter 7, "Digital Records and Archives in the Commercial Cloud," the trustworthiness of records has historically been grounded in the nature of the archive as a *physical place*. Given that public cloud providers typically offer no guarantees as to where specific data may reside, archivists must define new concepts, conditions, and terms of service that can continue to ensure proper chain of custody and the corresponding evidential value of electronic records.

To software manufacturers, on the other hand, the shift in control brought about by delocalization offers an extraordinary opportunity to resolve the long-standing problem of software distribution. Not only is the need to provide consumers with a physical copy of their software obviated by the Cloud, but the contractual relationship shifts from one of ceding ownership to one of providing a service. As Lothar Determann and David Nimmer eloquently demonstrate in chapter 8, "Software Copyright in the Cloud," legal scholars and practitioners have already struggled for years to reconcile fundamental concepts of copyright law with the specific material embodiment of software (including the inherent need for computers to make multiple working copies of the original software) and the thorny problem of distinguishing functionality from creative expression. The shift to the Cloud, however, might signify a turning point, and Determann and

Nimmer argue that its consequences might reach far beyond software to all downloadable content, including film, music, and literary works. Their chapter powerfully demonstrates how the computing infrastructure persists, not only in terms of physical wires and software abstractions, but also in terms of legal concepts carried over, for better or for worse, from otherwise forgotten episodes of technical history.

Finally, delocalization induces shifts not only in terms of control, but also in terms of *agency*. As Nicholas Bauch argues in chapter 9, "Bodies in the Cloud: A Geography of Electronic Health Data," laws and policies are increasingly recognizing that our cloud-based virtual representations operate in the world as functional extensions of ourselves, expanding our geographic presence beyond the confines of our mere biological bodies. Bauch coins the term *body-data* to recognize that electronic data, stored remotely in data centers and moving through digital networks, "contributes to the objecthood of something else (in this case, a human body) in a different location." The Cloud is Us, literally, and its geography, energy consumption, and waste are but an extension of our own.

On a historical scale, the gradual shift of computing from stand-alone tool to behind-the-scenes infrastructure has barely begun. It will take considerable time to achieve a level of ubiquity, integration, and invisibility on par with that of, say, the transportation infrastructure. As such, the chapters in this book are intended as starting points, to take stock of the situation and explore concepts and approaches that might prove useful in tackling this important transformation of computing. Obviously, many additional dimensions of cloud computing will benefit from further discussion and exploration. These include (to name just a few) standardization, as the inherently modular character of the Cloud puts increasing pressure on standardization as a market strategy and the governance of standardization bodies; power consumption, which, in the span of a few short years, has become the dominant design objective across all layers of computing, with implications for the public interest in green computing; and liability, as institutions as diverse as the financial sector, health care, and law enforcement come to depend on the Cloud for their day-to-day operations. As the Cloud becomes imbricated in the fabric of an ever-broadening array of individual and societal pursuits, the range of policy issues that it raises will continue to expand, with a corresponding need to continue and deepen the kind of interdisciplinary dialogue exemplified in the following chapters.

Notes

1. I capitalize the term *Cloud* to underline its symbolic quality, even as this symbol encompasses diverse and heterogeneous technical realities.

2. See Longstaff (2000) for a very useful meta-analysis of networked industries and their common characteristics from a regulatory standpoint, including bottlenecks, access, small versus large loads, and short versus long hauls.

3. On the concept of infrastructural dynamics, see Jackson et al. (2007), Bowker et al. (2010), and Sandvig (2013).

4. This should not come as a surprise since the signature technology of the Internet, packet switching, predominated over circuit switching precisely through the application of automated statistical analysis to its own traffic.

5. Cisco (2013) predicts that the sum of all forms of video (i.e., TV, video on demand, Internet, and peer-to-peer file sharing) will constitute approximately 86 percent of global consumer traffic by 2016.

6. See, for example, Bell, Hey, and Szalay (2009).

7. To cite one example: "The unprecedented evolution of computers since 1980 exhibits an essentially exponential speedup that spans 4 orders of magnitude in performance for the same (or lower) price. No other engineered system in human history has ever achieved that rate of improvement; ... Whole fields of human endeavors have been transformed as computer system capability has ascended through various threshold performance values." (Millett and Fuller 2011, 25).

8. I have argued (Blanchette 2011, 2012) that a focus on infrastructural forces and the material foundation of computing resources provides an appropriate pedagogical framework for teaching the historical evolution of computing over the current emphasis on mathematical abstraction.

9. Ironically, in many cases, the transfer of data sets to the Cloud can be cost-prohibitive, leading Ambrust et al. (2009, 16) to recommend the "FedEx disk option" that is, shipping them using a more traditional infrastructure.

10. An excellent overview of these considerations is provided by Badger, Grance, Patt-Corner, and Voas (2012), which builds on the work of Mell and Grance (2011).

11. The increasingly blurry boundaries between personal devices and the cloud should also be noted. While this has been the case for some time with respect to content (such as music, photos, and streaming content), it is also increasingly the case with respect to software itself. Both Google and Apple provide for automatic updating of software so that applications, operating systems, and cloud services are optimally synchronized with one another. In addition, Amazon's Silk Browser, first deployed with its Kindle Fire, distributes its processing needs between the Kindle's processor and Amazon's cloud infrastructure (Thomas, Jurdak, and Atkinson 2012).

12. See, for example, the classic statements by Barlow (1996) and Negroponte (1996), and more recently, Abelson, Ledeen, and Lewis (2008) and Gleick (2011) on the digital as the evolutionary end point of information.

13. See, for example, Barroso and Hölzle (2009) on the engineering side, and on the policy side, chapter 13 of Frischmann (2012) for its application of these concepts to network neutrality.

References

Abelson, Hal, Ken Ledeen, and Harry Lewis. 2008. *Blown to Bits: Your Life, Liberty, and Happiness after the Digital Explosion.* Boston: Addison-Wesley Professional.

Armbrust, Michael, Armando Fox, Rean Griffith, Anthony D. Joseph, Randy Katz, Andy Konwinski, Gunho Lee, 2009. Above the Clouds: A Berkeley View of Cloud Computing. Electrical Engineering and Computer Sciences, University of California at Berkeley, Technical Report No. UCB/EECS-2009-28. Available at http://www.eecs.berkeley.edu/Pubs/TechRpts/2009/EECS-2009-28.html.

Armbrust, Michael, Armando Fox, Rean Griffith, Anthony D. Joseph, Randy Katz, Andy Konwinski, Gunho Lee, (April 2010). A View of Cloud Computing. *Communications of the ACM* 53 (4): 50–58.

Badger, Lee, Tim Grance, Robert Patt-Corner, and Jeff Voas. 2012. Cloud Computing Synopsis and Recommendations. National Institute of Standards and Technology Special Publication 800–146. Available at http://www.nist.gov/customcf/get_pdf.cfm?pub_id=911075.

Baldwin, Carliss Young, and Kim B. Clark. 2000. *Design Rules: The Power of Modularity.* Vol. 1. Cambridge, MA: MIT Press.

Barlow, John Perry. 1996. A Declaration of Independence of Cyberspace. Available at https://projects.eff.org/~barlow/Declaration-Final.html.

Barroso, Luiz André, and Urs Hölzle. 2009. *The Datacenter as a Computer: An Introduction to the Design of Warehouse-Scale Machines.* San Rafael, CA: Morgan and Claypool Publishers.

Bell, Gordon, Tony Hey, and Alex Szalay. 2009. Beyond the Data Deluge. *Science* 323 (5919): 1297–1298.

Blanchette, Jean-François. 2011. A Material History of Bits. *Journal of the American Society for Information Science and Technology* 62 (6): 1042–1057.

Blanchette, Jean-François. 2012. Computing as if Infrastructure Mattered. *Communications of the ACM* 55 (October): 32–34.

Bowker, Geoffrey, Karen Baker, Florence Millerand, and David Ribes. 2010. Towards Information Infrastructure Studies: Ways of Knowing in a Networked Environment. In *International Handbook of Internet Research*, ed. Jeremy Hunsinger, Lisbeth Klastrup, and Matthew Allen, 97–117. Berlin: Springer.

Cisco. 2013. Cisco Visual Networking Index: Global Mobile Data Traffic Forecast Update, 2012–2017. Available at http://newsroom.cisco.com/documents/10157/ 1142732/Cisco_VNI_Mobile_Data_Traffic_Forecast_2012_2017_white_paper.pdf.

Clarke, Richard A., Michael J. Morell, Geoffrey R. Stone, Cass R. Sunstein, and Peter Swire. 2013. Liberty and Security in a Changing World. Report and Recommendations of the President's Review Group on Intelligence and Communications Technology. Available at http://www.whitehouse.gov/sites/default/files/docs/2013 -12-12_rg_final_report.pdf.

Dean, Jeffrey, and Sanjay Ghemawat. 2008. MapReduce: Simplified Data Processing on Large Clusters. *Communications of the ACM* 51 (1): 107–113.

Edwards, Paul N. 2002. Infrastructure and Modernity: Force, Time, and Social Organization in the History of Sociotechnical Systems. In *Modernity and Technology*, ed. Thomas J. Misa, Phillip Brey, and Andrew Feenberg, 185–225. Cambridge, MA: MIT Press.

Federal Communications Commission (FCC). 2010. The National Broadband Plan. Washington, DC. Available at http://transition.fcc.gov/national-broadband-plan/ national-broadband-plan.pdf.

Frischmann, Brett. 2012. *Infrastructure: The Social Value of Shared Resources*. Oxford, UK: Oxford University Press.

Fuller, Matthew. 2008. *Software Studies: A Lexicon*. Cambridge, MA: MIT Press.

Ghemawat, Sanjay, Howard Gobioff, and Shun-Tak Leung. 2003. The Google File System. *Operating Systems Review* 37 (5): 29–43.

Gleick, James. 2011. *The Information: A History, A Theory, A Flood*. New York: Pantheon.

International Business Machines Corporation. 1953. Principles of Operation: Type 701 and Associated Equipment. New York. Available at http://bitsavers.trailing-edge. com/pdf/ibm/701/24-6042-1_701_PrincOps.pdf.

Jackson, Steve, Paul N. Edwards, Geoffrey Bowker, and Cory Knobel. 2007. Understanding Infrastructure: History, Heuristics, and Cyberinfrastructure Policy. *First Monday* 12 (6).

Lanier, Jaron. 2010. *You Are Not a Gadget*. New York: Random House.

Lessig, Lawrence. 2001. The Architecture of Innovation. *Duke Law Journal* 51: 1783.

Longstaff, P. H. 2000. Networked Industries: Patterns in Development, Operation, and Regulation. Program on Information Resources Policy, Center for Information Policy Research, Harvard University. Available at http://www.pirp.harvard.edu/ pubs_pdf/longsta/longsta-p00-2.pdf.

Mell, Peter, and Tim Grance. 2011. The NIST Definition of Cloud Computing. National Institute of Standards and Technology, Special publication 800–145. Available at http://csrc.nist.gov/publications/nistpubs/800-145/SP800-145.pdf.

Millett, Lynette I., and Samuel H. Fuller, eds. 2011. *The Future of Computing Performance: Game Over or Next Level?* Washington, DC: National Academies Press.

Mosco, Vincent. 2014. *To the Cloud: Big Data in a Turbulent World.* New York: Paradigm.

Negroponte, Nicholas. 1996. *Being Digital.* New York: Random House.

Roscoe, Timothy. 2006. "The End of Internet Architecture." In *Proceedings of the 5th Workshop on Hot Topics in Networks.* Available at http://conferences.sigcomm.org/hotnets/2006/roscoe06end.pdf.

Sandvig, Christian. 2013. The Internet as Infrastructure. In *The Oxford Handbook of Internet Studies,* ed. William H. Dutton, 86. Oxford, UK: Oxford University Press.

Thomas, Bryce, Raja Jurdak, and Ian Atkinson. 2012. SPDYing up the Web. *Communications of the ACM* 55 (December): 64–73.

Weinman, Joe. 2012. *Cloudonomics: The Business Value of Cloud Computing.* Hoboken, NJ: John Wiley & Sons.

Wu, Tim. 2011. *The Master Switch: The Rise and Fall of Information Empires.* New York: Random House.

Zittrain, Jonathan. 2008. *The Future of the Internet—and How to Stop It.* New Haven, CT: Yale University Press.

1 Cloud Strategy and Economics

Joe Weinman

Much has been written about cloud computing from a technical perspective: virtualization, containers, automation, dynamic provisioning, live virtual server migration, and the like. However, the essence of the cloud may be abstracted away from specific technologies and examined from a strategic and economic perspective. Such a perspective may well be one of the most important; after all, a technology is not relevant unless it creates value for users, customers, businesses, or society.

Such abstraction requires a delineation of the essential characteristics of the cloud model, one not tethered to a specific physical embodiment in servers and storage, together with an assessment of the costs and benefits that may derive from such a model versus its alternatives. Such an analysis—from the perspective of underlying universals—can help inform the discussion regarding the cloud, as well as provide a commonsense check of some of the widely held assumptions and beliefs regarding the cloud ecosystem and its evolution. For example, demand aggregation can reduce resource requirements. The degree to which this will occur depends on the individual and joint statistics of the customer demand functions. Such an analysis, rather than being merely a mathematical diversion, has important implications for real-world value generation by cloud computing, the technology architectures required to unlock that value, and regulatory and policy frameworks that may accelerate or hinder delivery of the value; this analysis also suggests likely ecosystem evolution.

We will formally define a cloud shortly, but for now, we will merely observe that a broad variety of services across a range of industry segments meet customer needs by utilizing business models with similar attributes: serving a mix of customers through a pool of dynamically allocated, shared resources rather than dedicated ones; offering pay-per-use pricing (i.e., linear tariffs), rather than flat rates or "unlimited" pricing plans; and utilizing on-demand resources rather than reserved or dedicated ones. For example, hotel rooms are the cloud model for residences, in contrast to private homes; taxis or rental car services are the cloud model for automotive transport, versus private vehicles; coffee shops are the cloud model for caffeinated beverages, in contrast to personal coffeemakers. Moreover, banking and credit facilities constitute a cloud model for capital, in contrast to equity: the resource is money, and the pay-per-use pricing plan is the interest rate.

Clouds—whether computing or otherwise—can exhibit a number of counterintuitive characteristics and behaviors. As an example, one can save money even while paying more: the key is to differentiate between unit cost and total cost. After all, a midsize sedan might cost $10 a day to own, based on $300 per month in financing, leasing, or depreciation costs; that same sedan might cost four to five times as much per day from a rental car service. Nevertheless, it is a rational economic decision to use a rental car service when the demand is sufficiently unusual—say, during a vacation—or unexpected—e.g., due to one's own car being totaled. It's not the daily unit cost comparison that is relevant, but the total cost. In other words, value is generated not necessarily by the *price*, but by the *pricing model*: pay per use.

Another example: normally there is a marginal (i.e., additional) cost to acceleration: a Lamborghini Diablo costs more than a Toyota Camry. However, in a world of pay-per-use pricing appropriately exploited by parallelizable tasks, acceleration of results can be achieved at zero marginal cost. Consider transporting 100 passengers from point A to point B. A single taxicab can be used, in which case the time to transport 100 passengers is on the order of 100 times that for 1 passenger. Alternatively, 100 cabs can be used in parallel, requiring an elapsed time essentially identical to that of transporting a single passenger. In either case, the total cost is 100 times as much as that for a single cab ride, but in the second scenario, the elapsed time is reduced by a factor of 100.[1] Similarly, computing rented from the cloud can accelerate the computation of parallelizable tasks at zero marginal cost. This simple fact has profound policy implications because enabling companies to frictionlessly use public cloud computing resources can unleash innovation, but the same approach can also be used to cheaply crack formerly unbreakable codes.

At a macro level, cloud computing can have a transformational impact on consumers, employees, citizens, businesses, and governments. For businesses, for example, there are four generic strategies—"digital disciplines" (Weinman 2014)—that leverage the cloud and related technologies such as the Internet of Things (IoT) and big data, which can drive competitive advantage. One is information excellence; i.e., leveraging information in real time to optimize processes. Another is solution leadership: smart product and service delivery element connected to cloud services. A third is collective intimacy: using advanced algorithms against big data to create value for individual customers, such as via recommendation engines or patient-specific therapies. A final meta-strategy is accelerated innovation: using cloud-mediated idea markets, open innovation, and contests to accelerate the pace of innovation in processes, products, and relationships, and to shift from straight salaries for employees to contest economics for ad hoc subject matter experts.

In addition to a qualitative *strategic* perspective, one can examine the cloud from a quantitative and behavioral *economic* perspective. The rest of this chapter will explore the economics of the cloud—*Cloudonomics*, to use the neologism coined by the author (Weinman 2008)—by examining mathematical abstractions of cloud services, including the statistics and dynamics of cloud systems. Because a valid economic perspective requires a behavioral and cognitive perspective and consideration of emergent qualities as much as a rational quantitative analysis, this chapter will also touch on these topics.

Defining the Cloud, Abstractly

Many definitions of the cloud exist (Vaquero et al., 2009), but for the purposes of this discussion and its strategic and economic focus, five related attributes are essential, forming the convenient retronym CLOUD (Weinman 2012). A cloud may be defined as a Common, Location-independent, Online, Utility, on-Demand service. Resources are common; i.e., pooled and dynamically shared across multiple customers or workloads. They are location independent, in that one can use the cloud from anywhere without needing to know exactly from where the services are delivered. To enable both dynamic sharing and location independence requires online access via a network. Clouds have utility pricing: like electricity or water, usage is metered and payment is typically proportional to usage. Finally, cloud resources are available on demand: prior reservations are not needed, any more than a reservation is needed for electricity resources before flicking a switch to have power delivered from the electric utility. These attributes are domain independent: while they apply to cloud computing services, they equally apply to rental car services, hotel chains, retail chains (including food service), mobile communications services, electric utilities, and even labor pools and credit facilities.

While such domain-independent attributes can be expressed qualitatively, we can gain insight by analyzing them quantitatively, formulating a simple mathematical model of a cloud system comprising a cloud provider and its customers. Generally, we will assume a set of m customers $1, 2, \ldots m$, and a time-varying demand function for each of those customers $D_1(t), D_2(t), \ldots D_m(t)$, and thus an aggregate demand $D^+(t) = \sum_{i=1}^{m} D_i(t)$. The notation $D_k(t)$ just signifies that customer k has "demand" (i.e., resource requirements) that vary over time. For example, if the third customer needs a dozen resources on the first day, we would write $D_3(1) = 12$. The notation $D^+(t)$ just refers to the aggregate demand; i.e., the sum of the individual demands as it varies over time. It is a simple sum: if Mr. Jones wants two peaches on Tuesday and Mrs. Smith wants three that same day, a total of five peaches are needed.

Such demand functions are context sensitive, varying by industry, region, country, and culture. For example, demand for computing resources tends to be variable, and such variation depends on the industry segment. Retailers in China have their biggest spike on Singles' Day, whereas those in the West often have peaks near the end of the year due to holiday gift giving, but may also experience spikes due to promotions at that time (e.g., Cyber Monday), or at other times (say, an annual sale). News organizations may have randomly arriving spikes due to noteworthy events with characteristic exponential decays; weather sites may show steady growth due to impending hurricanes or decaying spikes due to tornadoes. Storage resources may also experience such variability but are more likely to exhibit monotonically nondecreasing growth as data accumulates (Mazhelis, Fazekas, and Tyrväinen 2012).

Of course, not only do individual and aggregate demands vary over time, but resources do as well. A cloud provider or individual customer may increase the quantity of resources it has available by purchasing new ones or restoring recently maintained ones to service, or it may experience a decrease (say, due to a natural disaster). Individual customer resources may be pooled through peer-to-peer sharing, or they may be viewed as pooled when aggregated and offered through a cloud service provider. Therefore, as with demand, we can specify functions for resources: $R_1(t), R_2(t), \ldots R_m(t)$, or resource pools, where $R^+(t) = \sum_{i=1}^{m} R_i(t)$; and a price for those resources, $P(t)$, which under a linear tariff follows $P(t) = kR(t), k > 0$. A *linear tariff* is just a pricing plan where the price is linearly proportional to the quantity purchased. If peaches cost \$2 each, then three peaches cost \$6. In this formula, k is the constant of proportionality; i.e., rate (e.g., \$2 per peach). Simply put, on-demand resource allocation is a colloquial way of saying that $\forall t, D(t) = R(t)$, and pay-per-use pricing is a colloquial way of saying that $\forall t, P(t) = kR(t)$—in other words, that the price is proportional to the quantity of resources allocated and used. Thus, the cloud model first and foremost aligns demand, resource allocation, and charging: $D_i(t) = R_i(t) = P_i(t) / k$. Conversely, if $D(t) \neq R(t)$, there is at least one point t_1 where either $D(t_1) < R(t_1)$ (i.e., there are excess resources), or $D(t_1) > R(t_1)$ (i.e., there is insufficient capacity to meet the offered demand). Such mismatches cause economic loss, through opportunity costs of capital that could be better deployed, or unserved demand which would generate revenue or otherwise be productive.

A cloud is defined as *common* when demand from two or more customers is served via a pool of resources that is shared concurrently, sequentially, or both. This contrasts with resources that are either owned by a customer or a service where resources are dedicated to a single customer, as in a long-term leasing arrangement. We will examine how such demand aggregation and resource pooling can generate value.

Service is *location independent*; the service is delivered ubiquitously and responsively regardless of where the user is and without regard to where the service provider's facilities are. Responsiveness, however, is domain dependent. We don't need to know where email servers or electric power plants are located, but we do expect these services to be responsive (i.e., meet the time constraints relevant to the situation). A delay of ten seconds for an email to arrive is generally not noticeable; a similar delay in illumination after flicking on a light switch would be. We will examine the cost and benefit implications of siting facilities to meet such constraints given a geographically dispersed set of users or customers.

Cloud services are *online*. Providing common resources to dispersed customers requires a network that connects the two. In the case of cloud computing, the network may be the Internet, connecting users or devices from the Internet of Things to cloud service provider data centers, or it may also be other data networks, such as virtual private networks (VPNs), wireless, or optical networks. In other domains, such as retail services or lodging, the network may by physical, such as highways and sidewalks. Interestingly, the network, which may generally be viewed as an enabler, has a cost that is required to achieve several of the other benefits. We will briefly examine some of the trade-offs in network architectures.

By *utility* pricing, we mean a linearly proportional usage-sensitive pricing scheme, or *linear tariff*, typically referred to in cloud computing as *pay per use*. Simply put, $P(t) = kR(t)$; i.e., the cost incurred is proportional to the resources used (the relief of this obligation depends on details such as billing and payment schedules). In contrast to owned, financed, or leased resources, which are dedicated to a user and whose costs are constant over time regardless of use, this charging model offers key advantages in a variety of contexts.

By *on-demand*, we mean the right quantity of the right resources at the right time. Simply put, $D(t) = R(t)$. In a computing context, this implies "near-instantaneous" provisioning and deprovisioning of resources such as computers, applications, storage, and networking capacity, which can have a very fine granularity, thanks to technologies such as containers, multitenancy or virtualization. This is in contrast to other approaches, such as reservations, queuing, or fixed capacity. In the reservation model, future capacity is reserved in advance; in queueing, current demand is deferred until capacity is available; and in fixed-capacity models, capacity remains the same regardless of the level of demand. Like a broken watch that is correct twice each day, fixed capacity may occasionally match an instantaneous level of demand, but variable capacity aligns better with variable demand, and on-demand capacity aligns best with variable and unpredictable demand.

The CLOUD model is *a* model of services, and one way to meet customer needs. It is not the only model or necessarily the best model. It is important to realize that one or more of these attributes may be inverted, as shown in table 1.1, and such inversions may be preferred by certain users or in certain contexts. Moreover, hybrids or mixed approaches often will be

Table 1.1
Cloud Attributes and Their Inversions

	Cloud	Not Cloud
Resource	Common	Dedicated
Geolocation	Location independent	Local; location-sensitive
Network-centricity	Online	Untethered
Charging	Utility	Flat rate; nonlinear tariff; free; freemium; etc.
Resource allocation	On-Demand	Reserved in advance; queued until resources available; excess demand dropped

economically optimal and meet constraints such as legacy architectures, existing contracts, or minimizing switching and migration costs.

These inversions can be beneficial in certain circumstances. For example, rather than common resources, resources may be dedicated to a specific user or customer. While the benefits associated with, say, sharing overhead costs or achieving economies of scale may thus be forgone, other benefits may be achieved, such as assured access to at least a certain (bounded) level of resources, lack of performance impacts from resource contention or pathological resource use by neighboring processes, and enhanced security through prohibition of shared access.

Rather than location independence, a service may be offered in only a single location, perhaps offering hedonic benefits associated with a unique experience or maximizing benefits associated with resource consolidation, which we will quantify shortly. Rather than being online, a service or resource may be off-net, enhancing security and avoiding networking costs. Rather than being available on demand, a service may require reservation requests, as with many restaurant reservations and committed reservations (as with nonrefundable airline tickets); or customers may queue, acquiring resources as they become available, such as waiting for a library book or an amusement park ride.

Resources that are available on demand offer greater flexibility to deal with unpredictable demand patterns, possibly at the expense of lower utilization or possible lack of availability. Those that are reserved in advance or offered based on best-efforts availability can achieve greater utilization and thus economic efficiency, but do so potentially at the expense of delays in servicing demand, potentially negatively affecting customer value.

And, rather than being utility-priced, there are numerous pricing approaches other than linear tariffs: flat rates, multipart tariffs, Shapley pricing, pay what you like (Fernandez and Nahata 2009), and a variety of free approaches, such as freemium (Anderson 2008) and third-party pays (e.g., advertiser-supported services or content). While pay per use can offer benefits in the presence of variable demand, flat rates can as well, smoothing payments and facilitating budgeting, as shown in figure 1.1. Health insurance, for example, is merely a means of charging a flat rate (the insurance premium) for a service with variable and unpredictable demand (the delivered health care). Even in the absence of risk and unpredictability, flat rates have value: a fixed-rate mortgage offers a smoothing of payments increasingly used to reduce the principal, versus what otherwise would entail constant principal with very large interest payments at the beginning of the loan and trivially small ones at the end.

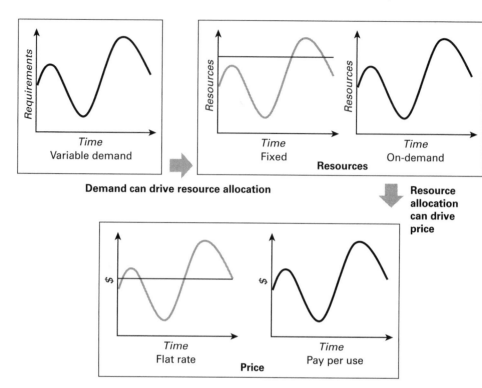

Figure 1.1
Pay-per-use versus flat-rate pricing. Image by the author.

However, flat rates can cause moral hazard or market failure if rational customers attempt to bypass the rules or exit the market when they realize they are paying an average rate for below-average consumption (Weinman 2010). This has important policy implications; consider the current Net Neutrality debate.

In short, the cloud model—whether applied to computing, hotels, rental cars, mortgage loans, or health care—is not in and of itself clearly superior. It is an option which offers trade-offs, whose value is often application dependent. Under the right conditions, the options offered in the cloud services model can be beneficial, as we shall see.

The Value of Common Resources

Consider two entities, each with varying demands for computing (or any other) resources. They can either choose to acquire their own resources (i.e., use a "do-it-yourself" approach) or rent them from a service provider. Suppose that each entity wants to be assured that it has sufficient capacity to meet demand and must "build to peak"; i.e., deploy enough capacity to handle its peak demand. In such a scenario, the value of common (shared) resources is largely driven by inverse relationships between the demand functions: fewer total resources are needed when demands are aggregated and resources are pooled if, when one entity is having a demand spike, the other is having a lull.

We can demonstrate this formally. Let $D_1(t)$ and $D_2(t)$ represent the demands. If resources are partitioned (i.e., not pooled), then assurance of sufficient capacity at all times requires that $R_1(t) \geq D_1(t)$ and $R_2(t) \geq D_2(t)$ for all t in the relevant range; for example, $-\infty < t < \infty$, or perhaps a one-year business planning cycle. Deploying a fixed quantity F of resources means that $R(t) = F$, and for it to be "built to peak" requires that $F_1 = R_1(t) = \max(D_1(t))$ for the first entity and a similar value for the second. If F^+ represents the fixed-capacity requirement for a service provider offering common resources to service aggregate demand, it is clear that $F^+ = \max(D_1(t) + D_2(t)) \leq \max(D_1(t)) + \max(D_2(t)) = F_1 + F_2$, or more simply, that $F^+ \leq F_1 + F_2$. In other words, in the presence of varying demand levels, in the worst case, the aggregate capacity required will be no more than the sum of the individuals, but it very well may be less.

Although the (public) cloud model implies the presence of a service provider, not all service providers offer a cloud model with dynamic allocation of resources. If a service provider exposes resources as a service, but still maintains a fixed quantity of resources dedicated to each customer, as often happens in information technology (IT) outsourcing and traditional managed services, there are various factors at work. On the one hand, the service provider may exhibit economies of scale based on volume purchasing power or lower costs for systems administration. On the other hand, the service provider has additional cost structure elements—information costs such as metering usage, transaction costs for order management or credit card fees, extending credit, management of receivables and uncollectibles, sales, and marketing—as well as a need to achieve a return on invested capital. If c_{sp} is the charging rate or price, which we'll consider to be a unit cost of such resources or services based on the resources of the service provider, and c_c is the cost for a customer to do it themselves, the service provider can create value in such a scenario only if $c_{sp}(F_1 + F_2) < c_c F_1 + c_c F_2$, implying, of course, that $c_{sp} < c_c$. This can happen, but it is not necessarily always the case.

However, if demand is aggregated and served out of a common pool of resources that are dynamically allocated to customers, it is *not* necessary for the unit cost from the service provider to be lower than the customer unit cost. This is because $\max(D^+(t)) = \max\left(\sum_{i=1}^{m} D_i(t)\right) \le \max(D_1(t)) + \max(D_2(t)) + \ldots + \max(D_m(t))$

To express this in words, the maximum capacity required to service the aggregate demand will never be more than the sum of the individual peak capacities required to service each of the demands. One frequently hears about the enormous economies of scale that cloud providers achieve. However, these economies are often conflated with factors that have nothing to do with scale per se, such as building data centers where power is cheap. Such techniques are also available to enterprises; moreover, should the costs of power shift, cloud providers who currently have advantaged power costs may find themselves disadvantaged: one shouldn't confuse recency of site selection and data center construction with inherent economies of scale. Other scale advantages may not be sustainable. For example, the ability to manage large numbers of servers may be a current advantage of the large providers, but management and administration technologies are diffusing. And, even if there are scale economies, there may be additional application-dependent costs required to leverage these benefits, the same way that saving money on ground beef at a wholesale grocer requires an expenditure of fuel and time to drive to the warehouse. Similarly, data transport requires an expenditure of capital to implement networks or a cost to acquire network services on a bandwidth or megabyte transferred rate, and a cost for delay—e.g., a loss of revenue, a negative customer or employee experience, or loss of productivity.

In short, economies of scale are neither necessary nor sufficient for cloud service providers to deliver economic benefits. However, even without such economies, the reduced total resource requirements inherent in dynamic resource allocation and demand aggregation *do* generate benefits.

How large are those benefits? It is traditional for economists and business analysts to refer to *economies of scale*—a reduction in unit costs at increased volume—in production and service operations. These are driven by factors such as increased purchasing power and the ability to distribute fixed costs, such as for product development, over more units. Many of those factors are at work with cloud computing service providers, as well as larger-enterprise IT shops. However, there is another important factor at work, which might be termed the *statistics of scale*—the characteristics of aggregation of diverse demands. The difference between multiple demands and a single demand is not just that there are more of them, it is that individual variations tend to cancel each other out. This means that a service provider can serve many customers with spiky, unpredictable demands, and rather than the problems of overcapacity and undercapacity being magnified by the number of customers, the variation tends to smooth out, leading service providers to have extremely high utilization and thus drive unit costs down by reducing waste associated with excess capacity and opportunity costs associated with insufficient capacity.

A simple analogy is any given individual's trip to a vacation destination, such as Las Vegas. Some people may travel there every spring, some once every few years, and others once in a lifetime. Hotels servicing millions of such customers don't have a million-fold-sized problem of such variability. Instead, their occupancy rate (i.e., utilization), is close to 100 percent.

To appreciate the *statistics* of scale, consider what happens as we aggregate an increasing number of demands. Let each demand $D_i(t), 1 \le i \le m$ be an independent, identically distributed random variable that is uniformly distributed on the [0,1] interval. Figure 1.2 shows 10 random samples from the aggregate demand, which is also a random variable $D^+(t) = \sum_{i=1}^{m} D_i(t)$ for m equal to 1, 10, 40, 100, 200, and 400. As can be seen in the illustrative example in figure 1.2, the sample sums become increasingly less variable. Mathematically, their coefficient of variation, a measure of variability compared to the mean, decreases as m increases. The

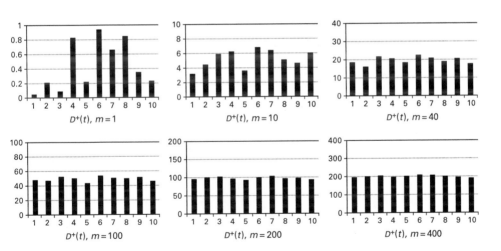

Figure 1.2
Reduction in the coefficient of variation through aggregation of increasing numbers of independent workloads. Image by the author.

higher the coefficient of variation, the more jagged a curve is, whereas the smaller the coefficient of variation, the flatter it is. We refer the reader interested in the calculations elsewhere (Weinman 2011d), and note here that the coefficient of variation of m aggregated independent identically distributed demands is only $1/\sqrt{m}$ as large as that of a single one, as illustrated in figure 1.3. Therefore, as m gets larger, the aggregate demand becomes relatively flatter. It is important that the demands be independent, or else there is less or no smoothing effect, depending on how correlated the demands are. From an economic perspective, this means that a customer with only one such demand (as shown in the upper-left side of figure 1.2) can expect to achieve only 50 percent utilization, whereas a service provider aggregating 400 such demands (as shown in the bottom-right side of figure 1.2) can expect to achieve close to 100 percent utilization.

The example shown in figure 1.2 is for a uniform distribution, where the peak is twice the mean. Other distributions have different peak-to-average ratios. For example, online retailers may have a peak-to-average ratio of 2 to 1, as Amazon.com has had, 3 to 1, as Target.com has had, or over 6 to 1, as Walmart.com has had. Other industries have even higher peak-to-average ratios. For independent demands with ratios such as those, rather than 50 percent utilization, they can expect single-digit percent utilization. However, if enough such demands are independent and aggregated, the service provider can still achieve 100 percent utilization in the limit.

This leads to an interesting effect: even if the unit cost of a resource from a cloud service provider is ten times that of an enterprise using its

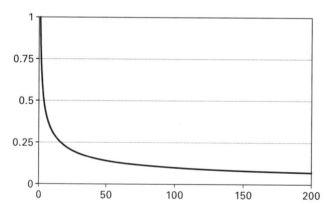

Figure 1.3
Behavior of $1/\sqrt{m}$. Image by the author.

own resources, the service provider may still be cheaper from a total cost perspective due to the pay-per-use model, including the lack of commitment or prepayment. It can be the case that "more is less" (Weinman 2008).

The $1/\sqrt{m}$ function is interesting for its implications on cloud ecosystem evolution and regulatory policy. As figure 1.3 shows, it means that a company can gain immediate benefits by aggregating workloads from its various business units, or even functions within a given business unit into a private cloud. Two workloads can reduce the penalty by 30 percent, and four by 50 percent. It also implies that a small or midsize cloud provider or facility can achieve nearly the utilization gains of a large one. One with 100 independent customers or workloads can get to within 10 percent $(1/\sqrt{100})$ of the penalty function of a large provider. When the workloads are correlated, there is no compelling benefit due to statistics of scale that a midsize provider offers, but the same is true for a large provider. While there are many forces influencing consolidation in industries, the statistics of scale suggest that midsize providers can compete based on a variety of attributes, such as customer intimacy, security, geographic proximity, or innovative pricing models, not just a requirement to "go big or go home." This may reduce the need for countervailing antitrust actions in the cloud computing infrastructure as a service industry.

Moreover, from a public policy perspective, the benefits of simple sharing are dramatic. It has been estimated that the average server utilization in an enterprise data center is in the single digits. Let's say that it is 10 percent (for ease in calculation). The utilization benefits inherent in demand aggregation into dynamically allocated resources would then result in a tenfold decrease in facilities, equipment, and possibly the power (and thus carbon footprint) required to power and cool all that equipment. Also, the corresponding software tooling available with the cloud can enhance labor productivity, and thus national competitiveness. Additional effects, such as time compression through platform as a service and automated provisioning, can drive productivity, competitiveness, and innovation.

While scale economies exist, the statistics of scale argument suggests that they are not necessary for service providers to generate real economic value. Assuming identical unit costs, service providers can generate value via statistical multiplexing—i.e., demand aggregation into dynamically allocated resources—achieving higher utilization than any individual customer. This reduces the costs of unused and thus unsold resources, which nevertheless must be incorporated into the cost structure.

It has also become popular to prognosticate that there will be only a handful of survivors in the cloud computing industry: other providers will either fail or be acquired. However, it isn't clear that architectures that are built on standard components will achieve substantial economies of scale in areas such as volume discounts relative to, say, midsize providers or large enterprises. Moreover, other current proprietary advantages would appear to be diffusing as management software vendors distribute cloud enablement tools, and best practices diffuse through "open-source hardware," such as the Facebook-initiated Open Compute Project.[2] This analysis shows that penalty functions associated with underutilized resources, a third source of potential advantage besides economies of scale and proprietary technologies, diminish rapidly and, as a percentage of cost, are virtually indistinguishable between midsize and large providers. It is thus likely that other sources of competitive differentiation will play a role in the emerging ecosystem, such as ease of use, customer relationships, or customization. As strategy icon Michael Porter has argued, industries tend to remain fragmented when there are low barriers to entry, an absence of economies of scale or experience curve effects, limited advantages to size in driving power over customers or suppliers, diverse market needs, etc. (Porter 1980). There are arguments for and against consolidation. On the one hand, there are economies of scale, brand power, heavy capital investment requirements, and heavy innovation investment requirements. On the other hand, standardized stacks (i.e., configurations of operating systems, hypervisors, web servers, database management systems, etc.) are reducing barriers to entry; scale-out architectures—i.e., data centers made of thousands or hundreds of thousands of servers—and automation and management technology diffusion reduce economies of scale and tend to minimize lock-in; and there are diverse customer needs in terms of IT, vertical industry, or functional expertise, and compliance requirements opening up opportunities for focused specialists.

The Value of Pay per Use

As discussed previously, clouds may exhibit economies of scale. The question of whether such economies of scale translate into prices lower than an enterprise's cost to provide such services itself is unclear and presumably depends on the specific cloud provider and the specific enterprise. Additional factors affect the cost structure for service providers, such as sales, general and administrative expenses, accounts receivable and uncollectables, margin requirements, and cross-subsidies. Moreover, even if there is a unit cost advantage, whether it is sustainable as technology enablers diffuse is another question.

However, it turns out that even if cloud services cost more, they still should be used, at least to serve some demand. The economic value of cloud services may or may not be based on unit cost advantages, but it can definitely be compelling based on pay per use. An example will help make this clear.

A midsize sedan can be financed, leased, or depreciated for $300 per month, which conveniently works out to about $10 per day. That same car, from a world-class, highly efficient service provider exhibiting massive economies of scale, might be four or five times as expensive. However, rational economic decision makers still rent cars, even at such a unit cost disadvantage. The deciding factor isn't the $40 or $50 per day for a rental car versus the $10 per day for an owned car during the few days of the rental, but the $0 per day for no rental car versus the $10 per day for an owned but unused car during the *non*-rental. If a resource tends to be sufficiently *unused*, it is fine to pay a premium during use so long as this premium is accompanied by the privilege of *not* having to pay for it during periods of nonuse. We can formalize this concept as described next.

The Interplay of Cloud Pricing with Demand Variability

Let the unit cost of a dedicated resource over a given unit time period—whether a car, capital, or a computer—be represented by c_r. For example, a car might cost $10 per day, a dollar might cost 3 cents per year, or a computer might cost $1 per day. Let the cost of a pay-per-use resource from a service provider be represented by $U \times c_r$; that is, U represents what we might call the *utility premium*. There are then three main cases:

- If $U < 1$, the pay-per-use cost is actually *lower* than the dedicated cost. This can happen due to multiple causes. For example, economies of skill or scale may lead a service provider to achieve cost efficiencies over a do-it-yourself approach. Even a poor service provider may have a better cost structure than a good small business. Alternatively, statistics of scale (or more precisely, the statistics of aggregated uncorrelated demand, as discussed previously) may enable a provider to achieve enhanced utilization, thereby eliminating wasted resources and, even in the absence of such economies, to offer a better price point than a customer can otherwise achieve. In yet another scenario, a provider may offer services under loss-leader or freemium pricing, thus offering a beneficial rate, at least for a time. Finally, a customer may have poor processes, lack competencies, have substantial overhead, or suffer from other issues; in other words, it is not that the service provider is so good, but that the customer is relatively inefficient.

- If $U = 1$, the unit costs are *identical* for the pay-per-use service provider and the do-it-yourself customer. However, we still note a salient difference: while the unit costs are identical when the resource is used and thus charged for, the pay-per-use model offers a cost of zero when the resource is not used, unlike the dedicated model.
- Finally, if $U > 1$, the cost of the resource from the service provider is *higher* than the dedicated resource. This is not a theoretical case, but one that matches real-world comparisons between well-run enterprise IT shop costs relative to service provider prices. Economies of scale arguments generally neglect to factor in the difference between economies of scale in the *cost* structure compared to all the elements that go into determining *price*, including sales, general, and administrative expenses and profit margin. As it will turn out, though, the value generated by cloud providers is not limited to cases where they offer unit cost advantages; a large part of it depends on the pay-per-use pricing structure. In other words, the price difference for resources when they are used is sometimes not as important as the price difference when they are *not*.

Elsewhere (Weinman 2011b), we provide a more formal analysis, but it turns out that the other major characteristic that affects the choice of owned resources sized to peak demand versus pay-per-use ones is the peak-to-average ratio of the demand curve, P / A. If this is large, the demand is "spiky"; if it is 1, it is perfectly flat. Note that the peak P is not to be confused with the pricing function $P(t)$. It is important to note that pay-per-use costs are proportional to $A \times U$ (the average demand times the utility premium), whereas do-it-yourself costs are proportional to the peak demand P over the same time period.

We can consider a variety of permutations:

- If demand is flat and pay-per-use resources are pricey, a do-it-yourself strategy is optimal. In other words, if $P = A$ and $U > 1$, then $P < A \times U$, so do-it-yourself costs less than the cloud.
- If there is no difference in pricing, but demand is variable, a utility option is better. In this case, $U = 1$ and $P > A$, so $P > A \times U$; i.e., the cloud is cheaper.
- If there is no difference in pricing and demand is flat, either option has equivalent cost. In this case, $U = 1$ and $P = A$, and thus it is straightforward to realize that $A \times U = P$. Risk management may then come into

play. If there is a possibility that demand will vary in the future, a pay-per-use solution is to be preferred. On the other hand, if it is more likely that a provider will raise prices than that demand will vary, do-it-yourself may be preferable. It should be noted, however, that demand variation is nearly certain (Weinman 2009) and that service providers have, over the past few years, been dropping prices (Kanaracus 2012). Of course, there is nothing to guarantee that prices (adjusted for technology-based price-performance improvements) will continue to drop once market share stabilizes. Consequently, while a quantitative analysis might suggest equivalence of either strategy, qualitatively, a cloud service provider appears to offer the best risk mitigation.

- We can generalize this to the case where $U = P / A$ (thus, trivially, $U = 1$ when $P = A$). In this case, $U \times A = P$; i.e., both scenarios cost the same. Again, the insights from the prior case regarding unpredictability apply.
- If demand has any shape and pay-per-use resources are relatively inexpensive, it is better to use the service provider. In other words, if $U < 1$, since it is certain that $A \leq P$, we know that $U \times A < P \times 1$.
- The most interesting case, where *more is less* (in other words, paying more in terms of unit cost can result in a lower total cost), is when the utility premium is lower than the demand is variable; i.e., $1 < U < P / A$. For example, a cloud provider might have a unit cost of twice what an enterprise can achieve, but the enterprise might have a still higher peak-to-average ratio, say, 4:1. In this case, $1 < U < P / A$, since $1 < 2 < 4$. Whenever $U < P / A$, we know that $U \times A < P$; i.e., pay per use is preferred.

In summary, it is not just unit cost that is of interest, but how it interacts with pay-per-use pricing in the context of demand variability.

Hybrids Are Typically Best   Up to now, we have looked at when a pure cloud approach is better or worse than a pure do-it-yourself approach, but it turns out that we can often do better by using a hybrid approach—a mixture of do-it-yourself, with fixed resources, and cloud, with pay-per-use resources. The detailed proofs are provided elsewhere (Weinman 2011b); here, we will just offer qualitative arguments. We can consider demand to fall into three major tranches, as illustrated in figure 1.4.

This figure shows a typical demand curve over time. For this curve, we can consider three tranches of usage. One tranche, shown on the bottom, is where there is relatively consistent demand for resources. At the other extreme, there is relatively infrequent demand for resources. And in between, there is an intermediate level of demand. Let us further assume

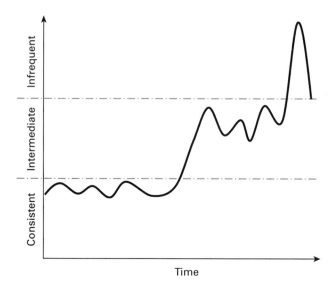

Figure 1.4
Tranches of frequency of resource utilization. Image by the author.

that $U > 1$; i.e., there is a premium for cloud services (there may not be, in which case clouds offer both lower unit costs and pay-per-use pricing—an unbeatable combination, all other things being equal).

Briefly, the portion of demand in the lower tranche, which is relatively consistent, has a peak-to-average ratio near 1, and we've already seen that when $U > 1$, such relatively flat demand is best served by owned resources. Conversely, the portion of demand in the upper tranche, which is relatively inconstant, has a really high peak-to-average ratio, and we've seen that when $P / A > U$, a cloud solution is best. The portion in the middle has the characteristic that it can be served just as well (i.e., at the same cost) by either pricing strategy. Regardless of where we choose to serve that demand, this kind of demand curve has a component that should be do-it-yourself and a component that should be served from the cloud.

The implication of this simple analysis is quite important: generally, a hybrid approach will be best. Most real-world demand curves will be a mix of some sort of relatively constant baseline demand and one or more spikes. The duration of demand at various levels for our analysis is invariant to interchanges in timing; in other words, a one-month-long demand peak in January and a one-month-long peak in June is no different than a two-month-long peak in November and December. In either

Table 1.2
Optimal Strategies Given Utility Premium and Peak-to-Average Ratio

	$U < 1$	$U = 1$	$U > 1$
$U \leq P / A$; i.e., the cloud is less premium-priced than the workload is spiky.	Cloud best	Cloud best	Cloud good; hybrid best
$1 < P / A \leq U$; i.e., the workload is less spiky than the cloud is premium-priced.	N/A	Don't care $(U = 1 \rightarrow P = A)$	Dedicated good; hybrid best
$P = A$; i.e., the demand is constant.	Cloud best	Don't care	Dedicated best

case, a build-to-peak strategy must build to that peak, and a pay-per-use strategy will incur peak resource charges for two months.

A summary of the best approach under various permutations is shown in table 1.2.

Complicating Factors Of course, one can add in other real-world complications that affect this type of analysis. One of these is transaction costs associated with increasing and decreasing capacity. However, a more important general issue is that a hybrid is more than a simple addition of pay-per-use resources to dedicated resources. Generally, we would like a hybrid to behave holistically. In a cloud computing context, this may entail data networks and so-called cloud operating systems or a cloud management layer. Pricing of these may be fixed (e.g., for owned networks or usage-insensitive bandwidth provisioning) or usage-sensitive (as with cloud costs per megabyte transferred), and the implications of these options are covered elsewhere (Weinman 2012, Mazhelis and Tyrväinen 2011, Mazhelis, Fazekas, and Tyrväinen 2012). However, it is to be noted that such costs will shift the break-even point (or zone) or even the viability of a hybrid solution. For example, it may not be worth deploying a $20 million network to save a nickel or two on compute or storage. In this case, we are back to selecting between a pure dedicated or pure pay-per-use solution.

The Value of Pay per Use in Parallelism To this point, we have explored the value of pay-per-use pricing for the resources that enable demand fulfillment. We assume that the demand is what it is, $D(t)$. However, there are other types of resource use in computation or in other domains. For example, one may wish to perform a computation comprising a serial portion and a parallelizable portion. In everyday life, child rearing includes serial and parallelizable portions. Making a baby is a serial process that largely has defied cycle time improvement, typically requiring roughly nine months from conception through completion.[3] On the other hand, making clothes for the baby can be parallelized: if each outfit takes an hour to cut and sew, one parent can make eight outfits in eight hours, but eight seamstresses can make eight outfits in one hour. In computation, some tasks are serial, but others are highly parallelizable, such as fulfilling web search queries. If 1 server would take 1 minute to respond to a query, then 10 servers only take 6 seconds, 100 would take only 600 milliseconds, and 1,000 would take only 60 milliseconds. Google has disclosed that they use 1,000 servers or more in parallel to respond to such queries (Shankland 2008).

In an owned or dedicated environment, acceleration can be costly. If search queries arrive conveniently spaced 1 minute apart, we can serve each one, with the abovementioned assumptions, on 1 server: each computation completes just as the next one arrives. The utilization of the system is now at 100 percent. However, suppose that we are trying to compete with Google. We buy 999 new servers, and now meet the competitive response time objective, but our utilization has dropped to 0.1 percent. Cycle time reduction for the compute process has led to massive capital expenditures and terrible utilization.

In a pay-per-use environment, however, acceleration is free. At 10 cents per hour, the 1,000 server hours cost $100 whether we use 1 server for 1,000 hours, 1,000 servers for 1 hour, or any combination thereof.

Implications Pay-per-use pricing generates clear value, whether alone or as part of a hybrid solution. It is common for vendors that offer on-premises solutions to argue for the merits of a private cloud, and service providers that offer public cloud solutions to argue the merits of a public cloud. However, for virtually all reasonable demand curves, and for virtually all realistic utility premiums, a hybrid solution is generally optimal, even after adjusting break-even points for additional pay-per-use costs, such as megabytes transferred, or fixed costs, such as dedicated networks.

There are additional factors suggesting that hybrid architectures are likely. For example, the cost to migrate legacy applications to cloud architectures/stacks or even cloud environments may be prohibitive, even if there were savings to be had in a pure cloud deployment. These applications or data warehouses have a gravitational effect, causing other applications to remain in proximity. Behavioral economic factors—such as the sunk-cost fallacy, which incorporates irreversible prior investments into decisions for the future, the endowment effect, which overvalues owned resources, and the need for control, where humans feel a need to control their environment—or sound mathematical reasoning may both contribute to a decision to keep at least some applications or portion of computing for applications in an enterprise data center, or at least on dedicated resources in a colocation facility; i.e., a shell of a data center that provides space, power, and network connectivity as a service.

Given that acceleration—speeding up the elapsed time for computing tasks—can be free in a pay-per-use environment, it is likely that the intensity of time-based competition involving computation will increase. More firms will attempt to acquire a competitive edge by accelerating cycle times. A good example of this is hedge funds or high-frequency traders, who will stop at nothing to shave a millisecond—or even tens of microseconds—off a total time through strategies such as proximity placement, optimized network routing, and parallel computing. But many other tasks, ranging from interactive applications such as search to long-running workloads such as seismic analysis, circuit simulation, or protein folding can be accelerated, potentially leading to a competitive edge in anything from product introduction to oilfield bidding. In markets with winner-take-all dynamics, it isn't a matter of an "edge," but survival. In addition, for some activities, such as web load testing, it isn't just a matter of speed, but the ability to deliberately employ thousands of processors to generate artificial demand. Again, renting them for a short period beats owning them and leaving them idle most of the time.

The Value of Location Independence

Cloud services should be available regardless of where you—the user—are and regardless of where they are delivered from. Moreover, such services should be delivered responsively (i.e., meet certain time constraints relevant to the context). For example, Starbucks coffee and McDonald's burgers are within a few minutes of hundreds of millions of people. The Bronx Zoo, however, while conceptually accessible to virtually anyone, is too distant to be of value to most.

Response time is not just a technical performance metric. It affects usability, customer and user experience, revenue, and labor productivity. For e-commerce vendors, subsecond delays have been associated with negative impacts on the order of billions of dollars (Hamilton 2009).

Conversely, speeding up response time has a beneficent effect: users can view more web pages, are more likely to stay on site as opposed to "bouncing" to a competitor, and are more able to complete purchases. For employee applications, faster response time means an ability to complete more tasks in a given time (i.e., enhanced labor productivity). Of course, adding up improvements in firm labor productivity ultimately affects national productivity.

To a first approximation, latency, which is for all intents and purposes roughly proportional with response time and to distance (whether worst-case or average), is proportional to the inverse square root of the quantity of nodes. Consider a planar area A covered by n nodes. Each node is at the center of a coverage area of radius r. Excluding factors such as the packing density η (eta) based on whether the covering is a circle covering (no point left uncovered, as in placing drop cloths before painting a ceiling) or a circle packing (attempting to cover a surface maximally, but with interstitial gaps—for example, with hockey pucks), but assuming that the covering is regular, it is clear that each node covers area πr^2, and thus $A \propto n \times \pi r^2$; that is, the area covered is roughly proportional to the number of circles times the area covered by each circle, as shown in figure 1.5.

For a given area, as we increase the number of nodes, since A and π are constants, it is clear that $1/n \propto r^2$; in other words, $r \propto 1/\sqrt{n}$. There are some trigonometric adjustments required for calculations on a sphere versus a plane; these are beyond the scope of this current treatment and are covered elsewhere (Weinman 2011e). This means that halving the latency (presumed to be proportional to the radius) requires quadrupling

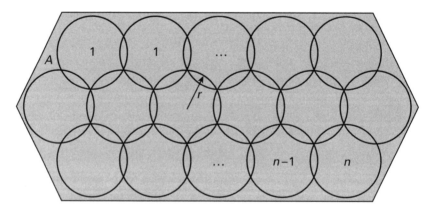

Figure 1.5
Planar area A covered is proportional to $n \times \pi r^2$. Image by the author.

the number of service nodes. This tactic has rapidly diminishing returns. At first, enormous response time improvements can be easily gained. On a planet such as Earth, going from one node to two will reduce worst-case terrestrial/subsea round trip latency by 80 to 100 milliseconds or so (based on a reduction of about 6,250 miles at a one-way optical fiber transmission speed of about 125 miles/millisecond). But at some point, reducing latency by only a couple of microseconds would require over 2 billion additional data centers. This is an important observation because it points to the economic difficulty of cloud services ever fully replacing end-point processing for highly interactive tasks. It also argues for the value of a globally dispersed footprint to serve a global user base. Many of the large cloud providers are investing in globally dispersed facilities, and enterprises are best served by employing these providers on a pay-per-use basis rather than investing in their own global footprint of data centers.

Tradeoffs between Consolidation and Dispersion   There are a variety of resource deployment strategies, as shown in figure 1.6.

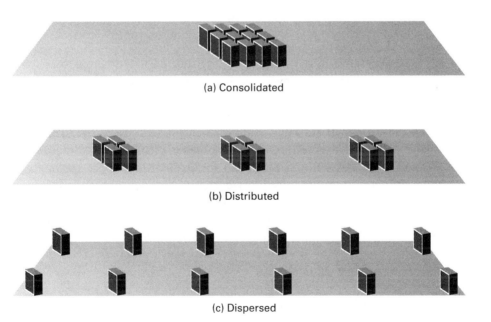

(a) Consolidated

(b) Distributed

(c) Dispersed

Figure 1.6
Consolidated, distributed, and dispersed resource deployment strategies. Image by the author.

Dispersion is beneficial in reducing latency and thus enhancing the customer experience and growing revenues. However, consolidation is useful for exploiting scale economies and achieving statistical multiplexing benefits, as discussed in above. Ultimately, there is no perfect answer. A single consolidated location would achieve some benefits; an aggressively dispersed architecture would achieve others. However, for a given quantity of resources, an optimal balance can be found that reduces total latency by minimizing processing latency through parallelization and network latency via proximity. Excluding stochastic factors such as network congestion, we can simply (and perhaps simplistically) express total latency as the sum of three terms: a fixed constant F, which includes the serial portion of the computational task; a network transport time N, which may involve multiple round trips; and a processing time P for the parallelizable portion of the computational task. On p processors, the parallelizable portion of the work is assumed to take P / p time. Using n service nodes, per these arguments, the network transport time may be assumed to take $N / \sqrt{n}$ amount of time. Given a fixed quantity Q of processors, where $Q = n \times p$, it turns out (Weinman 2011e) that the minimum total latency occurs when

$$n = \sqrt[3]{\frac{QN^2}{2P}}$$

To interpret this equation, when N is large relative to P (in other words, transport time dominates over processing time), the number of nodes should be larger as well, as it is a priority to get the transport time down. On the other hand, when P is large relative to N, resources are better spent in parallelization. To use a real-world example, consider Google search. If a single query takes a minute, this is hundreds of times longer than a worst-case network round trip on the Earth, which takes under 200 milliseconds. Hundreds of processors, then, are best deployed in a single location. However, if a thousand processors brings the processing time below the network transport time, it begins to make sense to focus on reducing the network transport time through geographic dispersion.

Implications

Investments in both processing time reduction via parallelization in consolidated facilities and latency reduction via dispersion can be useful. However, both exhibit diminishing returns. For "embarrassingly parallel" tasks (i.e., those that, unlike pregnancy, offer time compression opportunities through the employment of additional resources), gains diminish in accordance with $1/p$, as discussed previously. For latency reduction, gains diminish in accordance with the $1/\sqrt{n}$ principle. Generally, this means that dispersion becomes less and less relevant versus parallelization, assuming that the task can be accelerated via parallelization. If not, dispersion is the only tool in the toolbox.

From an economic perspective, dispersion generally offers unfortunate economics as a do-it-yourself strategy. The investment in additional nodes can be linear, whereas the payoff can become sublinear, even before considering real-world considerations such as cannibalization of existing branches or stores (i.e., nodes). For instance, opening a Starbucks across the street from an existing one will reduce the time needed to get coffee for those customers living or working across the street, but may also reduce the business at the existing one.

However, if a cloud service provider can be leveraged, the economics can exhibit similar indifference to dispersion, as we saw with pay per use for parallelization. Rather than cost being linear in nodes, the cost can be constant regardless of nodes. Consequently, benefits associated with dispersion can be had at zero marginal cost. Moreover, ancillary benefits, such as a reduction in network backbone traffic, may accrue when services are consumed locally. While network costs are dropping, processing and storage costs are dropping faster, implying that, in the limit, the network will account for 100 percent of the technology cost of a distributed computation (not including power, cooling, management, etc.). Consequently, dispersion will be important not only to enhance response time but also to reduce the total cost. This is not merely a theoretical observation; even large global telecommunications companies are actively pursuing content delivery technologies to reduce their (own internal transfer) costs of network transport.

This logic applies not only to distributing information services and information goods, but also physical goods, and it explains why consumer packaged goods firms generally distribute their wares using a bricks-and-mortar retail distribution cloud service provider (i.e., a retailer).

The Value of On Demand

On-demand resourcing implies that the right resources are being supplied in the right quantity at the right time. If $R(t)$ is the function describing the quantity of resources over time, we would prefer $R(t) = D(t)$. The right quantity of resources has value because one may associate a penalty with excess resources *and* with insufficient resources. The penalty associated with each excess resource may be viewed as the cost of the resource (say, as a monthly lease) or the cost of the capital tied up in the resource (based, say, on weighted average cost of capital or opportunity costs). The penalty associated with insufficient resources may be viewed as the lost customer revenue or employee productivity associated with the loss or delay of transactions. Depending on the workload, a transaction or activity not immediately served may be lost—as when a real-time voice over IP (VoIP) packet is dropped due to congestion, or a search query is not served within an acceptable time—or may be queued until resources are available, as in transcoding movies for later content delivery. Queues may have a variety of behaviors, such as balking (customers avoiding a long line), reneging (abandoning a long line when the wait becomes too much to bear), and penalty functions associated with delays or service level agreement (SLA) violations (Ellens et al. 2012).

Valuation is context dependent and relies on whether transactions are abandoned or merely delayed, whether unhappy customers create negative publicity, whether they actively switch to a competitor, and so forth.

A simple way to model such a system is to assume that there is a penalty cost for each excess resource, c_r, and a penalty cost for each insufficient resource, c_d. We can now look at several scenarios briefly.

- **Fixed-Capacity, Uniform Distribution of Demand, Symmetric Penalties:** Suppose that $D(t)$ is uniformly distributed on $[0,1]$ and $c_r = c_d$; i.e., there are equal penalties for undercapacity and overcapacity. If we were to pick a capacity of 0 or 1, the expected value of the penalty would be $.5c_r$. The minimum expected penalty is a capacity at the midpoint, in which case the expected value of the penalty is only $.25c_r$. This conclusion is straightforward to generalize to uniform distributions on other intervals.

- **Fixed-Capacity, Uniform Distribution of Demand, Asymmetric Penalties:** When $D(t)$ is uniformly distributed on $[a,b]$ and the penalties are asymmetric (say, $c_r \ll c_d$), we should err on the side of caution. Specifically, the minimum will be $a + [(b - a) \times c_d / (c_r + c_d)]$. This is a more likely case because IT resource costs are a small fraction of the total revenue that they generate. A \$2,000 server ($c_r = 2,000$) might well generate (or at least be associated with) \$1 million of revenue ($c_d = 1,000,000$). This theoretical optimum in the real world is typically exceeded with some safety margin. Another way to view this is that insurance against undercapacity is cheap.

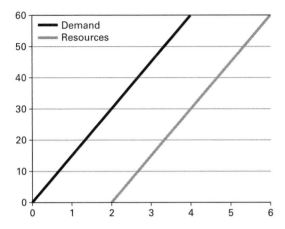

Figure 1.7
Monotonically increasing linear demand function with fixed resource provisioning delay. Image by the author.

- **Linear Demand Growth, Fixed Provisioning Intervals:** Let $D(t)$ be a linearly growing function of the form $at + b$. Let $R(t)$ be of similar form, but with a fixed resource-provisioning delay d, so that $R(t) = a(t - d) + b$ as shown in figure 1.7. In such a case, the penalty is directly proportional to the provisioning interval, so halving the provisioning interval halves the penalty. Reducing the provisioning interval to zero means there is zero penalty. To put it another way, virtually any speedup in provisioning generates a business benefit.
- **Exponential Demand Growth, Fixed Provisioning Interval:** Suppose that $D(t) = e^t$; that is, demand is exponentially growing. Let $R(t)$ reflect a fixed provisioning delay, again of duration d. Thus, $R(t) = e^{t-d}$, as shown in figure 1.8. Again, $D(t) > R(t)$, and demand exceeds resources. The gap is $D(t) - R(t) = e^t - e^{t-d}$. Unfortunately for whoever is in this situation, even though the provisioning delay is constant, the penalty grows exponentially, since the penalty is just $e^t(1 - e^{-d}) \times c_d$, which is an exponential term times a constant. Making things worse in the real world is that rather than being fixed, d grows as the gap does: the time to provision a virtual server is less than that to provision a physical one, which in turn is less than that to provision a rack or container, which is less than to site and build a data center. This type of exponential growth is typically seen during the early days of a hot startup—say, a social network, microblogging service, or online movie-streaming service. Under such growth conditions, it is very difficult to provision resources oneself,

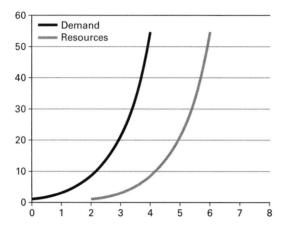

Figure 1.8
Exponentially increasing demand function with fixed resource provisioning delay. Image by the author.

leading many such startups to leverage the cloud (together with many other reasons, such as minimizing capital expenditures and mitigating customer acceptance risk).

- Other possibilities exist as well—for example, where $D(t)$ follows a random walk and therefore has an expected translation distance proportional to the square root of the number of steps, a situation covered in depth elsewhere (Weinman 2011a). This scenario turns out to have a penalty proportional to $\sqrt{d}$, so reducing the provisioning delay by a factor of 4 leads to a penalty cost reduction by only half.

Implications

The penalty cost associated with undercapacity or overcapacity depends on the nature of the demand function, the nature of the resource provisioning function, and the relative costs of excess or insufficient capacity, which may be identical or asymmetric. In a simple case, where resourcing is delayed a fixed time from a linearly growing demand curve, halving the delay halves the penalty. Often these days, we find businesses that are growing exponentially. In such a case, any fixed delay causes literally exponentially worsening problems. A number of well-known firms, such as Netflix and Zynga, during periods of exponential demand growth, pursued public cloud strategies because the public cloud could offer on-demand capacity. Only on-demand capacity can offer the needed flexibility to scale out and scale back during periods of variability, while reducing the penalty cost to zero. As described previously, however, if $U > 1$, generally a hybrid strategy will be cost-optimal.

Use Cases for the Cloud

Although cost comparisons are interesting, they don't tell the whole story with respect to valuing the cloud. There are a number of patterns, or use cases, where the cloud generates value in unique ways. For example, consider a large global social network or communication network. One cannot merely consider the relative unit cost of resources required for these setups; such networks *inherently* are cloud-centric. One cannot run a billion-user social network *privately* on a disconnected basis in one's garage, even if the costs were lower; the functionality requires the cloud. Companies and services such as Skype and YouTube illustrate the Communications pattern; eBay and Craigslist the Market pattern; Bitcasa the Repository pattern; and Amazon Web Services' Simple Storage Service (S3) the Replication pattern. We will explore some of these patterns and quantify their benefits and trade-offs in the next sections.

The Communications Pattern

Perhaps the most fundamental use case for cloud services is communication. This spans services such as Skype and Twitter, but also mobile telephony and even plain old telephone service (POTS) in keeping with our theme that implementation details are merely an annoying distraction from the underlying economics of the cloud

As shown in figure 1.9, there are also many different types of networks: fully connected full duplex (private two-way connections between each pair of nodes, as shown in figure 1.9a), broadcast (a single source node with multiple destination nodes as shown in figure 1.9b), and so forth.

As can be seen from figure 1.9a, a fully connected network on n nodes has order (n^2) connections, specifically $n(n-1)/2$. Moving to a hub-and-spoke network, as shown in figure 1.9c, reduces the number of needed connections by a factor of n. As networks grow, this is a dramatic improvement: a hub-and-spoke network with 1,000 nodes would need only 1,000 connections, whereas a fully connected point-to-point network would need almost 500,000. Assuming that connections require investments in network equipment and transport facilities, this is a very substantial difference.

However, there are other trade-offs to consider. Because transmissions sent through a central hub generally have to travel farther than those

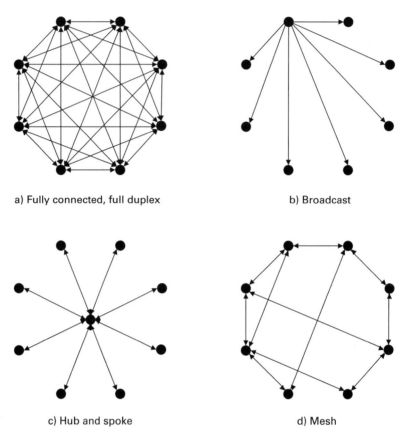

a) Fully connected, full duplex   b) Broadcast

c) Hub and spoke   d) Mesh

Figure 1.9
Some example networks: fully connected, broadcast, hub and spoke, mesh. Image by the author.

taking the shortest direct path, latency is increased when using a hub. For two points selected at random on a unit disk (a circle with radius 1 plus its interior points), the expected value of the point-to-point distance is $128/(45\pi) \cong .905$ (Burgstaller and Pillichshammer 2009), whereas the expected value of the distance traversing the hub is 4/3 (Weinman 2012), a nearly 50 percent penalty. This is before any additional real-world constraints, such as congestion at the hub, the need for repeaters or regenerators due to longer distances, optical-electronic-optical conversions, and the like. The investment in facilities is also worse for point-to-point, because although the distances traveled are shorter, there are many more connections (n times as many) traversing this roughly one-third shorter distance.

In short, excluding additional complicating factors such as congestion delays, bandwidth cost nonlinearities, routing anomalies, and so on, the cost-reduction value of a cloud service relative to fully connected, private point-to-point connections in a communications pattern can be viewed as proportional to the number of communicating nodes, but at the expense of about a 47 percent latency penalty. To the extent that the network enabling the cloud service is actually implemented as a mesh (figure 1.9d) somewhere between the extremes of pure hub and spoke (figure 1.9c) and fully connected (figure 1.9a) networks, the results moderate (i.e., lower savings, but with less of a latency penalty). These results match everyday experience: major airlines have multiple hubs, and passengers often have to wait to change planes due to the lack of point-to-point direct flights.

The Market Pattern

Clouds are often used to enable markets. Consider Amazon.com, eBay, and Craigslist, for example. One way to think of a market is as a trading network, and the prior analysis holds for costs to connect participants: a market reduces interactions by a factor of n by providing a hub. That is, a buyer doesn't need to individually canvas each seller but can merely query the market instead.

However, a more sophisticated analysis focuses on the marginal (net additional) value of a connection. In other words, if a buyer is already "connected" to nine sellers, what is the value of connecting to a tenth one? To put it another way, if one is looking for, say, a used Fender Stratocaster in good condition, how much of an improvement will one get in price by looking on eBay (a national/global marketplace) versus on the local Craigslist versus the community newspaper (/website) versus going door to door? These differences capture the value of the cloud in the Market pattern. Rather than assuming that each connection is identically valuable, we can consider the marginal value of an additional connection to a market participant.

The theory of order statistics helps answer the question. Briefly, suppose that every seller offers a good for sale at a price that is a random variable distributed on $[0,1]$. The expected value of the price from one seller is .5. It turns out that the expected value of the minimum price when there are n sellers is simply $1/(n+1)$. This harmonic series steeply falls for small values of n, then flattens out. To put it another way, a market doesn't need to have many participants to offer good value for customers, helping explain the longevity of local cloud-based marketplaces such as Craigslist.

Similar logic applies for the expected increase in price from multiple bidders.

If the price (or bid) dispersion is wide, however, the marginal benefit of an expanded market can be correspondingly large. Suppose that prices are normally distributed and therefore have the range $[-\infty, \infty]$. This is the way that a grilled cheese sandwich with an alleged image of the Virgin Mary can sell for $28,000 (Dabbagh 2010).

The Repository Pattern

Another use for the cloud is to maintain a single copy (or a small number of copies) of information, rather than every user or customer maintaining the copy. There is value to such deduplication, which trades off the cost of access for the cost of ownership and maintenance. In the offline world, such a scenario might involve checking out a book at a library versus owning it. In the digital world, it might involve streaming a movie or song from the cloud rather than maintaining a copy on your hard drive. Suppose that there are m users of such content, and the cost to maintain the content for a given time period is c_s. Then the cost to maintain the content across all users for that time is clearly mc_s. However, in the extreme, there is only one copy maintained in the cloud, and thus the cost would be just c_s (assuming that cost of cloud storage is the same as local, somewhat of a convenient oversimplification). However, there is a trade-off with access cost. If the cost for a customer to access the object is c_a, and the expected number of accesses per time period is k, then the savings on storage are traded off against the cost of access: $m \times k \times c_a$. The cost of access may be viewed as a reduction in the quality of the user experience due to delays associated with either the beginning of use (e.g., buffering time) or complete access (e.g., download time), modified by factors such as perceptions of wait time, which often have a nonlinear relationship to actual wait time, and behavioral economic factors such as hyperbolic discounting, a cognitive bias that overweights immediate gratification. Additional loss may arise from behavior such as balking or reneging. The cost of access may also involve the communications network required to access the information. Sometimes, for example, when there are fees per megabyte transferred, there is a hard-dollar cost. If the network is already provisioned, under capacity, and priced at a flat rate, then there is zero marginal cost.

The Replication Pattern

One use for the cloud is deduplication via the repository pattern. But the other is the reverse: selective duplication (i.e., replication), as when the cloud is used for backup. Let us exclude the fact that some backup services are currently offered for free, and assume that there is a cost c_s to maintain a copy of an object over a given time period, as before. Assume that the cost of a lost object is c_o, outages or other disasters are independent events, that the probability that a disaster occurs and thus that an object is lost in the given interval at a given location is P, and that the number of copies maintained of the object is n. Then the cost to maintain n copies is $n \times c_s$ and the likelihood that an object is lost because *all* copies are lost is p^n. Even for nontrivial P, enough copies can reduce the probability of loss to a sufficiently low level. To put it differently, one doesn't need to maintain *that* many copies to largely ensure that at least one is available. On the other hand, no matter how many copies we maintain, we will never actually achieve an absolute guarantee of data durability (i.e., object preservation). If the object is of high value (i.e., $c_o \gg c_s$—in other words, the cost of a lost object is much higher than that of the cost to store it), it certainly makes sense to maintain a few copies, since the expected value of the marginal benefit associated with the preservation of the data via replication is greater than the cost of maintaining the copies. Specifically, since the likelihood of loss is p^n, the reduction in the probability of loss from copying one object an additional $n-1$ times is $p - p^n$; therefore, maintaining n copies makes sense whenever $c_o \times (p - p^n) > (n-1) \times c_s$.

For this reason, many cloud services offer the ability to maintain multiple replicas of data. Additional considerations are that the cost of storage may vary between home or an enterprise data center and the cloud, and that the likelihood of a loss of data may vary. In addition, the assumption that losses of object copies are independent is not necessarily valid. Outages due to human error or technology problems at a given service provider will be correlated, and one can't rule out a deliberate attack to physical premises, a cyberattack that would destroy all digital copies, or provider bankruptcy.

Behavioral Economic Factors

A number of behavioral economic factors may affect cloud adoption positively or negatively. Broadly speaking, behavioral economics addresses cognitive biases and fundamental, repeatable, predictable errors in thinking that humans (and other primates and even nonprimates) make, in contradistinction to a classical viewpoint of humans as rational optimizers. These biases may be due to what Herbert Simon called "bounded rationality," the insight that people have neither perfect information nor unlimited mental resources to make optimal decisions; or due to what Dan Ariely calls "predictable irrationality" (Ariely 2008), often the mental equivalent of an optical illusion. Next, we briefly cover some relevant cognitive biases and anomalies as they relate to the cloud.

Common resources and a service model correspond to a lack of ownership. However, ownership is associated with the *endowment effect,* where customers value goods that they own more than they do equivalent goods that they don't. In one experiment, people with similar psychographic profiles who desired an asset—Duke University basketball tickets—were willing to pay an average of about $170 for them; those who owned the same asset were willing to sell them for an average of $2,400 (Carmon and Ariely 2000). Moreover, humans—and other animals—exhibit a need for control. A lack of cognitive control—awareness of the environment and intended actions—or behavioral control—ability to affect future actions— has been associated with stress, illness, and premature death (Rodin and Langer 1977). These effects rightly or wrongly may create a bias toward ownership versus service models.

Pay-per-use pricing typically includes a lack of upfront commitment. The zero-price effect is relevant to the cloud's no-commitment model, which eliminates upfront costs. Customers have been shown to prefer to receive a free $10 gift certificate rather than pay $7 for a $20 gift certificate, even though the latter is a better value (Shampanier, Mazar, and Ariely 2007). One may draw parallels from this to the cloud: customers are likely to prefer service offers that are at least initially free, even if for-fee services or resource ownership are better values.

On-demand resources are aligned with biases such as hyperbolic discounting and instant gratification, sometimes called the *present bias,* which irrationally overweight immediacy. This bias is favorable toward cloud services: rather than wait for the IT department to schedule a feature or allocate compute resources, a user may acquire it instantly via software as a service, build it quickly via platform as a service, or acquire the resources through on-demand infrastructure as a service.

Utility pricing (i.e., pay per use) is rational, but it is also antithetical to the flat-rate bias, an often irrational preference for flat-rate over pay-per-use pricing. This includes traditional unlimited cell phone plans versus pay-per-use plans such as pay-per-text message, pay-per-voice call minute, or pay-per-megabyte or per-gigabyte-transferred plans.

The flat-rate bias has been traced to several factors (Lambrecht and Skiera 2006). First is the *insurance effect,* which includes a desire to avoid variation in sequential bills, as well as potentially loss aversion, a core cognitive bias in which a dollar of loss is more painful than a dollar of gain is pleasurable. This is not just a human cognitive bias: capuchin monkeys are reference dependent and loss averse—and even in the presence of equal risk and equal payoffs, they prefer situations where payoffs are expressed as a gain (Chen, Lakshminarayanan, and Santos 2006). A monkey given one treat and half the time given another is delighted; one given two treats and half the time having one taken away becomes violent, even though the expected value received in both scenarios is 1.5 treats. Second is the *taxi-meter effect,* where the present pleasure of consumption is lessened due to present awareness of pain of loss associated with payment. Another is the *convenience effect,* wherein paying a flat rate can reduce the cognitive and hard-dollar information costs associated with tariff selection. Finally, there is the *overestimation effect,* where customers overestimate future consumption, thus incorrectly (albeit rationally given the faulty prediction) select a plan which they expect to minimize payment. Moreover, the flat-rate bias is not completely irrational, given unusual cases such as a $200,000 mobile phone bill due to the roaming fees for a few videos (Fraser 2011). It is worth noting that there also exists a *pay-per-use bias,* where customers eschew flat rates to their detriment.

Pricing continues to be an area of innovation for cloud providers. For example, Amazon Web Services introduced a program called "spot instances," a means of offering dynamic pricing for yield management. Google introduced "sustained-use pricing," which offers a discount for maintaining a consistent level of usage (Google 2014). Pay-per-use versus flat-rate pricing has a few additional characteristics to note. In a system with rational, optimizing customers with dispersed levels of usage and both flat-rate and pay-per-use providers, the dynamics tend to favor the pay-per-use provider(s). This is because lighter users will choose the pay-per-use plan, resulting in an increase to the flat-rate price that must be charged, driving additional users to pay per use, and so on (Weinman 2010). Moreover, consideration of the behavior of systems with flat rates calls into question oft-cited arguments regarding quality uncertainty, information asymmetry, and market failure (Akerlof 1970). Briefly, rather than a buyer lacking information regarding the quality of a product and willing to buy only at the average quality level; a provider offering a flat rate based on average consumption lacks the ability to decide not to serve the customer— even with perfect information regarding consumption levels—which can lead to market failure (Weinman 2010). In short, even though consumers mostly have a flat-rate bias, there are numerous issues with flat-rate pricing that the cloud tends to circumvent.

There are many ways to price for goods and services. Pay per use is one. Flat rate is another. However, there are also two-part tariffs, three-part tariffs, "pay what you like," lifetime unlimited, Paris Metro, Shapley, congestion, and a variety of auctions such as English, Dutch, and Vickrey. Free is also a pricing strategy, used in everything from cross-subsidies such as razors and razor blades; freemium, where a certain level of service is free but additional levels cost hard dollars; or other approaches, where a few paying users support many nonpaying ones (Anderson 2008).

Simply focusing on pay-per-use versus flat-rate pricing offers a number of interesting lessons from both a behavioral economic and system dynamics perspective. Pay per use via a linear tariff is arguably the most logical pricing strategy. After all, if we visit a fruit stand, we don't expect to pay anything if we don't buy any apples. We expect to pay the price of one apple when we buy one, two apples when we buy two, and so on (excluding volume discounts; i.e., block-declining nonlinear tariffs). Flat rate is simpler to implement, as no measurement of consumption is required, but leads to a number of distortions. For example, under a flat rate, we pay even if we don't consume, and the marginal cost of additional consumption is zero, leading to issues such as *moral hazard,* where customers waste resources without care because they don't incur a marginal cost for such use.

Suppose, however, that we consider a duopoly with perfect competition, where one provider offers flat-rate plans priced to the average consumption of their customer base and the other offers a pay-per-use plan. Assume that customers with dispersed levels of consumption are permitted to switch plans at will, based on rational self-interest. Light users on the flat-rate plan realize that they can save money via pay per use; heavy users on the pay-per-use plan realize that they can same money via flat rates. Over time, the average consumption of flat-rate customers increases, causing a rate increase, disenfranchising a new tranche of light users. It may be proved that such a system evolves to an end state where the only customers of the flat rate plan are the heaviest users, who will actually pay the same under either plan. Counterintuitively, even though each customer switches to save money, the total revenue in the system remains constant.

Such a dynamic, however, is based on several assumptions: rational users, rational providers who won't sell at a loss to gain share, no grandfathering of prior rate plans, no switching costs, no measurement costs, consumption dispersion, perfect competition providing no profit margin cushion for pricing, etc. In other words, theory must be carefully applied to practice.

Summary

Cloud computing may be viewed from a number of perspectives, such as computational complexity (Weinman 2011c), technology such as virtualization, security and privacy, and public policy (Yoo 2011). One important perspective is that of strategy and economics, where minimizing costs and maximizing financial and business value may be explored. The characteristics of clouds, and the way that a common, location-independent, online, utility, and on-demand service behaves, may be analyzed abstractly, economically, behaviorally, and empirically. Such services exhibit a number of nuanced characteristics economically, for example, it may be perfectly rational to pay a higher unit cost for some resources under pay-per-use pricing to achieve a lower total cost in the presence of variable demand; acceleration of certain types of highly parallelizable workloads can be achieved at zero marginal cost; dispersion of nodes for latency reduction has rapidly diminishing returns; and economies of scale are neither necessary nor sufficient for service providers to generate a quantifiable customer value proposition. Moreover, markets offering pay-per-use pricing and flat rates can have interesting system dynamics, assuming rational active customers with dispersed consumption levels, which interact with a variety of behavioral economic considerations that can either hinder or accelerate cloud adoption. Finally, although traditionally the cloud has been valued based on its ability to reduce cost or increase "business agility," a number of cloud-based patterns such as communications and markets generate value in more profound ways. The economics of cloud services systems, in short, can be a fascinating object of study and are amenable to formal quantitative methods, as well as more qualitative assessments from the behavioral and cognitive sciences. Such economics, in turn, must be considered in the development of regulatory and policy frameworks for the cloud. For example, if pay per use is a key means by which the cloud delivers value and flat rates cause problems such as moral hazard, there are implications regarding network service pricing and traffic prioritization. If IT is strategic, can create wealth, and can drive productivity, as is often the case, it is in a nation's self-interest to eliminate barriers to the diffusion and implementation of IT and to invest in IT infrastructure We are seeing this realization dawn in various countries and regions; for example, the European Commission's Horizon 2020 initiative is the European Union's largest-ever investment: 80 billion euros, including areas such as information and communication technologies (European Union 2014). If the use of cloud computing—both private and public—can optimize resource utilization and speed time to market, then it also can enhance firm and national competitiveness and should be promulgated. On the other hand, cloud computing is not a monolithic good, as various events ranging from privacy intrusions to security breaches have shown, so achieving the right balance of maximal benefits while minimizing issues is an appropriate matter for policy review and fine-tuning.

Notes

1. This discussion is intended to be illustrative and qualitative; it excludes passenger load times, traffic congestion, single taxi round trip and refueling times, etc.
2. See http://opencompute.org.
3. However, simultaneous multiple gestation of twins, triplets, etc., is a parallel process.

References

Akerlof, George. 1970. The Market for "Lemons": Quality Uncertainty and the Market Mechanism. *Quarterly Journal of Economics* 84 (3): 488–500.

Anderson, Chris. 2008. "Free: Why $0.00 Is the Future of Business," *Wired*, 16 (3; February). www.wired.com/techbiz/it/magazine/16-03/ff_free.

Ariely, Dan. 2008. Predictably Irrational: The Hidden Forces That Shape Our Decisions. New York: HarperCollins.

Burgstaller, Bernhard, and Friedrich Pillichshammer. 2009. The Average Distance between Two Points. *Bulletin of the Australian Mathematical Society* 80 (3): 353–359.

Carmon, Ziv, and Dan Ariely. 2000. Focusing on the Forgone: How Value Can Appear So Different to Buyers and Sellers. *Journal of Consumer Research* 27 (December): 360–370.

Chen, M. Keith, Venkat Lakshminarayanan, and Laurie R. Santos. 2006. How Basic Are Behavioral Biases? Evidence from Capuchin Monkey Trading Behavior. *Journal of Political Economy* 114 (3): 517–537.

Dabbagh, Omar. 2010. "12 Weirdest eBay Auctions," *PCWorld*, June 20, 2010. www.pcworld.com/article/199332/12_weirdest_ebay_auctions.html.

Ellens, Wendy, Miroslav Zivkovic, Jacob Akkerboom, Remco Litjens, and Hans van den Berg. 2012. "Performance of Cloud Computing Centers with Multiple Priority Classes," 2012 IEEE Fifth International Conference on Cloud Computing, (June) pp. 245–252.

European Union. 2014. http://ec.europa.eu/programmes/horizon2020/en/what -horizon-2020

Fernandez, José, and Babu Nahata. 2009. "Pay What You Like," April 2009. mpra.ub.uni-muenchen.de/16265/.

Fraser, Patrick. 2011. "Help Me Howard: $201,000 Cell Phone Bill," WSVN Channel 7 News, October 17, 2011. www.wsvn.com/features/articles/helpmehoward/ MI93365.

Google. 2014. "Introducing Sustained Use Discounts—Automatically Pay Less for Sustained Workloads on Compute Engine," (April 4). http://googlecloudplatform .blogspot.com/2014/04/introducing-sustained-use-discounts.html

Hamilton, James. 2009. "The Cost of Latency," Perspectives: James Hamilton's Blog. http://www.perspectives.mvdirona.com/2009/10/31/TheCostOfLatency.aspx.

Kanaracus, Chris. 2012. Amazon Web Services Enacts "Significant" Price Cut. *Computerworld* (March 6). http://www.computerworld.com/s/article/9224916/Amazon _Web_Services_enacts_39_significant_39_price_cut.

Lambrecht, Anja, and Bernd Skiera. 2006. Paying Too Much and Being Happy about It: Existence, Causes, and Consequences of Tariff-Choice Biases. *JMR, Journal of Marketing Research* 43 (May): 212–223.

Mazhelis, Oleksiy, and Pasi Tyrväinen. 2011. "Role of Data Communications in Hybrid Cloud Costs," 2011 37th EUROMICRO Conference on Software Engineering and Advanced Applications (SEAA), (Aug. 30–Sept. 2), pp. 138–145.

Mazhelis, Oleksiy, and Pasi Tyrväinen. 2012. Economic aspects of hybrid cloud infrastructure: User organization perspective. *Information Systems Frontiers* 14 (4): 845–869.

Mazhelis, Oleksiy, Gabriella Fazekas, and Pasi Tyrväinen. 2012. "Impact of Storage Acquisition Intervals on the Cost-Efficiency of the Private vs. Public Storage," 2012 IEEE Fifth International Conference on Cloud Computing, pp. 646–653 (June).

Porter, Michael. 1980. Competitive Strategy: Techniques for Analyzing Industries and Competitors, 196–200. New York: Free Press.

Rodin, Judith, and Ellen J. Langer. 1977. Long-term effects of a control-relevant intervention with the institutionalized aged. *Journal of Personality and Social Psychology* 35 (12): 897–902.

Shampanier, Kristina, Nina Mazar, and Dan Ariely. 2007. Zero as a Special Price: The True Value of Free Products. *Marketing Science* 26 (6): 742–757.

Shankland, Stephen. 2008. "We're All Guinea Pigs in Google's Search Experiment," CNET News, May 29. http://news.cnet.com/8301-10784_3-9954972-7.html.

Vaquero, Luis, Luis Rodero-Merino, Juan Caceres, and Maik Lindner. 2009. A Break in the Clouds: Towards a Cloud Definition. *Computer Communication Review* 39 (1): 50–55.

Weinman, Joe. 2008. "The 10 Laws of Cloudonomics," Gigaom.com, September 7, 2008. http://gigaom.com/2008/09/07/the-10-laws-of-cloudonomics.

Weinman, Joe. 2009. "Peaking through the Clouds," Gigaom.com, June 25, 2009. http://gigaom.com/2009/06/25/peaking-through-the-clouds.

Weinman, Joe. 2010. "The Market for Melons: Quantity Uncertainty and the Market Mechanism," September 6, 2010. http://joeweinman.com/Resources/Joe_Weinman _The_Market_For_Melons.pdf.

Weinman, Joe. 2011a. "Time Is Money: The Value of On-Demand," January 7, 2011. http://www.joeweinman.com/Resources/Joe_Weinman_Time_Is_Money.pdf.

Weinman, Joe. 2011b. "Mathematical Proof of the Inevitability of Cloud Comput-ing," January 8, 2011. http://joeweinman.com/Resources/Joe_Weinman_Inevitability _Of_Cloud.pdf.

Weinman, Joe. 2011c. "Cloud Computing Is NP-Complete," February 1, 2011. http://www.joeweinman.com/Resources/Joe_Weinman_Cloud_Computing_Is _NP-Complete.pdf.

Weinman, Joe. 2011d. "Smooth Operator: The Value of Demand Aggregation," February 27, 2011. http://joeweinman.com/Resources/Joe_Weinman_Smooth _Operator_Demand_Aggregation.pdf.

Weinman, Joe. 2011e. "As Time Goes By: The Law of Cloud Response Time," April 12, 2011. http://www.joeweinman.com/Resources/Joe_Weinman_As_Time_Goes_By .pdf.

Weinman, Joe. 2012. Cloudonomics: The Business Value of Cloud Computing. Hoboken, NJ: John Wiley & Sons.

Weinman, Joe. 2014. "Strategies for Thriving in the Networked Economy of Things," http://blogs.sap.com/innovation/innovation/strategies-thriving-networked -economy-things-01252574.

Yoo, Christopher. 2011. Cloud Computing: Architectural and Policy Implications. *Review of Industrial Organization* 38 (4): 405–421.

2 Finding Security in the Clouds

Marjory S. Blumenthal

The cloud has been getting a lot of attention as a new way of organizing computing and communications. The benefits of cloud computing—in terms of costs, speed (of activity, of change, of innovation), and elasticity (that is, ease of ramping usage up or down)—have broad appeal; they are increasingly noted for small and medium-sized enterprises and entities in developing nations (both categories having comparatively limited means),[1] as well as individuals, from students to people starting new businesses. Vocal proponents include, in addition to major cloud-service vendors, trade associations and other industry groups, academic technologists, and business and technology consultants. In 2011 alone, TechAmerica, the Computer and Communications Industry Association, and the Software & Information Industry Association published reports promoting the development and use of cloud systems and exhorting government restraint—and that was just in the United States.[2] As cloud use has spread and become more accepted, the discussion has been shifting from *whether* to *how*.

The US government itself became a proponent, thanks to the championship by its first federal chief information officer (Vivek Kundra), who produced a federal cloud computing strategy published by the White House (Kundra 2011)—and then left the government to work for a major public cloud provider.[3] Federal adoption of the cloud has promised simplification of government information technology (IT) operations, as well as more nimble adaptation of IT-based activities. The National Institutes of Standards and Technology (NIST), a component of the Department of Commerce, has engaged in an intensive and inclusive process of developing key definitions, reference architecture, and a road map[4] for developing cloud technologies and services; NIST has a tradition of convening broad groups of stakeholders to discuss and agree on directions for new forms of IT, both for use within the US government and for broader use in the economy and globally. In addition, the Department of Commerce has, in conjunction with the National Telecommunications and Information Administration (NTIA), engaged the private sector through an Internet Policy Task Force (IPTF; discussed later in this chapter). Finally, the Department of State engages in international forums and bilateral and multilateral negotiations addressing cloud and other information services as elements of international trade and commerce.[5] This strong, multipronged support from the Obama administration helped to legitimize cloud computing in the United States, thereby further stimulating the marketplace for cloud services.[6] The 2013 disclosures by Edward Snowden of previously secret US government activities (Greenwald 2013) perturbed the market and the government context, but the long-term trend toward more use of the cloud continues.

The cloud-computing narrative has evolved steadily. Often, cloud computing is discussed as a logical, if not inevitable, step in the evolution of computing systems, beginning with centralized time sharing and continuing through contemporary, Internet-based distributed systems and, most recently, the rise of mobile computing and communications, which are generating quantitative and qualitative change in the nature and use of computing systems. Increasingly, cloud computing is linked to the concept of utility computing and the vision of people accessing computing as they would a utility such as electricity. While cloud computing is discussed in terms of its variants (infrastructure, platform, and software as a service—abbreviated IaaS, PaaS, and SaaS, respectively), the utility concept connects to the generalization of "everything as a service" (Joint and Baker 2011). When looking at the cloud through a security lens, its linkage with the concept of a utility—which connotes services such as electricity that are delivered through what have become recognized as critical infrastructures—motivates the questions of whether, when, or how cloud computing might be considered critical infrastructure.

This chapter builds on the author's prior consideration (Blumenthal 2011) of security issues associated with cloud computing—in particular, the public cloud—to contemplate critical infrastructure prospects for the cloud as a thought exercise. It draws from technical, business, and policy literature, as well as conversations with different kinds of experts.

Cloud Security in Context

Attention to security is growing within the cloud-computing narrative, and it is increasingly nuanced. A notable illustration is the evolving guidance from the Cloud Security Alliance (CSA), which in version

3.0 added "Domain 14" on security as a service (CSA 2011)[7] and then proceeded, through a corresponding working group, to solicit input and to develop implementation guidelines. Industry-based groups have situated advocacy for the cloud in the context of changes in the structure and conduct of business. An example is the phenomenon of "de-perimeterization" of enterprises.[8] This is an evolution of connections to the outside world at many levels and for many processes, which limits an enterprise's ability to provide security through some kind of barrier between outside and inside. The process began prior to the emergence of cloud systems, which themselves vitiate traditional notions of perimeters. The phenomenon implies a need for different security strategies than those that have been needed when perimeters seemed more meaningful (Hardy 2014). Proponents continue to acknowledge that the cloud may not be for everyone, or for all data or applications (Norton and Boulton 2014).

As documented previously, there are a number of ways in which the cloud can function as a platform for malice, either through inadvertence, acquiescence, or even bad intentions (Blumenthal 2011). Circumstances reflect the state of the art of the technology, which is continuing to evolve relatively rapidly and features some risks associated with such fundamental aspects as multitenancy and the nature of hypervisors (Blumenthal 2011; Bellovin 2014). The essence of cloud use is the sharing of the underlying computing hardware by users and uses; *multitenancy* refers to the fact that there may be multiple users of a given server, for example, and a *hypervisor* is the software that controls the assignment of hardware to different users and uses, which may be dynamic to allow the service provider to use the hardware efficiently. A cloud security challenge is making sure that one user (tenant) cannot explore or interfere with what another user is doing.

Circumstances also reflect the states of the market and the law, which are evolving, but which at present can be considered to lack the strongest incentives for providers to do as much as they might to enhance security for their users.[9] The public cloud is a source of externally provided—outsourced—services. Although it is sometimes suggested that the history of outsourcing provides ready models for legal mechanisms and motivation for customer comfort, at least one interpretation suggests that legal differences could put cloud users at a disadvantage compared to users of conventional outsourced services (Joint and Baker 2011). A longtime concern about outsourcing is dependence on someone else's personnel. Although the Snowden disclosures were not connected to the cloud, the global attention that they received may be the best cautionary tale in years about the risks from insiders going rogue. Meanwhile, people with malicious intent are as responsive as others to the appeal of the cloud, and by 2014, evidence had begun to emerge about cyberexploitation and cyberattacks being mounted from public cloud environments.[10]

At the heart of the matter are the providers of public-cloud services and their users, who depend substantially on these providers. Cloud advocates point to the benefits of scale economies achievable by providers (at least large and vertically integrated ones). Large systems can avoid the complexity and inconsistency of multiple (especially legacy) systems.[11] Scale provides economies in everything from monitoring for irregularities (e.g., spam filtering in cloud-based email) to hiring and training of key personnel (Molnar and Schechter 2010)[12] (promising growth in managed security as a business). Scale also improves functionality—spam filtering, intrusion detection, and other activities based on big-data analytics work better with more data. These observations lead some to argue that large cloud providers can manage security better than individual users managing their own data centers.[13]

Skeptics, however, point to the potential downside of size. One obvious concern is that along with capability, vulnerability grows with the aggregation of content and activity at a given provider. This is an illustration of a traditional security concern (the "big, fat target") and a concern that began to be discussed in the late 1990s—the risks of a technological monoculture (Schneider 1998). A successful attack on a major public-cloud provider would be a major incident with broad ramifications. Another concern is what comes with growing market power. In mid-2014, NIST responded to a related concern, the difficulty of moving data from one provider to another (vendor lock-in), by creating a working group to address data portability across cloud platforms (Brown 2014); an industry association focusing on the interests of corporate users of public clouds published guidance on portability (and interoperability with customer facilities) in late 2014 (Cloud Standards Customer Council 2014). Vendors may capitalize on market power in different ways. For example, in early 2012, the announcement and later implementation by Google of plans to scan and analyze customer traffic across its services, all of which are supported by cloud technology, illustrated the potential for a large provider to trigger privacy concerns.[14] It remains to be seen how large and powerful leading providers will become or, more generally, how the organization of the public-cloud-supplying industry will evolve as it matures.

The shape of the public-cloud industry and the scale of major providers have become issues for international deliberation. As introduced, the cloud concept is fundamentally location-independent, with economies inhering from the provider's ability to balance and distribute load algorithmically and dynamically. Early leadership of US-based firms (e.g., Google, Amazon, and Salesforce.com), combined with both international competition and differing regional frameworks for the treatment of online content (e.g., for privacy protection in Europe or for speech control in China), have fed the debate about the propriety or desirability of customers seeking to limit the cross-border travels of their data and applications. These concerns were aggravated first by opportunistic rumormongering by non-US entities about the potential for US government exploitation of access to the clouds run by US-based firms.[15] The Snowden disclosures seemed to corroborate those concerns, fueling a major marketplace perturbation and spurring providers around the world to develop and promote their security.

Although the 2011 articulation of a US international strategy for cyberspace is Americentric, it links interoperability, free trade, and joint attention to security.[16] It also underscores the importance of international collaboration for security, complementing earlier collaboration through the Organisation for Economic Cooperation and Development (OECD) and elsewhere.[17] Prior to the Snowden disclosures, US providers had begun to call for international cooperation and coordination in support of an international cloud marketplace. This has become a focus for high-level bilateral negotiations with the European Union, Japan, and Australia, as well as multilateral activity.[18] The situation became more complex and more contentious as a result of the Snowden disclosures, which gave ammunition to those favoring localization of content and a more Balkanized Internet environment. Meanwhile, NIST is leveraging its pioneering work in characterizing cloud technology and issues through participation in related international standards-development activity (e-tech 2014).

What would it mean to look at the public cloud as critical infrastructure? The question is becoming more important, assuming that (1) the market for public cloud systems will continue to grow, (2) incentives problems—a chronic challenge for cybersecurity—are likely to persist (even if they improve somewhat),[19] and (3) progress in security remains slow given enduring challenges in cybersecurity and introduction of new challenges associated with the cloud. The following discussion addresses that question for the purpose of furthering the analysis (without advocating one way or the other).

Critical Infrastructure in Context

As the name suggests, critical infrastructure is particularly important to the functioning of an economy, society, or country.[20] Critical infrastructure discourse emerged in the mid- to late-1990s with the President's Commission on Critical Infrastructure Protection (PCCIP 1997). Among other things, PCCIP served to focus some of the conversations within government, as well as expanding those between government and industry, about cybersecurity. Although cybersecurity concerns were acknowledged by government and industry in the 1990s, constructive activity was bounded in the face of rapid growth in commercial Internet activity, the race to introduce new software and software-based services, and enthusiasm about national and global information infrastructure (Blumenthal 1999).

US public policy attention to critical infrastructures has been driven by governmental concern to protect public interests in a context in which the infrastructures are largely owned privately. (Greater public ownership, control, or both simplify matters in other countries.) That tension between public and private interests is fundamental to government attempts to promote, as levers of critical infrastructure protection policy[21] and (to some extent) practice, public-private partnership and public-private information sharing, as well as to facilitate relevant private-private information sharing. Various mechanisms for partnership and sharing have been proposed and tried, generating cumulative experience but less than commensurate impact, as evidenced by repeated proposals for new or modified mechanisms often relating to partnerships and information sharing. As even the Department of Homeland Security (DHS) acknowledges, "[a]lthough articulating the value proposition to the government is easier to achieve, it is often more difficult to articulate the direct benefits of participation for the private sector" (DHS 2009).[22]

Over the past almost two decardes spanning multiple presidencies, the policy framework for critical infrastructure protection—including the list of designated critical infrastructures and approaches to associated sectors—has evolved with Executive Orders and other presidential directives, legislation, and the emergence and evolution of the DHS.[23] Some of these steps were prompted by the terrorist attacks of 9/11, which breathed life and urgency into discussions of critical infrastructure and its protection in addition to spawning related bureaucracy. The issuance of Executive Order 13636, "Improving Critical Infrastructure Cybersecurity," in February 2013 (Executive Order 13636) has been characterized by some as a response to the difficulty—extending over a decade—of enacting legislation in this arena (Fischer et al. 2013).

Notwithstanding time and experience with the concept, defining critical infrastructures seems to remain an art[24] that is subject to politics as well as policy, with implications for resource allocation as well as innovation.[25] In the late 1990s, PCCIP, together with preparations to handle the so-called Y2K problem, potential software issues as the calendar approached the year 2000 (Mitchell 2009), helped to enlarge the set of technologies and industries beyond, in particular, conventional (and regulated) telecommunications that were deemed critical by government. (It is worth noting that concerted action was comparatively easy to achieve for Y2K because not only was there a specific time when a problem was predicted to occur, but also the kind of problem was relatively well understood.) The challenges of achieving a holistic approach endure; some of the historic siloed treatment of telecommunications security and cybersecurity persists.

(Inter)dependence

Critical infrastructures do not stand alone. Among the more capital-intensive critical infrastructures today, certain ones—electric power and telecommunications—are themselves fundamental to the Internet and cloud computing (and, of course, telecommunications depends on electricity). All critical infrastructures today, whether delivering a physical service (e.g., water, transportation systems) or something less tangible (e.g., banking and finance) can be described as significantly depending on IT generally.[26] This circumstance has grown over time and continues to grow, with sensors (and actuators) increasingly equipped with processing capability and connected to networks for longer-distance communication, including the Internet. Thus, for example, the proliferation of electronic equipment for diagnostics and for delivering treatments, as well as for administrative information management, makes health care more dependent on computers, telecommunications, and electricity. This trend already presents a growing cybersecurity challenge,[27] which may be compounded by how cloud computing is adopted in the sector. As more patients—that is, people—embrace wearable devices or use smartphones to collect and analyze personal health-related information, often using cloud-based services, dependence on the cloud will grow, and with it perceptions of criticality (Barcena, Wueest, and Lau 2014).

Dependence of any critical activity on the Internet, per se, can arouse concern, given the openness that is associated with both its benefits and some of its side effects. In the limit case, dependence on public cloud and other external services risks "pervasive connectivity leading to the point where the Internet itself can become the corporate network" (Dorey and Leite 2011). Indeed, the DHS already considers the Internet a key resource (DHS 2009, p. 32).

Some cloud services themselves depend on other cloud services (Mulazzani et al. 2011). All cloud services depend on power infrastructures, even if they have built some of that infrastructure themselves. Power outages have already compromised cloud services (Bradley 2011).

As these observations suggest, critical infrastructure is in part about dependencies (in the engineering sense) and interdependence generally. Ironically, in the months preceding the Fukushima nuclear disaster in 2011, a Japan-based organization, the Global Inter-Cloud Technology Forum,[28] pointed to the potential for federated clouds to assist one another by sharing resources in the event of a crisis—interdependence can be helpful as well as a source of risk (which, of course, is why systems evolve with dependencies in the first place). In the meantime, it is not surprising that a new line of disaster-recovery-as-a-service offerings has emerged—it signals that some people may use one cloud to back up what they do in another.[29]

Given the concerted effort in the US federal government to adopt the cloud, joint efforts of government and industry have begun to address potential risks associated with government—itself a kind of critical infrastructure—becoming more dependent on cloud services, which are themselves dependent on other services. There are certifications of provider offerings under long-standing federal frameworks,[30] and as of mid-2012, there is a framework designed for federal users of cloud services, the Federal Risk and Authorization Management Program (FedRAMP), "a government-wide program that provides a standardized approach to security assessment, authorization, and continuous monitoring for cloud products and services."[31] Whether FedRAMP proves to be a positive force or just another box to check for providers remains to be seen. Implementation has been slow.

The growing complexity of critical infrastructure has led to a growing emphasis on risk management; complete prevention of problems, long desired by cybersecurity experts, is recognized as unrealistic. Risk management requires identification and analysis of risks, which in turn requires identifying and analyzing vulnerabilities and potential threats, which are the key determinants of risk. A detailed exploration of how to think about cloud-related risks was developed in Europe in 2009 by the European

Network and Information Security Agency (ENISA) as both interests in and questions about the cloud began to grow; it remains the guidance from that source (ENISA 2009).

The US Cybersecurity Framework for critical infrastructure (and associated road map) developed in response to Executive Order 13636 illustrates the emphasis on risk management (NIST 2014). That framework is aimed at the private sector. Also providing a kind of framework, aimed at public and private sectors, is the National Infrastructure Protection Plan, which calls for risk management that integrates cyber, physical, and human elements (DHS 2013). It illustrates how contemporary discourse about critical infrastructure protection has begun to emphasize resilience, a quality that the public cloud could help to foster even as it generates new questions. Within the federal government itself, risk management is central to the implementation of the Federal Information Security Management Act of 2002 (FISMA), which, like its predecessors, remains a work in progress—rigorous analysis of vulnerabilities and threats is hard, and it needs continual monitoring and updating (GAO 2013).

NIST security guidance to federal agencies addresses risks to federal agencies from use of the public cloud as a kind of external service, suggesting additional measures such as encrypting content to be stored by a cloud provider (NIST 2013, p. 20). Interestingly, commentators have begun to speculate about the potential for cloud insurance—notwithstanding the failure of an effective cybersecurity market to grow—and at least one product has been announced (Kelly 2012).

Industrial Anxieties

Although criticality may be an indicator of importance, industry is clearly leery of a designation that carries with it a variety of burdens.[32] In particular, there is a higher security bar associated with critical-infrastructure protection than for protection of more conventional enterprises or infrastructures.[33] Those expectations come with a variety of costs, and possibly greater expectations of liability. The emergence of the "key resources" concept (as in "critical infrastructure and key resources," part of the elaboration of the critical infrastructure concept in the first decade of the twenty-first century) reflects such concerns. It allows industry and government to focus protection efforts on the most critical or key resources rather than take the more costly route of securing an entire infrastructure at the highest level. For example, the Internet Protocol (IP) backbone is a key resource for major communications providers; their services depend on its operation. More generally, key resources for communications and information services are often aggregation points, such as undersea cables or large data centers, which imply that more is at risk if such points are compromised.

Among the enduring challenges for policy makers is the heterogeneity of the industry landscape, including within such sectors as telecommunications and information services. Conventional telecommunications providers (given traditional regulation and both government-specific and broader public interests in access to communications) have historically been at the government table to discuss reliability, interoperability, and security. They have a history of interacting with the Federal Communications Commission (FCC) and state public utility/service commissions, and their leadership has been engaged in dialogue with government about the reliability of telecommunications through such special bodies as the National Security Telecommunications Advisory Committee.[34] Newer information service providers have not, however, a reality that has vexed policy making relating to cybersecurity beginning with the rise of the Internet as a commercial venue in the 1990s and then the rise of social media in the following decade.[35]

The fact that major public-cloud providers—which may be only a few years old—do not have much history of coordination and cooperation with government complicates prospects for a path forward that is collaborative between government and industry. This divide reflects company and industry history with government regulation: Not surprisingly, companies and industries (e.g., conventional telecommunications) that have had a history of government regulation have seemed more responsive to government overtures than those that have not, which is not to say that further regulatory attention has been welcome.[36] Whatever progress had been made through outreach by government officials and through companies' own recognition of the growing challenge of cybersecurity was confounded by the Snowden disclosures, which undermined trust in the federal government.

Prior to those disclosures and capitalizing on positive business attitudes toward the early Obama administration, the quest for an effective public-private balance and the politics of industry-government collaboration were demonstrated by the IPTF developed by the Department of Commerce (IPTF 2011). That task force argued that a critical infrastructure designation is at least premature for the information services addressed—it addressed the issue proactively or, perhaps, preemptively. Its June 2011 report introduced the "Internet and Information Innovation Sector (I3S)" (inviting comment on the concept), which it expressly excluded from consideration as critical infrastructure:

The I3S includes functions and services that create or utilize the Internet or networking services and have large potential for growth, entrepreneurship, and vitalization of the economy, but would fall outside the classification of covered critical infrastructure as defined by existing law and Administration policy. Business models may differ, but the following functions and services are included in the I3S:

- provision of information services and content;
- facilitation of the wide variety of transactional services available through the Internet as an intermediary;
- storage and hosting of publicly accessible content; and support of users' access to content or transaction activities, including, but not limited to application, browser, social network, and search providers.

The I3S is comprised of companies, from small business to "brick and mortar-based firms" with online services to large companies that only exist on the Internet, that are significantly impacted by cybersecurity concerns, yet do not have the same level of operational criticality that would cause them to be designated as covered critical infrastructure. (IPTF 2011, 2–3)

Whereas the 2002 National Strategy for Homeland Security referred to the "information and telecommunications sector" (US Office of Homeland Security 2002, 30), the IPTF approach is consistent with the 2009 and 2013 National Infrastructure Protection Plans (DHS 2009, 2013), which combine IT and communications for sector oversight but identify two sectors, echoing the DHS practice of separating telecommunications and cyber.

The IPTF discussion differentiated information services from core and underlying telecommunications services; it acknowledged dependency but focused on a difference in kind for the industries in question. There was a clear interest in protecting and preserving relatively rapid innovation in this new sector, with an assumption that telecommunications moves more slowly and is perhaps irredeemably subject to regulation—it is a critical infrastructure. The distinction evokes memories of debates from the 1980s and 1990s about enhanced services (Computer Inquiry II) and the implications of layered service models for telecommunications providers and their regulation (Telecommunications Act of 1996).[37]

Although not clearly explained by the task force, the rationale for distinguishing the I3S and treating it liberally can be attributed in part to a division of labor among agencies, with two components of the Department of Commerce, NIST and the NTIA, focusing on commercial and ostensibly noncritical industries, and DHS focusing on critical infrastructure, which is acknowledged to depend on the Internet and "core telecommunications." Ironically, the report acknowledged public input that was not only critical of a number of government players, but also requested fewer points of contact for the private sector.[38] Unfortunately, the history of US government and cybersecurity has long featured divides among agencies focusing on the economy and those focusing on security; divide and conquer may be practical for some purposes, but it may also perpetuate policy compromises and shortcomings.

A key IPTF assumption, evident in a variety of Obama administration activities, seemed to be that "certain industries are important to innovation and economic growth and may be more responsive to flexible structures for promoting security that is in their own interest" (IPTF 2011, 9). Consistent with the noncritical designation, the recommendations of the IPTF report focused on consensus standards, voluntary codes of conduct, disclosure (of practices, security incidents, and so on), and public education, with third-party assessment of compliance or quality of effort. With regulation eschewed as likely to chill innovation and growth, there was a call for incentives instead. At the same time, there was recognition that past incentives have not worked well and that many incentives proposed to the IPTF were not practicable. As with repeated calls for public-private partnership and information sharing in critical-infrastructure discussions, these calls for incentives-based approaches do not explain why success would be more likely this time. There was also a call for federal development of "a broadly stated, uniform set of cyber management principles for I3S entities to follow," something encouraged by a variety of public and private entities beginning at least in the 1990s.[39]

In one of the few places in the IPTF report where the cloud is singled out, technology is flagged as an important mechanism for protection: "As more computing services are based in the cloud and move further away from centralized enterprises, automating security will likely become even more important than it is today." (IPTF 2011, 18) Enhanced cybersecurity was thus linked to reducing dependence on human discretion and decision making by both cloud providers and users. After all, it continues to be the case that even when good guidance about cybersecurity is available, it is often not used—even in critical infrastructures (GAO 2011). That is a reason that automated support has become an interest in cybersecurity research circles.[40]

Scaling Up: Just a Matter of Time?

Cloud services continue to evolve: they are comparatively new, their aggregation points—although fundamental to the business model—are not as large as they may become (while being comparatively distributed), and they are not necessarily critical to some or all of their users and customers. These observations support the interests of those seeking to nurture this young capability and associated industry. An obvious question is about possible tipping points: When do such facilities become so big and important to the economy that they are deemed critical? The concept is being explored already in Europe, where follow-up to 2009 guidance on cloud-related risk assessment (ENISA 2009) included an examination of the criticality of cloud services, as well as their implications for governance. This diagnosis was positive:

From the scenarios and the data about uptake and incidents we draw a number of conclusions. Cloud computing is critical: Cloud computing usage is growing and in the near future the vast majority of organizations will rely on some form of cloud computing services. This makes cloud computing services critical in themselves. When cyber attacks and cyber disruptions happen, millions of users are affected. Cloud computing is being adopted also in critical sectors, like finance, energy, and transport. (ENISA 2013)

Both the public-cloud industry and the user base will grow; market forecasts, while clearly speculative, call for dramatic growth,[41] and the encouragement for cloud use by such major IT users as the US federal government can only further that growth. Indeed, former federal-cloud champion Vivek Kundra had not only called for the closure of hundreds of data centers as part of his cloud-promoting strategy, he also envisioned consolidation into "three major federal data centers, Digital Fort Knoxes" (Lipowicz 2011)—the metaphor alone evokes criticality, albeit in a government-controlled context. Vendors have been honing offerings over the last few years: Amazon Web Services has launched AWS GovCloud (US) Region, "an isolated AWS Region designed to allow US government agencies and customers to move sensitive workloads into the cloud by addressing their specific regulatory and compliance requirements."[42] Google has promoted Google Apps for Government at the federal and state levels,[43] and Microsoft, with the longest history of any public-cloud provider in working with government, targets government clients with its offerings, too.[44,45]

International trade policy has homed in on three aspects of cloud services, each of which could be seen as having at least the potential for criticality: privacy, security, and localization or restriction of the free flow of information (common for financial services and governmental entities) (Berry and Reisman 2012). One of the most important developments arising from the Snowden disclosures was an increase in concerns about privacy, especially in the United States. The cloud has become the platform of choice for mobile apps and for a growing body of data generated by embedded sensors, including those in smart devices in the home or the external environment, which may be Internet-connected and which involve cloud platforms for key service-related software and integration of data from customers, ostensibly to deliver and improve various services (President's Council of Advisors on Science and Technology 2014). Publicity about associated big data and what can be gleaned from big-data analytics has raised questions about what happens to data about individuals and their behavior that are stored in the cloud.

Concerned about calls for localization, cloud-service-provider lobbying against requirements for data to be stored in a given jurisdiction on the grounds that it is contrary to a global economy, with some governmental support in international negotiations (Perine 2012), reinforces the expectations that individual public-cloud providers will grow. As noted previously, the Snowden disclosures have fueled challenges to the growth of US providers, who have been global leaders, but even if the result is a larger number of major providers, growing demand as well as scale economies are consistent with the growth of individual providers. Hence, as with conventional utilities decades ago, it is likely to be only a matter of time— with attendant growth in scale—before large public-cloud services become seen more broadly as critical, given how much (information, processes, or both) they may aggregate and how much users may come to depend on them.[46]

Adding to the potential for concern is the prospect of the Intercloud, which hinges on the realization of the potential for cloud providers to interconnect, especially horizontally (there is already vertical connection through which specialized service providers such as Dropbox piggyback on larger providers such as Amazon [Mulazzani et al. 2011]). The Intercloud will create new capabilities, and in so doing, it will build in new dependencies and possibly create new security concerns. In addition to work to develop technical standards to support interoperability of cloud systems generally,[47] there is specific work relating to the federation of cloud systems that could support all manner of exchanges between clouds (Villegas et al. 2012; Rochwerger et al. 2011). Federation could have a number of impacts on the eventual shape of the cloud-provider industry. For example, it could support the emergence of services that specialize in a given service layer and of brokers that foster connections between providers of different kinds of services in the context of a larger, multilayer, and multiservice marketplace.[48] Whether interconnection enhances service availability (by providing redundancy) depends on the specifics of the architecture; more generally, both architecture and operations will affect the implications of the Intercloud for security and reliability. Even if dominant providers resist interconnection and openness, some degree of interconnection is likely, bringing with it even greater interdependence.

Conclusion

Government officials and industry leaders, as illustrated by the IPTF, make a strong case that it is premature to constrain the young cloud services industry, which could happen with the chilling and distorting effects of premature regulation. Although US critical infrastructure protection policy has emphasized voluntarism and respected the free-enterprise tradition, it has aspects of regulation and it may reinforce other regulatory regimes.[49] Entities deemed to be critical infrastructure are subject at least to regular expectations for vulnerability assessments and reporting, which add to costs.[50] Greater attention to the supply chain for technology underlying public cloud services, given the growing appreciation for the supply chain as a factor in cybersecurity,[51] could also add cost. Supply-chain elements include the hardware (e.g., servers and chips) and software that a public-cloud provider uses to deliver its services, and attention to the supply chain implies understanding who made the component, how, and where, as well as an ability to test whether it does what it is supposed to do (and nothing else).

In the United States, a separate development could add reinforcement to any new contemplation of regulation: in mid-2014, FCC chairman Tom Wheeler suggested that one avenue for maintaining "network neutrality" for the Internet—a response to growing economic and societal dependence on the Internet—is to consider applying conventional telecommunications regulation (Wheeler 2014). Open Internet Order (FCC 2015) reclassifying mobile broadband as a telecommunications service subject to regulatory oversight with "forbearance" (i.e., limited expected scope of regulatory attention); impacts will depend on how any legal challenges are resolved. This new controversy illustrates the continuing challenge presented by privately owned infrastructures that are important to the public interest.

Monitoring societal dependence on the public-cloud-services industry to understand what aspects of it may become critical and when that seems to be happening—that is, when we have hit a tipping point—would be a logical complement to US government leadership in fostering cloud adoption. It would also be consistent with the history of public policy relating to critical infrastructure,[52] which has featured iterated planning by individual sectors and overall, attention to cybersecurity within all critical infrastructures, the promotion of information sharing for mutual learning about risks among government and business entities,[53] and the spread of critical infrastructure protection as a concern around the world (ENISA 2012).

US cloud providers leery of regulation can leverage Americans' popular and political ambivalence about the appropriate posture of government toward cybersecurity and critical infrastructure protection.[54] It will be interesting to see whether the industry groups that have been so quick to advise governments on the value of cloud services to the economy (and the importance of allowing providers to reach their potential) will acknowledge the value of monitoring success as measured by growing dependence on the public cloud, with all that that may imply about protecting that accomplishment (DHS 2013).

Notes

This work was supported in part by ONR award number N000140910037. Constructive feedback on an early draft from Eric Burger and Roger J. Cochetti is gratefully acknowledged, as well as constructive conversation with John C. Nagengast and Chris Boyer and feedback from Steven Bellovin, Ari Schwartz, Jeffrey Glick, and Charles Nelson on a later draft. Responsibility for the content remains that of the author.

1. See, for example, Banerjee et al. (2011), and also Friedman (2011). Among start-ups, observers have noted the popularity of such cloud-based services as QuickBooks for accounting, Google Analytics for business intelligence, Salesforce.com for CRM, and Dropbox for storage. See McKendrick (2011).

2. See Cloud2 (2011), Computer and Communications Industry Association (2011), and Software & Information Industry Association (2011). Also in 2011, a cross-industry group dedicated to providing customer (user-organization) perspectives on cloud systems, security and standards was organized, the Cloud Standards Customer Council. Among other things, that Council has provided guidance on negotiating public-cloud security protections, an attempt to help balance the knowhow of vendors. See Cloud Standards Customer Council (2013).

3. Kundra left the government after two-and-a-half years, going first to Harvard University and then to Salesforce.com, a leading SaaS vendor. See Henschen (2012) and Ravindranath (2014).

4. See the NIST Cloud Computing document site at http://collaborate.nist.gov/twiki-cloud-computing/bin/view/CloudComputing/Documents.

5. For example, the European Union–United States Trade Principles for Information and Communication Technology Services calls for "free flow of information across borders" (Office of the United States Trade Representative 2011). More broadly

among developed nations, the Organisation for Economic Cooperation and Development (OECD) principles for Internet policy making call on nations to "promote and enable the cross-border delivery of services" (OECD 2011).

6. The high-level and high-impact support echoes the Clinton administration's support for "information infrastructure," which was eventually characterized as support for the Internet.

7. See the implementation guidelines at https://cloudsecurityalliance.org/research/secaas/.

8. The term *de-perimeterization* has been attributed to the Jericho Forum. See https://www.opengroup.org/jericho/deperim.htm and https://www.opengroup.org/jericho/cloud_cube_model_v1.0.pdf.

9. See, for example, Molnar and Schechter (2010), Joint and Baker (2011), and Villegas et al. (2012).

10. For example, a US small-business innovator tracked a cybersecurity problem to a Chinese public-cloud platform. According to an article discussing the experience, "It's common that these attacks come through cloud computing services. A quarterly threat assessment by the private Internet security firm Solutionary ... said that 'the cloud has become a preferred mode for attackers' and that 'use of major hosting provides [*sic*], such as Amazon or Google, allows malware distributors to originate traffic from trusted address spaces that ... would not likely draw suspicion based on IP addresses alone" (Mufson 2014).

11. This is the motivation for the US government, especially the Department of Defense. See, for example, Censer (2010) and Shachtman (2012).

12. "The good news is that the same forces concentrating data in enormous datacenters will also aid in using collective security expertise more effectively" (Song 2012).

13. One specialized illustration of the appeal of large vendors that can handle growing business volume securely is the growth in the number of universities moving from their own delivery of basic online services (email, calendar, and some office-productivity applications) to using Google's offerings (Google Apps for Education, http://www.google.com/apps/intl/en/edu, and with respect to security specifically, http://www.google.com/apps/intl/en/edu/privacy.html).

14. See Google's privacy policies at https://www.google.com/policies.

15. See, for example, Stokes (2011) and Rauf (2011).

16. "The United States will work internationally to promote an open, interoperable, secure, and reliable information and communications infrastructure that supports international trade and commerce, strengthens international security, and fosters free expression and innovation. To achieve that goal, we will build and sustain an environment in which norms of responsible behavior guide states' actions, sustain partnerships, and support the rule of law in cyberspace." (White House 2011, 8).

17. "The United States will facilitate cybersecurity capacity-building abroad, bilaterally and through multilateral organizations, so that each country has the means to protect its digital infrastructure, strengthen global networks, and build closer

partnerships in the consensus for open, interoperable, secure, and reliable networks" (ibid., 14).

18. For example, the Transatlantic Economic Council lists cloud computing as an area of cooperation in its Joint Statement issued on November 29, 2011. See Transatlantic Economic Council (2011).

19. See Blumenthal (2011) for incentives challenges relating to cybersecurity and cloud providers.

20. The Critical Infrastructures Protection Act of 2001 defines the term *critical infrastructure* as "systems and assets, whether physical or virtual, so vital to the United States that the incapacity or destruction of such systems and assets would have a debilitating impact on security, national economic security, national public health or safety, or any combination of these matters." 42 USC §5195c(e) See also the DHS website discussion of critical infrastructure protection at http://www.dhs .gov/files/programs/critical.shtm.

21. See, for example, the various iterations of the National Infrastructure Protection Plan and related documentation on the DHS website at http://www.dhs.gov/ national-infrastructure-protection-plan.

22. Note that the latest version is DHS (2013).

23. An overview can be found in Moteff (2011).

24. The DHS maintains (and evolves) a national inventory of critical infrastructures and key resources, along with "basic information about the relationships, dependencies, and interdependencies among various assets, systems, and networks."

25. According to the Congressional Research Service, "There is some debate among policy makers about the implications of an ambiguous or changing list of critical infrastructures. Ambiguity about what constitutes a critical infrastructure (or key resource) could lead to inefficient use of limited homeland security resources. For example, private sector representatives state that they need clear and stable definitions of asset criticality so they will know exactly what assets to protect, and how well to protect them. Otherwise, they risk protecting too many facilities, protecting the wrong facilities, or both. On the other hand, arbitrarily limiting the number of critical infrastructures a priori due to resource constraints might miss a dangerous vulnerability. Clear 'criticality' criteria will also be important if federal agencies intend to implement and enforce any potential future security regulations related to critical infrastructure." See Moteff and Parfomak (2004).

26. Whereas conventionally critical infrastructures may have been defined in part by specialized technologies, which may still be important, the convergence of so many industries and processes on the use of often general-purpose as well as specialized information technologies [e.g., supervisory control and data acquisition (SCADA) systems) raises its own questions about vulnerabilities.

27. See, for example, O'Harrow (2012) and Zetter (2014).

28. See http://www.gictf.jp.

29. See, for example, Cisco discusses Disaster as a Service at http://www.cisco. com/c/en/us/td/docs/solutions/Hybrid_Cloud/DRaaS/1-0/DRaaS_1-0.html;and

Microsoft acquired a Disaster as a Service entrepreneur to incorporate the capability into its Azure cloud offering: http://azure.microsoft.com/blog/2014/07/16/azure-site-recovery-now-offers-disaster-recovery-for-any-physical-or-virtualized-it-environment-with-inmage-scout-2/.

30. See, for example, Brodkin (2011).

31. See the US General Services Administration FedRAMP portal: http://cloud.cio.gov/fedramp.

32. This discussion focuses on cybersecurity and related objectives. There is an additional set of issues (e.g., universal access of some kind) associated with utilities, inasmuch as most conventional critical infrastructures are also regulated public utilities, but that topic is outside of the scope of this chapter.

33. That higher bar is one reason why a prominent cybersecurity study group (of which the author was a member) focused key recommendations on critical infrastructures. See CSIS Cybersecurity Commission (2008).

34. See http://www.dhs.gov/nstac.

35. Progress has been made, as evidenced by the company roster currently involved in the National Coordinating Center for Telecommunications (http://www.dhs.gov/national-coordinating-center-communications) and the membership of the National Security Telecommunications Advisory Committee (https://www.dhs.gov/nstac-members).

36. Historically, regulated enterprises have personnel and practices attuned to coping with regulation; engaging with government personnel is comparatively familiar and understandable for their management.

37. Telecommunications Act of 1996, codified at 47 USC.

38. "This echoed a theme throughout the comments that the federal government ought to work hard to constrain and, wherever possible, reduce the federal points-of-contact on cybersecurity issues, so that coordination is less fragmented and less daunting to the public" (IPTF 2011, 34–35).

39. For example, the concept of Generally accepted System Security Principles (GSSP) was advanced in 1991 to foster better practices in developing and using computer systems (CSTB 1991).

40. The US government coordinates support for cybersecurity research, including efforts aimed at automating cybersecurity, and documents that support through the Networking and Information Technology Research and Development (NITRD) Program (NITRD 2014).

41. For example, in spring 2012, market researcher IDC forecast that cloud-related revenue could exceed $1 trillion by 2015. See McCafferty (2012).

42. http://aws.amazon.com/govcloud-us.

43. http://www.google.com/enterprise/apps/government/benefits.html.

44. http://www.microsoft.com/government/en-us/Guides/Pages/cloud-computing.aspx.

45. http://www.microsoft.com/government/en-us/products/Pages/azure.aspx.

46. To carry the thought exercise further, one might consider the case of social media. Most people's immediate reactions are to dismiss the possibility of Facebook, Twitter, and other similar sites becoming critical infrastructure. But an argument can at least be made that systems used by large segments of populations and businesses, including some leaders, to communicate and to plan are growing in importance to society and the economy. Tampering with them—not just physically, but also by manipulating the information presented—could cause problems. Of course, social media may represent the most popular use of cloud computing (in the literal sense), and they also are highly dependent on the actions of their providers, who structure the kinds of interactions that users experience and who do not offer to individual consumers the kinds of negotiated agreements the large organizational users can forge with their cloud service providers. Such long-term prospects for social media were explored during the Summer Hard Problem Program of the Office of the Director of National Intelligence in 2010 (in which the author participated).

47. For example, the Institute for Electrical and Electronics Engineers (IEEE) Standards Association features a Cloud Computing Initiative, which is developing a road map and standards relating to the portability of data and applications and to interfaces for interoperability among clouds. See Kowalenko (2012).

48. With federation, one layer might request services of a lower layer in either the local or a different provider. All providers need not implement every layer, consistent with multiple service suppliers connected to satisfy a single application request, implying the possibility of specialized providers of single layers—see Villegas et al. (2012).

49. The Congressional Research Service analysis of Executive Order 13636 makes this point—see Fischer et al. (2013).

50. As noted earlier, the CSIS Cybersecurity Commission argued for critical infrastructure sectors to be in the vanguard for more stringent cybersecurity efforts.

51. Dependence concerns extend down to the building-block level. Government and industry both have concerns about the supply chain since the security of a service can depend on how it is delivered. At issue are components, pieces of equipment incorporating components, and systems built from pieces of equipment—nested dependencies. Companies like AT&T, as well as at least some federal government agencies, use trusted-vendor programs, leveraging their market power as large customers.

52. Not to mention the history of government attention to providers of IT goods and services that have achieved large market shares.

53. Executive Order 13636 focused on information sharing, and the Obama administration has encouraged information sharing for cybersecurity generally. See, for example, http://www.whitehouse.gov/blog/2014/04/10/getting-serious-about -information-sharing-cybersecurity.

54. "There is limited support for government mandates, but there is no broad-based call for government to stay away, even among Republicans." See Nakashima and Cohen (2012).

References

Banerjee, Prith, 2011. Everything as a Service: Powering the New Information Economy. *IEEE Computer* 44 (3), 36–43.

Barcena, Mario Ballano, Candid Wueest, and Hon Lau. 2014. "How safe is your quantified self?" Version 1.0, July 30, Symantec. Available at http://www.symantec. com/connect/blogs/how-safe-your-quantified-self-tracking-monitoring-and -wearable-tech.

Bellovin, Steven M. 2014. "Clouds and Virtualization." Unpublished manuscript.

Berry, Renee, and Matthew Reisman. 2012. Policy Challenges of Cross-Border Cloud Computing. *Journal of International Commerce and Economics* 4 (2): 1–38.

Blumenthal, Marjory S. 2011. Is Security Lost in the Clouds? *Communications & Strategies*, Quarter 1 (81): 69–86.

Blumenthal, Marjory. 1999. The Politics and Policies of Enhancing Trustworthiness for Information Systems. *Communication Law and Policy* 4 (4): 513–555.

Bradley, Tony. 2011. "Lessons from Amazon Cloud Lightning Strike Outage." *PC World*, August 10. Available at http://www.pcworld.com/article/237673/lessons_ from_amazon_cloud_lightning_strike_outage.html.

Brodkin, Jon. 2011. Amazon Cloud Earns Key FISMA Government Security Accreditation." Arstechnica.com, September 15. Available at http://arstechnica.com/ business/news/2011/09/amazon-cloud-earns-fisma-government-security -accreditation.ars.

Brown, Evelyn. 2014. "NIST Seeks Members for Three New Cloud Computing Working Groups." *NIST Tech Beat*, June 23. Available at http://www.nist.gov/itl/ antd/cloud-062314.cfm.

Censer, Marjorie. 2010. "Federal Government Moves Forward with 'Cloud-First' Plan for New Technology." *Washington Post*, December 5. Available at http://www .washingtonpost.com/wp-dyn/content/article/2010/12/05/AR2010120503320. html.

CSIS Cybersecurity Commission. 2008. *Securing Cyberspace for the 44th Presidency. CSIS Commission on Cybersecurity for the 44th Presidency.* Washington, DC: Center for Strategic and International Studies.

CSTB. 1991. *Computers at Risk: Safe Computing in the Information Age.* In Computer Science and Telecommunications Board, National Research Council. Washington, DC: National Academy Press.

Cloud Security Alliance (CSA). 2011. *Security Guidance for Critical Areas of Focus in Cloud Computing v3.0.* Available at http://www.cloudsecurityalliance.org/guidance/ csaguide.v3.0.pdf.

Cloud Standards Customer Council. 2013. *Cloud Security Standards: What to Expect & What to Negotiate.* October. Available at http://www.cloudstandardscustomer-council.org/Cloud_Security_Standards_Landscape_Final.pdf.

Cloud Standards Customer Council. 2014. *Interoperability and Portability for Cloud Computing: A Guide.* November. Available at http://www.cloudstandardscustomer council.org/CSCC-Cloud-Interoperability-and-Portability.pdf.

Cloud2. 2011. *Cloud First, Cloud Fast: Recommendations for Innovation, Leadership, and Job Creation.* Commission on the Leadership Opportunity in US Deployment of the Cloud, TechAmerica Foundation. September 21. Available at http://www.techameri cafoundation.org/cloud-commission.

Computer and Communications Industry Association. 2011. *Public Policy for the Cloud: How Policymakers Can Enable Cloud Computing.* July. Available at http://www.ccianet.org.

Department of Homeland Security (DHS). 2009. *National Infrastructure Protection Plan.* Washington, DC. Available at http://www.dhs.gov/xlibrary/assets/NIPP_Plan.pdf.

Department of Homeland Security (DHS). 2013. *NIPP 2013: Partnering for Critical Infrastructure Security and Resilience.* Washington, DC. Available at http://www.dhs.gov/publication/nipp-2013-partnering-critical-infrastructure-security-and-resilience.

Dorey, P. G., and A. Leite. 2011. Commentary: Cloud Computing – A Security Problem or Solution? *Information Security Technical Report* 16 (3): 89–96.

e-tech. 2014. "Standards in the Cloud: Interview with Don Deutsch, Chairman of ISO/IEC JTC 1/SC 38, Distributed Application Platforms and Services." *e-tech,* January/February 2014. Available at http://www.iec.ch/etech2014/etech_0114/tech-7.htm.

European Network and Information Security Agency (ENISA). 2009. *Cloud Computing Risk Assessment.* European Union Agency for Network and Information Security. Available at http://www.enisa.europa.eu.

European Network and Information Security Agency (ENISA). 2013. *Critical Cloud Computing: A CIIP Perspective on Cloud Computing Services.* February 14. Available at https://www.enisa.europa.eu.

Executive Order 13636. 2013. Improving Critical Infrastructure Cybersecurity. 78 *Federal Register* 11739, February 19. Available at http://www.whitehouse.gov/the-press-office/2013/02/12/executive-order-improving-critical-infrastructure-cybersecurity.

FCC. 2015. "FCC Adopts Strong, Sustainable Rules to Protect the Open Internet." Press release, Federal Communications Commission. Available at: http://www.fcc.gov/document/fcc-adopts-strong-sustainable-rules-protect-open-internet.

Fischer, Eric A. 2013. *The 2013 Cybersecurity Executive Order: Overview and Considerations for Congress. Report R42984.* Washington, DC: Congressional Research Service.

Friedman, Thomas L. 2011. "One Country, Two Revolutions." *The New York Times,* SR11, October 22.

Government Accountability Office (GAO). 2011. *Critical Infrastructure Protection: Cybersecurity Guidance Is Available, but More Can Be Done to Promote Its Use. GAO-12–92.* December. Washington, DC: Government Accountability Office.

Government Accountability Office (GAO). 2013. *Federal Information Security: Mixed Progress in Implementing Program Components; Improved Metrics Needed to Measure Effectiveness. GAO-13–776,* September 16. Washington, DC: Government Accountability Office.

Greenwald, Glenn. 2013. "NSA collecting phone records of millions of Verizon customers daily." *The Guardian,* June 5.

Hardy, Quentin. 2014. "Computing Goes to the Cloud. So Does Crime." *The New York Times,* December 3, F6.

Henschen, Doug. 2012. "Salesforce.com Hires Former U.S. CIO Vivek Kundra." *InformationWeek.* January 16. Available at http://www.informationweek.com/applications/salesforcecom-hires-former-us-cio-vivek-kundra/d/d-id/1102288.

Internet Policy Task Force (IPTF). 2011. *Cybersecurity, Innovation, and the Internet Economy.* US Department of Commerce Internet Policy Task Force. Available at http://www.nist.gov/itl/upload/Cybersecurity_Green-Paper_FinalVersion .pdf.

Joint, Andrew, and Edwin Baker. 2011. Knowing the Past to Understand the Present—Issues in the Contracting for Cloud-Based Services. *Computer Law and Security Review* 27 (4): 407–415.

Kelly, Susan. 2012. "Cloudy Coverage? Cyber policies may fall short for cloud computing." *Treasury & Risk,* June 11. Available at http://www.treasuryandrisk .com/2012/06/11/cloudy-coverage.

Kundra, Vivek. 2011. *Federal Cloud Computing Strategy.* The White House. February 8. Available at http://www.cio.gov/documents/federal-cloud-computing-strategy .pdf.

Kowalenko, Kathy. 2012. "Standards for Seamless Cloud Computing." *The Institute.* June. Available at http://theinstitute.ieee.org/benefits/standards/standards-for -seamless-cloud-computing.

Lipowicz, Alice. 2011. "Kundra Describes Vision of Three Huge Federal Data Centers." *Federal Computer Week Circuit Blog.* February 24. Available at http://fcw.com/blogs/ circuit/2011/02/kundra-3-federal-data-centers.aspx.

McCafferty, Dennis. 2012. Cloud to Create Jobs Boom. *CACM* 55 (5): 11.

McKendrick, Joe. 2011. How Cloud Computing Is Fueling the Next Startup Boom. *Forbes* (November 1). Available at http://www.forbes.com/sites/joemckendrick/2011/11/01/cloud-computing-is-fuel-for-the-next-entrepreneurial -boom.

Mitchell, Robert L. 2009. Y2K: The Good, the Bad, and the Crazy. *Computerworld* (December 28). Available at http://www.computerworld.com/article/2522197/it -management/y2k--the-good--the-bad-and-the-crazy.html.

Molnar, David, and Stuart Schechter. 2010. "Self Hosting vs. Cloud Hosting: Accounting for the Security Impact of Hosting in the Cloud." Paper presented at Ninth Workshop on the Economics of Information Security (WEIS 2010), Cambridge, MA, June 8.

Moteff, John D. 2011. *Critical Infrastructures: Background, Policy, and Implementation. Report RL 30153.* Washington, DC: Congressional Research Service.

Moteff, John, and Paul Parfomak. 2004. *Critical Infrastructure and Key Assets: Definition and Identification. Report RL32631.* Washington, DC: Congressional Research Service.

Mufson, Steven. 2014. "Why are global cyberspies so desperate to get inside this algae farm?" *Washington Post,* July 13, pp. G1, G5.

Mulazzani, Martin, 2011. "Dark Clouds on the Horizon: Using Cloud Storage as Attack Vector and Online Slack Space." In *Proceedings of the 20th USENIX Conference on Security (SEC'11),* USENIX Association, Berkeley, CA, 5–5.

Nakashima, Ellen, and Jon Cohen. 2012. "Poll Shows Nuanced Views on Cyber-threats: Government's Role at Issue." *Washington Post,* June 7. A3.

National Institutes of Standards and Technology (NIST). 2013. *Security and Privacy Controls for Federal Information Systems and Organizations.* NIST Special Publication 800–53 (Revision 4). National Institute of Standards and Technology, US Department of Commerce.

National Institutes of Standards and Technology (NIST). 2014. *Framework for Improving Critical Infrastructure Cybersecurity, Version 1.0.* National Institute of Standards and Technology, February 12. Available at http://www.nist.gov/cyberframework/upload/cybersecurity-framework-021214.pdf.

NITRD. 2014. *FY15 Supplement to the President's Budget.* NITRD National Coordination Office, March. Available at http://www.whitehouse.gov/sites/default/files/microsites/ostp/NITRD_FY15_Final.pdf.

Norton, Steven, and Clint Boulton. 2014. "Why Big Firms Delay Using Cloud." *Wall Street Journal,* July 17, p. B6.

Office of the United States Trade Representative. 2011. "United States–European Union Trade Principles for Information and Communication Technology Principles." Press Release, April, available at: http://www.ustr.gov/about-us/press-office/ press-releases/2011/april/united-states-european-union-trade-principles-inform.

O'Harrow, Jr. Robert. 2012. "Health-Care Sector Vulnerable to Hackers, Researchers Say." *Washington Post,* December 25. Available at http://www.washingtonpost.com/ investigations/health-care-sector-vulnerable-to-hackers-researchers-say/2012/12/25/ 72933598-3e50-11e2-ae43-cf491b837f7b_story.html.

Organisation for Economic Cooperation and Development (OECD). 2011. "Communiqué on Principles for Internet Policy Making." OECD High-Level Meeting on the Internet Economy, June 28–29. Available at http://www.oecd.org/ dataoecd/40/21/48289796.pdf.

President's Commission on Critical Infrastructure Protection (PCCIP). 1997. *Critical Foundations: Protecting America's Infrastructures.* Washington, D.C. October. Available at http://fas.org/sgp/library/pccip.pdf.

Perine, Keigh. 2012. "Businesses to W.H.: Stem Tide of Data Flow Rules." *Politico* (June 7): Available at http://www.politico.com/news/stories/0612/77190.html.

President's Council of Advisors on Science and Technology. 2014. *Report to the President—Big Data and Privacy: A Technological Perspective.* Washington, DC: White House Office of Science and Technology Policy. Available at http://www .whitehouse.gov/sites/default/files/microsites/ostp/PCAST/pcast_big_data_and _privacy_-_may_2014.pdf.

Rauf, David Saleh. 2011. "PATRIOT Act Clouds Picture for Tech." *Politico* (November 29). Available at http://www.politico.com/news/stories/1111/69366.html.

Ravindranath, Mohana. 2014. "A Cloud-Computing Pioneer Looks to the Government." *Washington Post,* June 9, p. A11.

Rochwerger, Benny, 2011. Reservoir—When One Cloud Is Not Enough. *IEEE Computer* 44 (3): 44–51.

Schneider, Fred. B. (ed.) 1998. *Trust in Cyberspace.* Washington, DC: National Academy Press.

Shachtman, Noah. 2012. "Military Networks 'Not Defensible,' Says General Who Defends Them," *Wired,* January 12. Available at http://www.wired.com/ dangerroom/2012/01/nsa-cant-defend.

Song, Dawn, Shi, E. Fischer, I. and Shankar, U. 2012. Cloud Data Protection for the Masses. *IEEE Computer* 45 (1): 39–45.

Software & Information Industry Association. (2011). *Guide to Cloud Computing for Policymakers.* July 26. Available at http://www.siia.net.

Stokes, Jon. 2011. "Microsoft Pushes Back on EU Cloud Concerns as European Rivals Move In." *Wired,* December 14. Available at http://www.wired.com/2011/12/ microsofts-pushes-back-on-eu-cloud-concerns-as-european-rivals-move-in.

Transatlantic Economic Council. 2011. "Joint Statement." November 29, Washington DC. Available at http://trade.ec.europa.eu/doclib/docs/2011/november/tradoc _148385.pdf.

US Office of Homeland Security. 2002. *The National Strategy for Homeland Security.* Washington, DC, July 16.

Villegas, David, 2012. Cloud Federation in a Layered Service Model. *Journal of Computer and System Sciences* 78 (5): 1330–1344. 10.1016/j.jcss.2011.12.017

Wheeler, Tom. 2014. "Finding the Best Path Forward to Protect the Open Internet." *Official FCC Blog,* April 29. Available at http://www.fcc.gov/blog/finding-best-path -forward-protect-open-internet.

White House. 2011. *International Strategy for Cyberspace: Prosperity, Security, and Openness in a Networked World.* May. Available at http://www.whitehouse.gov/sites/ default/files/rss_viewer/international_strategy_for_cyberspace.pdf.

Zetter, Kim. 2014. "It's Insanely Easy to Hack Hospital Equipment." *Wired.* April 25. Available at http://www.wired.com/2014/04/hospital-equipment-vulnerable.

3 Reliability and the Internet Cloud

William Lehr[1]

Introduction

The Internet is becoming the new PSTN[2], at the same time as it is evolving into the Internet Cloud[3] (a public utility for networked computing resources). These concurrent transitions will simultaneously increase the saliency of and complexity of ensuring reliability, which is a key defining dimension for any telecommunications service.

Understanding the nature of this challenge requires bridging divergent views of reliability as the concept has been considered in the Internet, what it has meant in the telephony-centric PSTN, and what it will mean in the evolving Internet Cloud of the future. This will have cross-layer implications for the entire Internet cloud computing ecosystem, where the term *layers* refers not just to protocol layers in an information technology (IT)–architecture sense, but the industry/market structure, business processes, and regulatory environment in which the Internet Cloud will exist.

This chapter will review how the challenge of ensuring reliability will evolve and what this will mean for policy makers and industry stakeholders. The challenges of ensuring high levels of reliability for critical infrastructure are not unique to the Internet, and much can be learned from other domains, although the legacy PSTN provides an obvious touchstone. This text will help frame the discussion of ensuring reliability in an Internet cloud ecosystem and interpret some of these lessons in light of current directions in future Internet architectures.

The next section traces the co-evolution of the PSTN and the Internet and the implications for the Internet ecosystem. Public utility regulation of the PSTN has shifted toward increased reliance on market forces, while at the same time, the Internet has been emerging as a more complex and capable replacement. Like two rivers flowing into one another, these two trends confront the convergence of network ecosystems with distinct technical, regulatory, and market legacies. Subseguent sections address the added complexity of ensuring reliability in the emerging Internet Cloud; and then focus on the special problem posed by the transition to a hyper reliable core routing architecture. The final section reviews the main conclusions and highlights the need for further research.

The Changing Internet Ecosystem

In this section, I describe how the Internet has evolved from a best-effort network into a platform for cloud computing services. In realizing this evolution, the Internet is in the process of becoming the new PSTN, a basic, essential infrastructure for our information economy. This transition has important technical, market structure, and regulatory implications.

From Telephone Network Application to the Internet Cloud Utility

Since its origins in the 1960s, the Internet has evolved from an application supported on top of the PSTN into *the* platform for all global electronic communications.[4] As a consequence of this evolution, the Internet has experienced exponential growth in its capacity, capabilities, and the volume of traffic and diversity of applications that it now supports.

In the 1990s, the Internet emerged as the first successful mass-market platform for data communications, adding the third crucial element needed to realize the world of pervasive *cloud* computing that is rapidly emerging. The other two legs were the concurrent PC revolution that delivered mass-market computing resources to users' desktops and the growth of mobile telephony that brought personalized mass-market communication services.

Mass-market access to networked computing resources proved sufficiently compelling to spur exponential growth in electronic commerce and investments in telecommunications infrastructure and complementary goods and services all across the information and communications technology (ICT) value chain. New ventures with novel business models like Amazon, Google, and eBay—among many others—have become mainstays of the business landscape, changing markets and business processes across the economy.[5] Unfortunately, realization of the Internet's potential was hampered by the slow speeds of dial-up access connections, the lack of mobility support, and the limited capabilities of user devices, applications, and the Internet in those days. These limitations contributed to the dot-com bust of 2000, when ambitious hopes for growth collided with real-world challenges.

With the migration to broadband and now mobile broadband, with more capable devices (like tablets, eBook readers, connected TVs, and smartphones), with enhanced interactivity through technologies like Web 2.0, and with the expansion in Internet-supported services such as social networking, interactive multimedia, and video conferencing, the Internet has become increasingly ubiquitous throughout society and the economy. With Moore's-Law–driven advances in computing, storage, and communications technology, it is now possible to foresee a future of pervasive computing in which everyone is connected always and everywhere and where all manner of activities may be computing-assisted.[6]

This future is sometimes referred to as the *Internet of Things (IoT)*, and its fullest realization would merge the real and virtual worlds.[7] Such a scenario will require embedding computer intelligence in all sorts of devices and network elements, rendering end-to-end computing/communications systems smart. Such systems underlie visions of "smart X," where X can include grids,[8] infrastructure (highways, buildings, transport grids, etc.),[9] supply chains,[10] health care,[11] and other areas. These ICT-augmented intelligent systems are a central element of national strategies for economic growth and environmental sustainability.[12]

The Internet is a central element in this vision of pervasive computing/communications resources. Whether the Internet's role should be principally to provide the telecommunications services needed to connect intelligent devices at the edges, such as central processing units (CPUs) and storage in data centers; or whether such services and resources should be embedded in the Internet is a question of active debate among network researchers, industry participants, users, and policy makers.[13] Ignoring for the moment where the smart functionality should be located (and who should control or own the assets that support it), it is clear that there are many things that today's Internet does not handle well that might be better addressed if the Internet's functionality were expanded. This includes things like better support for (1) trust (security, privacy); (2) context-differentiated services for quality of service (QoS), location awareness, or other "context"-related differentiators in service characteristics[14]; (3) network management, to allow better dynamic resource allocation; and (4) cloud-based computing and storage resources. Much of this functionality is already supported via a hodgepodge of Internet add-ons and fixes provided as value-added services by participants in the Internet value chain. Meanwhile, as part of the Future Internet Architecture (FIA) program of the National Science Foundation (NSF), several teams of network researchers are seeking to expand the range of intelligent functionality to support finer-grained, context-dependent resource assignment, including support for shared computing and storage resources.[15]

Enabling on-demand access to computing and storage resources via the Internet is a motivating characteristic of cloud computing. There are a growing number of taxonomies for describing the emerging markets for cloud computing services. A common one identifies three tiers of access: software as a service (SaaS), platform as a service (PaaS), and infrastructure as a service (IaaS).[16]

Some of the essential attributes that characterize the cloud computing vision include:[17]

- On-demand access to resources (storage, computing, network, etc.)
- Dynamic scaling of capacity (whether up or down)
- Broad network access (flexible "anywhere" access support)
- Resource pooling (shared resources via virtualization)
- Measured services (pay-as-you-go support for on-demand resources)

There are several economic benefits of enabling such functionality. On-demand access to resources allows better dynamic matching between resource needs and capacity. From a business/economic perspective, this can translate capital (fixed) costs for excess capacity into operating (variable) expenses, with users paying only for the capacity they need and use. These savings can also translate into savings in power and other shared operating costs. Whether opting for cloud-based services to meet users' needs for computing/communication services is a good decision obviously depends on how the cloud services are provided and priced relative to available alternatives. At least in principle, there may be significant scale and scope economies realizable from relying on shared resources to meet heterogeneous (and uncorrelated in time and location) demands.[18]

In addition to cost or resource utilization benefits, cloud-based resources may offer benefits in supporting flexible access with support for thin-client, mobile,[19] or ad hoc usage[20] and enhancing service reliability. When services are distributed in a highly connected cloud, there are many more routes to support robustness in the face of one- or multiple-link failures.

Indeed, the reliance on such resource sharing was fundamental to the economic design of the PSTN as a general telephone utility. The PSTN relied on shared transport and switching to allow anyone-to-anyone telephone calling. The cloud utility model generalizes that model to include computing and storage resources. As I discuss further later in the chapter, this generalization implies increased complexity.

From Service to Basic Infrastructure

The expansion in Internet capacity and capabilities described previously has been driven by (and in turn helps drive) the virtuous cycle of service demand and supply growth. The Internet has grown to a global scale, with adoption approaching saturation in mature markets and with exponential growth in per-subscriber and aggregate traffic. More users are using the Internet for a wider range of applications for a wider range of activities in our social and economic lives. In light of this transformation, the Internet is appropriately regarded as essential basic infrastructure.

As with electric power, roads, water, and the telecommunication services supported by the PSTN, policy makers recognize that ensuring universal access to reliable Internet service is essential for the health of the economy and society. This means that there is an enduring public regulatory interest in ensuring the health of the Internet ecosystem and its broad availability (universal access) for all citizens and businesses. This responsibility and its relevance for the overall economy is explicitly articulated in the National Broadband Plan in the United States.[21]

Recognizing that there is an enduring public (regulatory) interest, however, does *not* mean that the appropriate model for regulating the Internet cloud is legacy PSTN regulation.[22] Even in the absence of the growth of the Internet, telecommunication regulators would be continuing the decades-long project of dismantling and overhauling traditional PSTN regulation and transitioning from a command-and-control public utility model for regulation to one that relies ever more on market forces.[23]

This transition was motivated by the recognition that competition was viable in a wider range of PSTN elements and services (making reliance on market forces a more reasonable alternative), while the burdens of enforcing legacy PSTN rules became increasingly intractable. In addition to the deadweight costs of regulatory bureaucracy and the attenuated incentives for efficient resource allocation that the lack of a profit motive implies for government operations,[24] there is a fundamental information asymmetry: regulated firms generally know much more about market and technical trends and conditions and are much more agile at adapting (unless constrained by cumbersome regulations) than the regulators. As the environment gets more complex and information asymmetries amplify, the case for allowing regulated firms greater discretion increases. This allows firms more scope to optimize in the face of a dynamic environment—but it also potentially increases the risk that firms with market power might abuse that power to harm the public interest. If competition is sufficiently viable and robust, then the delegation of regulatory authority to markets instead of via direct regulation is a win-win proposition: overall efficiency is enhanced, while regulatory costs are reduced.

In contrast to the PSTN, the Internet remains largely unregulated. It began as an application that existed on top of the PSTN, implemented in equipment and software owned and operated by users. The Internet was designed as a peer-to-peer packet data transport network that required only very limited intelligence in the network to support end-to-end connectivity at the network layer. (However, there was a lot of network intelligence in the PSTN underlying the Internet in order to support reliable end-to-end network management.) Most of the incremental invest-ment to create the Internet was in user equipment and applications at the edge, but most of the total investment was still associated with the telecommunications infrastructure of the PSTN. Nevertheless, the Internet, like the markets for computer equipment, software, and services, has remained largely unregulated. In the 1990s in the United States, there were thousands of access Internet service providers (ISPs), and although there were only a large handful of Tier 1 ISPs, most analysts regarded the Internet as robustly competitive and pointed to the Internet's record for rapid growth and graceful scaling to meet new challenges in the absence of regulation as strong justifications for preserving its unregu-lated character. Also, there was limited political support for regulating the Internet while policy makers were struggling with the transition from legacy PSTN regulation to competition in all telecommunications services.

In transitioning from the voice telephony PSTN to the Internet, the basic circuit-switched paradigm is being replaced with packet switching. By itself, this change induces changes in PSTN regulations because many of the legacy rules (e.g., QoS, interface demarcations, and interconnec-tion rules) are often technology-specific. Voice telephony is now just another application on the Internet, such as voice over IP (VoIP). The central office switches are replaced with routers,[25] the copper wires with fiber and wireless,[26] and the centralized control of Signaling System 7 (SS7) with distributed or decentralized Internet routing and network management. In addition to swapping out legacy technologies with newer and more capable ones, the range and QoS offerings have expanded. The legacy Internet has been enhanced by adding new functionality. This includes support for additional access network infrastructures below the narrow waist of the Internet Protocols (IPs), such as IP on fiber rather than Synchronized Optical Networking (SONET), mobile wireless, ad hoc networks, etc.; and additional networking support in overlays above, such as routing, security, content delivery, etc.[27] Customer premise equipment such as PCs, smartphones, and modems/DVRs, as well as servers at the edge of the network[28]—collectively known as *edge boxes*— and software applications (e.g., browsers and client applications) have become more capable, adding new features like support for end-to-end encryption, modified congestion control, support for caching, and other functionality that is intended to enhance the quality of the user experience even in the face of the variable performance of the best-effort[29] Internet.[30]

These trends have blurred the traditional boundaries between end-host (peer) and network-based functionality.[31] Relative to the voice-only PSTN, figuring out what technical functions belong where and how to regulate them poses a much more complex problem for regulators. *Ceteris paribus,* this increased technical and marketplace complexity strengthens the preference for relying on market forces relative to direct regulatory oversight.[32]

At the same time, and with the relaxation of regulatory restrictions, intermodal facilities-based competition has emerged between telephone, cable, satellite, and mobile service providers as the scope of services that can be supported on each platform has converged (so each can offer a mix of voice, video, and data services). New types of all-IP providers like Global Crossing and Level 3 have emerged. Deregulation also eliminated line-of-business restrictions that limited the ability of local telephone companies to compete in markets for Internet services. As these providers expanded their Internet offerings, the boundary between Internet and telecom assets blurred. Today, the legacy access providers, who were also the dominant facilities-based providers of PSTN infrastructure, are among the largest ISPs. Meanwhile, new types of service providers, like Akamai, Google, Facebook, Netflix, Twitter, and Amazon, have emerged that rely on and interconnect with the ISPs; they provide Internet functionality but are not typically regarded as ISPs.[33]

This new environment presents policy makers with a quandary. On the one hand, the Internet is no longer just an application on the PSTN but is the new PSTN, and that means that there is a heightened public interest in regulating the Internet.[34] This increased interest is a direct result of recognizing that the Internet is essential infrastructure that subsumes the societal-economic role of the legacy PSTN. The question is not whether a public policy agenda is necessary, or even principally what such an agenda should entail, but rather how it should be realized.[35] On the other hand, the Internet ecosystem is fundamentally more complex than the telephony-centric world of the old PSTN, the inefficiencies of legacy PSTN regulation are well understood, and the prospects for the viability of competition across the Internet ecosystem remain uncertain. The largest access providers, content providers, and overlay network functionality providers have increased their market shares, but many performance indicators suggest that competition remains robust. At this point, it seems reasonable to expect that reliance on market forces will remain the dominant model for regulating the Internet.[36]

Although primary reliance on markets to govern the Internet as the new PSTN may be inevitable or even desirable, it is important to remember that market failures may arise in multiple ways. Market power may be excessive (competition is not vigorous enough) or competition may fail to be efficient for a number of other reasons. For example, there may be fundamental nonconvexities that preclude existence of a sustainable pricing equilibrium under competition (e.g., marginal cost pricing fails to recover long-run incremental costs[37]); or information imperfections may preclude equilibria supporting efficiency-enhancing quality differentials (e.g., a "lemons" problem[38]); or incomplete contracts [e.g., a lack of enforcement mechanisms for service level agreements (SLAs)] may prevent coordination even when it is in everyone's best interest to do so (e.g., a potential free-rider or Prisoner's Dilemma problem).[39] *Ceteris paribus,* increased complexity would suggest an increase both in the desire for more reliance on market forces and greater potential for market failures of multiple types.

This is not meant to imply that the increased complexity of the Internet (relative to the Internet of old and relative to the telephony PSTN) warrants more direct regulatory intervention, but only that our decision to rely on market forces comes with a challenge: *Markets are not unregulated—they are regulated differently.*

In the next section, I focus on the policy challenge of ensuring reliability in the new environment of the Internet cloud. Ensuring the reliability of essential infrastructure is an obviously important policy goal, and examining what this means in the Internet and a regulatory environment that favors market-based solutions (as opposed to direct regulatory interventions or strong ex ante regulation) highlights some of the larger regulatory challenges confronting telecommunications policy makers.

Reliability and the Policy Challenge

Reliability means different things in different contexts.[40] At the highest level, the concept of *reliability* implies that systems behave consistently as we expect them to. Generally, we also assume that a reliable system is one that performs well. A common metric for reliability is *availability*, which is the amount of time that a system is expected to be in service. It is often expressed as a statistical time measure (e.g., mean time to failure) or the percentage of time over some period that the system is available for service (i.e., free of failures). In accepting a public interest in the Internet as basic infrastructure, it is obvious that this implicitly implies an obligation to ensure an appropriate level of reliability.[41]

Reliability in Legacy Telephone Networks and the Internet

What constitutes a failure depends on what the system is supposed to do. The legacy fixed-line PSTN was designed to support anytime/anyone-to-anyone voice telephony. Because telephone service was regarded as critical infrastructure (i.e., for business, for public safety, and for daily life), it was expected that out-of-service events would be infrequent for individuals and extremely rare for large groups of individuals (or for big chunks of the PSTN). It was expected that the telephone-calling experience would be relatively homogeneous and of "good audio quality" across calls (at different times and between any two parties with fixed-line phones).[42] Absent excessive line noise or the occasional fast-busy signal resulting from switch congestion, fixed-line telephony provided over the PSTN achieved a very high standard of reliability. It was not uncommon for fixed-line telephony to continue to work even when storms disrupted electric service.[43]

This high-availability standard for the PSTN was consistent with the view that the telephone network was essential infrastructure. It was generally accepted that businesses could not function without telephones and lives depended on continuously available telephone service (e.g., the ability to call an ambulance in an emergency). Achieving this goal motivated the end-to-end design of legacy telephone networks.

The design of the PSTN was optimized to support voice-grade end-to-end circuits with tight technical performance characteristics and low blocking probabilities (i.e., fast busy signals should be infrequent). Interface standards imposed tight latency[44] bounds to ensure that end-to-end latency did not exceed 200 milliseconds, the threshold for real-time voice telephony to be viable. Core components of the PSTN, like telephone switches, were designed for five nines (99.999%) reliability, or less than 6 minutes of out-of-service time per year. This required full (1 + 1) redundancy for core switch and other critical network components. That is, there were full-capacity hot spares ready to assume the load if the active unit failed. If the probability of one failing is p, and the failures are independent, then the probability of both failing at the same time is p^2. Adding redundancy provides significant gains in terms of enhanced availability but comes at a significant cost in terms of increased capital intensity. That expenditure is warranted when a prolonged outage of a single central office switch would pose significant harm on a large number of telephone subscribers.

Meeting the rigorous technical requirements of supporting voice telephony with the desired high standard for reliability, given the state of technology at the time, required significant centralized, hierarchical control. The out-of-band SS7 network was put in place to support such control, allowing networkwide resource allocation. In addition, the desire to ensure ubiquitous coverage and connectivity required significant, ongoing capital investment as the national (and soon global) PSTN was being established. To manage the technical and economic challenges of supporting the PSTN, it was long believed that monopoly provisioning was desirable. It was only over time, with the advance of technology and market growth, that the technical design requirements and economics of the PSTN were rendered compatible with increased competition and the decentralization and distribution of control that that implied.

With mobile telephony, users historically have been tolerant of much more variable performance. Although the quality and coverage of mobile telephony services have improved substantially since they first emerged in the 1980s, and in many contexts are as good as or better than fixed telephony services today, it was not uncommon for calling to be unavailable in many locations (i.e., coverage was limited), congestion problems were not uncommon, and call quality could be quite variable (e.g., dropped calls were a common occurrence). Even with these deficiencies, however, mobile telephony had a compelling value proposition. Mobile telephones allowed calling where no fixed telephones were available and allowed users greater personal control over their calling.[45] Also, competition was built into mobile telephony from the start, with two operators licensed initially in each market in the United States. Although the technical architectures for each provider were hierarchical and centrally managed, control of core assets was inherently more distributed and decentralized (across service provider networks). A cost of this arrangement was that roaming across provider networks introduced additional quality degradation and might incur additional user charges.[46] On the other hand, competition allowed users service choices and helped drive down prices, both of which might be regarded as important quality improvements. Viewed in this light, mobile telephony may be seen to be not so much *less* reliable as *differently* reliable than fixed-line telephony. As I will explain shortly, a similar interpretation was applicable to the Internet.

The purpose of the Internet was to support asynchronous data communications rather than voice telephony. The Internet was not expected to meet the same sort of availability standards as the PSTN. In its original incarnation, it was a research network designed to support data communications between mainframe computers—and while this was important, it was not viewed as essential basic infrastructure, with the accompanying public interest mandate that that term implies. The Internet was not supporting business operations or other mission-critical functionality. The best-effort packet-delivery model provided a graceful way for asymmetrically sized and delay-tolerant datagrams to share transport capacity. Simple, lightweight IPs (the "narrow waist") allowed interoperable data connections between heterogeneous peers over variable-capacity transmission links without requiring much in the way of intelligent support from the network. Compared to the complex switches at the core of the PSTN, the routers that switch packets are simple packet-forwarding devices. Routers were not typically designed with 1 + 1 redundancy, and with their greater simplicity, they were far less expensive than PSTN switching equipment.

The Internet was not designed to meet tight latency bounds but to ensure data connectivity across variable-quality data links. The packets would get from source to destination, but they may take a while and follow different routes along the way. In achieving this goal, the Internet did not require significant intelligence from the routers that forwarded packets. They just needed to know where next to send arriving packets. Control and network intelligence were highly decentralized and distributed. There was no provision for centralized information sharing about the overall state of the Internet. When the network was congested, routers buffered packets, and when buffers overflowed, packets were dropped—and end-to-end latency increased. When the network was not congested, sending hosts were permitted to increase their data rate until either they completed sending the desired data or the dropping of packets indicated that congestion was occurring somewhere downstream and sending hosts should slow down and resend packets. This variable-bit-rate capability allowed applications like VoIP or streaming video (e.g., YouTube) to take advantage of higher-bit-rate opportunities to send improved quality audio and video or faster-than-needed delivery to support buffering to smooth performance when slower-than-needed data rates were available.

By continuously expanding the capacity of links throughout the Internet and moving to bigger and faster routers, the best-effort Internet was able to scale to meet exponential traffic growth without realizing debilitating end-to-end latency problems. When congestion threatened, it generally proved more efficient to simply expand capacity than to introduce significant network intelligence to support QoS differentiation. VoIP services like Skype, which used better codecs, are able to offer better-quality audio than legacy telephony, and can be easily extended to introduce interactive multimedia like videoconferencing or text/file sharing. The potential to expand functionality was an original driver for computer-based telephony, but in the 1990s, when mass-market VoIP services took off, there was the added attraction of "free" telephone calling.[47]

Over time, and as noted previously, the architectures of legacy electronic communication networks and the Internet have converged. Historically, silo-based service provider networks have moved toward a common architecture, with the broadband Internet as the common platform. While single-service, best-effort transport is still the dominant mode for exchanging Internet traffic between ISPs, the Internet ecosystem has grown substantially more complex, both from a technical and business/industry structure perspective. New technical functionality and service capabilities are being supported as intelligence and cloud-based services grow.

Reliability in the Internet Cloud

Whereas the legacy Internet was a general-purpose utility packet transport network, the emerging cloud is that, plus a platform for utility computing and storage, which adds complexity. More users with different goals in using the Internet (e.g., to make telephone calls, to watch movies, or to access emergency services) in different ways (e.g., real-time or delay-tolerant) and with different tolerances for performance-based prices may legitimately have very different perspectives on what constitutes an appropriate level of reliability.

Lehr et al. (2011) discussed what this means for broadband reliability, suggesting at least three ways in which a consumer might regard their broadband service as reliable: (1) performance metrics (e.g., probability bit rates are in some expected range, potentially exceeding some minimum threshold that would identify a service failure event); (2) connectivity metrics (e.g., the ability to connect to Internet servers); and (3) core service availability metrics [e.g., availability of core services like email or Domain

Name System (DNS)]. As was common with traditional telephony service monitoring, data could be tracked across a large sample of subscribers on competing service provider networks and benchmarked against appropriate standards. With millions of subscribers and service events occurring all the time, even a very high standard of service reliability will yield statistically significant samples of failure events that might be used to track service quality.

From a policy perspective, the challenge of ensuring adequate broadband reliability amounts to a customer-protection activity, akin to ensuring truth in advertising, product safety, and a well-functioning market of quality-differentiated services.[48] An extensive framework of standards, regulations, and reporting requirements were established over time to provide such customer-protection oversight for legacy telephone service. The need for such oversight was motivated in no small part by the almost $8 billion annual subsidy program that was designed to promote and secure affordable universal service for basic telephony service.

With the transition to broadband and a new technology encompassing an expanded range of services and involving a large number of new players that previously had been exempt from legacy telecom regulation, the challenges of designing and implementing such a consumer protection policy framework for the Internet cloud is daunting. Moreover, because management and the ownership of assets is more decentralized and distributed in the Internet cloud (and hopefully will remain so if viable competition is to be sustained), there will be multiple competing and complementary providers of key components for the end-to-end system. Diagnosing performance problems, assigning responsibility, and implementing remediation is more challenging in such an environment. As our earlier work on speed measurement pointed out, end-to-end performance may suffer because of problems in the user's home network (e.g., a misconfigured PC or poor WiFi access connection), the last-mile access network, or problems farther upstream (e.g., a congested content server).[49] And Internet speed measurement is much easier than evaluating Internet reliability.

As discussed in Lehr, Bauer, and Clark (2012), the added complexity will perforce drive us to rely on market forces rather than legacy PSTN regulatory models. Accomplishing that goal will depend critically on the markets' abilities (potentially aided by policy makers) to aggregate and disseminate appropriate information to users and service providers across the value chain if the markets are to work efficiently and, should market failures require regulatory intervention, permit regulators to intervene effectively.

With respect to access to cloud computing or storage resources that may be made available in data centers distributed across the Internet, like raisins in a muffin or intrinsic to the fabric of an FIA,[50] appropriate standards for reliability will need to focus on not just availability, but also consistency and accuracy of access, with heightened requirements for data security and protection. Legacy data centers were built from meshes of multiple computers that provided N + M redundancy. Data was replicated across multiple computers and drives, with smaller N and larger M providing greater protection and security, but at a higher cost in committed resources. With large N and small M, data was stored over many computers, any of which could fail with a fairly high frequency (like low-end routers in the Internet) without threatening a loss of data. Over time, data centers have evolved into rack-mounted systems where multiple CPUs share more reliable and efficient power supplies. While this offers performance improvements, it requires backup rack power supplies (i.e., 1 + 1 redundancy for certain key data center components) since the failure of these new, more powerful power supplies would no longer mean the loss of a single CPU, but all the CPUs supported by that rack. The data centers begin to look like large computers themselves.

Reliable access to data is further achieved by distributing copies of the data across multiple data centers. A fire that destroys a data center in Seattle, therefore, would leave the one in New York intact and ready to use. On the other hand, a user in New York could generally access the data from the data center in New York more quickly than from Seattle. Providing such redundancy presents fundamental challenges that are embodied by the CAP theorem, which says that you can guarantee, at most, two out of the three desirable properties of distributed databases: consistency, availability, and partition tolerance. When someone makes a change to the data in New York, that change needs to be reflected in the database in Seattle. Ensuring that the two copies of data are consistent, while allowing users to access the same data (partition tolerance) at the same time (high availability), is not possible.[51] Many database service providers sacrifice consistency (serve the latest available version of the database) to enable high availability. As the Internet's services expand to include cloud-based resources, appropriate metrics will need to properly capture such trade-offs.

While it seems likely that market forces will provide the principal mechanism for managing reliability in the customer protection sense, it important to remember that there are many ways in which markets might fail, and the range of potential failures is exacerbated by the increased distribution and decentralization of control and functionality across enterprises and user networks and equipment. It is far from clear what intelligence or functionality should be placed where, what may need to be regulated, and what should be insulated from the market distortions that regulation imposes. As noted previously, today much of the focus for broadband regulation is on last-mile access providers who may be deemed to have market power. In the future, it is not unreasonable to hypothesize that important functionality might be provided by data center service providers, the entities that provide identity management services for authenticating users and services, or some other critical functionality associated with accessing cloud resources. It is far from clear what (if any) regulatory entities have or should have jurisdiction over which firms. While Google (cloud resources), Akamai (content delivery network), and Verizon (last-mile access and transport) all provide complementary services that may each be critical for the reliable operation of the Internet cloud, only Verizon as a telecommunications service provider is subject to significant regulatory oversight from the Federal Communications Commission (FCC). These providers do not have explicit agreements with each other that help ensure the reliability of the overall Internet. When service failures occur, figuring out where the problem arose and who is responsible is quite complicated. Neither the alternative of regulating everyone nor the alternative of deregulating everyone seem desirable, but retaining asymmetric regulation distorts market incentives and potentially adversely affects innovation and investment.

The problem of designing an appropriate customer protection framework to ensure appropriate reliability in the Internet cloud does not have a single solution. It will require collaboration among multiple regulatory authorities, such as competition authorities like the Department of Justice, communications regulators like the FCC, and commerce regulators like the Federal Trade Commission (FTC), as well as key stakeholders. These key stakeholders will include the service providers, as well as users and other government interests like the security/public safety communities and international trade and standardization communities. It will remain a work in progress.

In the next section, I consider some of the special problems associated with ensuring reliability in the Internet core.

Reliability in a Hyperreliable Core

Today's data centers composite multiple computers that are each much faster and with denser storage than those that were in service only a few years ago. The 1 Gigabit Ethernet (GigE) links that were put in place between servers in the data centers after 2000 are being upgraded to 10-GigE connections. The increase in capacity at the edges drives a concurrent need for even higher-capacity connections in the core. This is driving the demand for 40-GigE links and beyond, as well as the ability to switch packets across links at line speeds.

Today, among the largest core routers currently deployed are the Cisco CRS-1s. These "carrier-grade" routers are deployed by large service providers and enterprise customers to support traffic switching in the core of the Internet. The CRS-1 is expandable to support up to 72 40-Gbps line cards, for a total switching capacity of 92 Tbps.[52] When fully loaded, these boxes consume thousands of watts of power, imposing significant air conditioning loads and requiring strong structures to support the routers and all the associated paraphernalia. These boxes are much closer to the telecom switches of old in complexity, cost, and infrastructure requirements than to the low-cost, simple packet-forwarding routers of old. If one of these boxes is out of service, then the volume of traffic and potential loss to businesses and users could be extremely large. Like the old switches, these megarouters need 1 + 1 redundancy capabilities to ensure adequate reliability.

To continue to meet the needs for increased traffic growth and keep ahead of the ever-expanding capacity of edge networks (i.e., data centers and customer premises),[53] router functionality needs to be spread over multiple boxes since the power density for a single box is getting too high.[54] This requires developing a distributed software architecture that is sufficiently reliable and robust that it can look to the other network elements that rely on these core routers as if it were a single router. Allowing capabilities for deploying software updates, routine router maintenance, and changes or additions to router feature sets—all tasks that are critically important in today's dynamic cloud service markets—poses significant technical challenges. The goal is to design systems that offer even better than five nines reliability—in effect, that approach 100% availability.[55]

From a policy perspective, meeting such a goal of hyperreliability presents a number of interesting problems. When systems get that reliable, potential failures may be so rare as to appear as "black swans."[56] The rarity of such "black swan" reliability failure events poses a number of challenges for efficient markets. First, estimating the probability of such rare events is very difficult. Reasonable analysts might have widely different estimates. Moreover, predicting the potential harm or costs from moderating either the harm (in the unlikely event of a failure) or reducing the likelihood of a failure (making a rare event rarer still) is even more difficult. With such a large potential space for valuation differences, it may be difficult to contract over and credibly commit to appropriate ex ante or ex post actions directed at ensuring system reliability.

Second, and in light of these information problems, there are strong incentives to free-ride or otherwise evade commitments. For example, one way to achieve such high reliability is to provide better than 1 + 1 redundancy, but it is less expensive to simply claim that you have secured the additional redundancy than to actually make the necessary investments to achieve it.[57] An analogous phenomenon incurred in financial markets when bankers sold each other portfolio insurance that ultimately failed to provide the risk protection that it was represented to provide. Ensuring that all the participants and components correctly implement the procedures and processes required to ensure the high degree of reliability is very difficult.

Coglianese and Mendelson (2010) discuss some of the regulatory approaches that may be required to help ensure reliability of components that require hyperreliability. One of the things that policy makers can do is audit the processes employed by firms—asking questions such as: Do they have architectures and business operational plans that might reasonably be expected to deliver the anticipated levels of reliability? Do they have audit processes to make sure that the plans and architectures are being followed? Do they have processes in place to learn and adapt if they find that earlier assumptions or plans require modification? In the event that a failure occurs, do they have credible response plans? Do they have the resources they need to address this?

The focus of regulation cannot be on outcome performance since bad outcomes (failures) are not supposed to be observed (except extremely rarely), and enforcement triggered by such outcomes is not credible and so cannot influence ex ante behavior. The focus of regulation needs to be on the inputs and processes used.

In the legacy PSTN, this problem was confronted in the 1980s when a series of well-publicized software bugs in SS7 resulted in widespread outages. In response, the industry engaged in industry self-regulation efforts, forming the Network Reliability Council (NRC). The NRC provided a forum for industry participants to formulate and share best-practice plans and coordinate on reliability (and recovery) planning. Such industry self-regulation efforts are a common response to a heightened perception of risk from extremely rare catastrophic events. Other examples include the

Bhopal chemical plant disaster in 1984 and the Three Mile Island nuclear reactor meltdown in 1979. In the former case, significant loss of life actually occurred, while in the latter, it was threatened but did not come to fruition. Interestingly, the subsequent efforts at industry self-regulation coordinated by policy makers in response was more successful in the case of nuclear power than for the chemical industry.[58] One potential reason for this was the presence of a shared sense of fate with nuclear power (i.e., another disaster would spell doom for the entire industry) that was lacking in the chemical industry (i.e., chemical firms operate in distinct markets that would allow those not affected by a disaster to avoid responsibility). An interesting question is whether the Internet cloud might look more like the chemical industry than the nuclear power industry.[59] Addressing these and other issues will present policy makers with difficult challenges in the years to come.

Conclusions

The Internet is morphing into a cloud computing utility. It has evolved from a packet transport network riding on top of the PSTN to become *the* platform for all electronic communications, and increasingly the host to general-purpose computing and storage resources. In assuming this role, the Internet becomes basic infrastructure and thereby attracts an enduring public interest in ensuring its universal accessibility and availability.

Relative to the PSTN and Internet of old, the new cloud-utility Internet is substantially more complex and important to our economy and society. As the ICT world evolves toward a future of pervasive computing, toward the world of the IoT, the Internet cloud will host an ever-growing range of services that are mission-critical to the daily lives and business interests of all citizens.

This new environment will entail a heightened interest in ensuring the reliability of Internet services analogous to the earlier public policy interest in ensuring reliability in the legacy telephone network. By contrast, however, control is much more decentralized and distributed at the technical, business, and regulatory levels in the Internet cloud.

Regulatory trends in recent decades favoring markets over public-utility style regulation for telecommunications, the increased complexity of the Internet ecosystem, and the growth of markets make it likely that the principal responsibility for managing Internet reliability will depend on market forces, with regulators potentially helping to steer markets when failures are detected. While prospects for market failures may increase with the Internet cloud, identifying these and managing them will pose strong challenges.

The policy challenge of ensuring Internet reliability may be divided into the customer protection challenge of ensuring adequate reliability in retail services and the need to ensure against systemic failures in a hyperreliable core. These two focus areas are equally complex but distinctly different in the types of challenges they confront.

Addressing both reliability challenges will require ongoing collaboration across the value chain and will require new forms of performance monitoring and metrics. Policy makers, industry analysts, and other stakeholders are only now beginning the difficult task of engaging the multidisciplinary expertise required to address these significant challenges.[60]

Notes

1. In completing this work, Dr. Lehr would like to acknowledge support from NSF Awards 1040020, 1040023, and the MIT Communications Futures Program. All opinions expressed herein are those of the authors alone.

2. PSTN is an acronym for the Public Switched Telecommunications Network, and it is used in this chapter as shorthand for the legacy networks originally deployed and managed to support universal access to telephony and the associated matrix of regulatory policies and services that evolved as a consequence. Historically, telephone networks were circuit-based, fixed, wired networks, and because telephony was regarded as an essential service and telephone networks were considered a natural monopoly, telecommunications networks were widely regulated as public utilities. In the United States, the precursor to today's PSTN was the Bell Telephone System.

3. The term *cloud* refers to future telecommunication networks that provide an expanded set of in-network services such as access to computing resources, online storage, and other higher-level services, in addition to traditional data transport services. The legacy Internet was a (packet) transport network overlaid on the PSTN. With the addition of expanded functionality, today's Internet is able to support a much richer set of services. There are multiple technical and business model architectures for describing the future of cloud computing and networking, and several are discussed elsewhere in this volume. As used here, the term *Internet cloud* refers to enabling this enhanced range of services in the public Internet with the same sort of universal access implicit in an expanded vision of the PSTN: that is, as a public utility that is universally accessible for general data communication applications.

4. The discussion in this section parallels the discussion in Lehr, Bauer, and Clark (2012).

5. Over time, many of these online businesses have augmented the basic transport and connectivity (addressing) functionality of the Internet, enabling it to evolve into a platform for global electronic commerce. It is hardly coincidental that companies like Amazon and Google are now leading providers of cloud computing and storage infrastructure and services.

6. The assistance may or may not require human interaction or awareness, may be passive or active, and increasingly will involve direct machine-to-machine (m2m) interaction.

7. For example, in a report prepared for the European Commission, Botterman (2009) describes IoT as "a world-wide network of interconnected objects uniquely addressable, based on standard communication protocols," or, more widely: "Things having identities and virtual personalities operating in smart spaces using intelligent interfaces to connect and communicate within social, environmental, and user contexts." Instead of just imagining a world with computing/communications "*anytime, any place* connectivity for *anyone,*" we will have a world where such connectivity is extended to "*anything*" (see ITU 2005).

8. See the Department of Energy at http://energy.gov/oe/technology-development/ smart-grid.

9. See "Smart Roads, Smart Bridges, Smart Grids," *Wall Street Journal,* February 17, 2009.

10. See "The Smarter Supply Chain of the Future: Global Chief Supply Chain Officer Study," IBM, 2009, http://www-935.ibm.com/services/us/gbs/bus/html/gbs-csco -study.html.

11. See "Connected Health," Cisco Healthcare Solutions, 2012, http://www.cisco. com/web/strategy/docs/healthcare/11CS3289-ConnectedHealth_AAG_R2.pdf.

12. See "Strategy for American Innovation," White House, February 2011, http:// www.whitehouse.gov/innovation/strategy. One of the key building blocks is identified as "develop an advanced information technology ecosystem ... a 'virtual infrastructure'" that encompasses the "critical information, computing, and networking platforms that increasingly support our national economy." Alternatively, see "Connection Technologies to Play Critical Role in Building Sustainable Future—UN," United Nations, February 7, 2012, http://www.un.org/en/development/desa/news/ sustainable/connection-technologies-to-play-critical-role-building-sustainable -future.html.

13. For example, see Thierer (2006), Odlyzko (1998), Lucky (1997), and Isenberg (1997).

14. Traditionally, much of the discussion over QoS differentiated services has focused on the need to address differential requirements for latency or other technical service attributes. For example, delay-tolerant applications like email may be better supported than delay-intolerant applications like telephony over a best-effort Internet service in the face of congestion, inducing some to advocate using technologies like MultiProtocol Label Switching (MPLS), Differentiated Services (DiffServ), or other techniques to support more fine-grained (service-specific) service

provisioning. However, "context" may be thought of more broadly as a characteristic of the type of application (telephony versus email), the identity of the parties communicating, the time and location of the communication, or anything else that might make it appropriate to manage the resources used to support the activity more effectively.

15. See Jianli, Paul, and Jain (2011) for a survey of Internet architecture research.

16. For further elaboration, see the Introduction to this volume, Zhu (2010), Armbrust et al. (2009), and Rimal, Choi, and Lumb (2010). Microsoft Office and Google Apps are examples of SaaS; Microsoft's Azure and Google App Engine are examples of PaaS; and Amazon's Elastic Cloud (EC2), Rackspace, and IBM Computing on Demand are examples of IaaS offerings.

17. See chapter 1, "Cloud Strategy and Economics," in this volume and Mell and Grance (2009).

18. Note that if demands are strongly correlated in time and location (everyone wants the same computing resources at the same time), then sharing will not efficiently address the peak capacity challenge.

19. Mobile clients may also be thin clients because of their device power, portability, and other inherent design constraints. Thin clients may make it easier to port applications to new devices, especially as the range of connected entities in an IoT world expands.

20. The term *ad hoc* here refers to unplanned or disruption-prone applications. If you cannot predict where and when you will need resources, your only option may be to provision on the fly. Demand-and-supply (capacity) shocks may be the cause of such uncertainty. A natural disaster is an example of just such a shock.

21. See FCC (2010). President Barack Obama has affirmed this position. Speaking for his administration, Susan Crawford commented in a speech on May 14, 2009 that "Broadband is the new essential infrastructure" (see http://www.broadcasting-cable.com/article/232506-President_Obama_Focused_On_Broadband.php). Similar positions have been adopted in Europe, where the European Commission concluded that "widespread and affordable broadband access is essential to realize the potential of the Information Society" (see http://ec.europa.eu/information_society/eeurope/2005/all_about/broadband/index_en.htm); in Australia, where a government report concluded that "ubiquitous, multi-megabit broadband will underpin Australia's future economic and social prosperity" (see http://ict-industry-reports.com/wp-content/uploads/sites/4/2013/10/2006-Broadband-Blueprint-DCITA.pdf); and in Japan, where the Japanese have joined with regional partners to "enable all people in Asia to gain access to broadband platforms" by 2010 (see http://www.soumu.go.jp/main_sosiki/joho_tsusin/eng/Resources/asia_broadband.pdf).

22. Legacy PSTN regulation includes a complex mix of retail and wholesale service, technology, and price regulations. These include universal service, QoS, interconnection, carrier-of-last-resort, duty-to-serve, public access, unbundling, line-of-business restrictions, and other regulations that constrained the investment, operating, and service offerings of telecommunication network operators.

23. The secular trend from end-to-end monopoly regulation of the PSTN has been led by the United States, but it is a mostly global phenomenon. A growing number of national PTTs (push-to-talk services) were privatized beginning in the 1970s, and the rise of cellular mobile telephony, the entry of cable television into telecommunication services, and the emergence of Internet-based alternative service models such as VoIP have lead regulators to increasingly rely on market forces instead of public utility–style regulations to manage communication network and service markets. In the United States, the process from public utility regulation of the end-to-end telephone network toward markets has progressed in stages, with the opening to competition of customer premises equipment (1960s), long-distance telephone service (1980s), and local telephone service markets (1990s); and the transition from rate of return to price cap; and the detariffing and deregulation of a growing range of services, including broadband services (beginning in the twenty-first century).

24. Government bureaucrats lack profit incentives and market discipline that can give rise to X-inefficiency (Leibenstein, 1966).

25. These switches were essentially special-purpose computers, and today, the functionality of legacy central office switches may be emulated in soft switches hosted on Internet servers.

26. There is still a lot of copper wire in use, and much of the outside plant investment is in conduit and other assets that remain important even today. Moreover, the transition to fiber or other very-high-capacity last-mile technologies like cable (with DOCSIS 3.0) reignites questions about last-mile bottlenecks and market power.

27. See Lehr et al. (2006).

28. For example, gateways to corporate or home networks often have firewalls, storage, and other IT intelligence that makes them increasingly able to host or assume functionality that previously or alternatively might be handled by network-embedded resources and intelligence.

29. The original IP is based on best-effort packet delivery service on a per-link basis and did not provide support for service quality guarantees. Ensuring end-to-end delivery verification and QoS (e.g., latency was not excessive) was left to higher-level client software. With best-effort delivery, packets might be dropped or delayed, posing a challenge for the support of real-time services such as voice telephony, which becomes unusable if the latency delays are too long. Augmentations to the original protocol suites to enable differentiated packet delivery and other QoS enhancements have expanded the range of services that may be reliably supported over the Internet.

30. See Bauer, Clark, and Lehr (2011) for a discussion of how faster-than-real-time broadband service may be used by streaming media applications to compensate for variable performance over time.

31. The traditional Internet architecture severely limited the amount of intelligence required between end-host clients at either side of an end-to-end

communication. Simplifying the support required from routers along the path between clients and pushing most of the intelligence to the clients at the edges of the network helped lower router costs and facilitated interoperability and interconnection, but at the expense of in-network functionality. Putting more intelligence and capabilities in the network shifts the control, management, and costs associated with such functionality from the user's clients and host machines to software and machines operated by the network operators and their value-added partners.

32. The debates over net neutrality regulation illustrate that there is a lack of consensus as to how best to regulate the Internet—whether by relying on the hand of market forces or by framing stronger, interventionist rules. However, system complexity and information asymmetries pose significant challenges for crafting public utility–like regulatory rules. Indeed, it was precisely such issues that helped motivate the transition from legacy rate-of-return regulations toward price-cap regulations in the 1980s. The increased complexity of the new PSTN environment and the Internet ecosystem and the secular trend away from public utility regulation in recent decades both mitigate in favor of increased reliance on market forces relative to the public utility models of old; however, this does not mean that some form of activist regulation might not be warranted or likely. Broad trends do not imply monotonic progress.

33. See Labovitz et al. (2009) for a discussion of the Arbor Networks Traffic Study, which documents the rise in recent years of the "hyper-giants" as the Internet ecosystem has expanded.

34. See Lehr, Bauer, and Clark (2012) for further discussion of some of the regulatory issues that are on the FCC's current and prospective regulatory agenda.

35. A fundamental role of government is to ensure that the citizens have affordable access to essential infrastructure. This may require the government to take a lead role in providing such infrastructure (e.g., roads and highways, which are seldom privately owned) or a more mixed or attenuated role, as in the provision of electric power or basic telecommunication services. With respect to the latter in both cases, there has been a transition toward market-based models in recent years, but regulatory oversight remains significant.

36. I say *will* to avoid offering an opinion here as to the desirability of more direct regulatory intervention. I believe that a strong case might be made for limited forms of regulatory interventions under certain conditions, but precisely what these might be would take the discussion too far afield for this chapter.

37. Fixed, sunk, or shared costs may be a sufficient share of total costs as to preclude any sustainable pricing equilibrium under competition.

38. See Akerlof (1970).

39. A free-rider or Prisoner's Dilemma problem may be solved if the players were allowed to form contracts about their actions.

40. See Lehr, Bauer, Heikkinen, and Clark (2011) for a discussion of broadband reliability.

41. Reliability is simply a dimension of service quality. Indeed, when viewed with the appropriate generality, it might be viewed as a superset of other quality dimensions.

42. Like other basic infrastructure, most users do not think about quality in this instance unless there is something wrong (such as potholes in the road, power surges that burn out electric appliances, water that tastes bad, or dropped telephone calls)—and then they notice in a hurry. This ability to "take the infrastructure for granted" is a design goal.

43. The copper telephone lines were powered.

44. Latency is an end-to-end delay. If round-trip delays exceed more than 250 milliseconds, real-time voice telephony is no longer feasible, and speakers default to a "walkie-talkie" mode of communication, in which each party waits until the other party has finished talking before speaking again.

45. When away from a user's home fixed-line telephone, pay phones, credit cards, or "borrowing" another person's fixed-line telephone were cumbersome alternatives to mobile telephony.

46. For example, second-generation (2G) digital handsets initially roamed using analog Advanced Mobile Phone System (AMPS), an older and lower-quality first-generation (1G) technology.

47. Legacy long-distance telephone calls were typically priced on a per-minute basis that included significant additional, regulatory-mandated "access" charges. For international calls, these so-called settlement charges could be quite large. With flat-rate (volume-insensitive) dial-up Internet subscriptions used over flat-rate telephone lines, which became the norm in the United States in the 1990s, using VoIP either end to end or in a network provided an arbitrage opportunity to bypass those charges.

48. Broadband services are offered in quality/usage tiers, with higher-priced tiers providing greater quality and volume of service.

49. See Bauer, Clark, & Lehr (2010).

50. For example, the FIA NEBULA Project (Smith et al., 2011) is an architecture for a hyperreliable cloud that would offer a sufficiently reliable and secure service to support remote monitoring and control of a diabetic's insulin pump via the cloud. And MobilityFirst (http://mobilityfirst.winlab.rutgers.edu/) would provide support for disruption-tolerant networking and access to in-network storage and computing resources spread across the Internet.

51. Strictly speaking, *partition tolerance* refers to the ability of the system to endure partitioning without failure. That is, the distributed database will continue to work even if the distinct database servers cannot communicate with each other (i.e., the distributed database system is partitioned).

52. http://www.cisco.com/en/US/products/ps5842/index.html.

53. The Internet is a network of networks. At the edge are access and customer networks (e.g., enterprise and home networks), which are distinguished from the core networks at the center that provide connectivity and services to these edge

networks and their customers. The demarcation of core and edge is not precise, but generally, the capacity of core routers and transport links (which aggregate the traffic of many edge networks and users) is significantly greater than what is commonly seen in edge networks.

54. Today's core router is tomorrow's edge router. The big service providers like Sprint, AT&T, and Level 3 migrate the core routers that they purchased a few years ago to the edge as they upgrade their cores to take advantage of recent advances in the technology. The opportunity to do so extends the life of equipment purchases, which reduces the economic cost.

55. Many of these issues are being addressed as part of the FIA NEBULA project in the design of the NCore, a hyperreliable core routing architecture (see Smith et al., 2011).

56. Taleb (2007).

57. Varian (2004) presents a simple model that shows how incentives to invest in the optimal level of reliability often fail to exist.

58. See Coglianese and Mendelson (2010).

59. Just as the PSTN of old was more heavily regulated than the Internet cloud of today, the nuclear power industry is significantly more heavily regulated than the chemical industry.

60. See Lehr (2012).

References

Akerlof, G. 1970. The Market for Lemons: Quality Uncertainty and the Market Mechanism. *Quarterly Journal of Economics* 84 (3): 488–500.

Armbrust, M., A. Fox, R. Griffith, A. D. Joseph, R. H. Katz, A. Konwinski, G. Lee, D. A. Patterson, A. Rabkin, and I. Stoica. (2009) "Above the Clouds: A Berkeley View of Cloud Computing," Technical Report UCB/EECS-2009–28, EECS Department, University of California, Berkeley.

Bauer, S., D. Clark, and W. Lehr. (2011) "Powerboost." In *Proceedings of the 2nd ACM SIGCOMM Workshop on Home Networks* (August, pp. 7–12). ACM.

Bauer, S., D. Clark, and W. Lehr. (2010), "Understanding Broadband Speed Measurements," MITAS Working Paper, June 2010, available at http://papers.ssrn.com/sol3/papers.cfm?abstract_id=1988332.

Botterman, M. (2009), "Internet of Things: An Early Reality of the Future Internet Workshop Report," prepared for the European Commission, Information Society and Media Directorate, May 10, 2009. Available at http://ec.europa.eu/information_society/policy/rfid/documents/iotprague2009.pdf.

Coglianese, C., and E. Mendelson. (2010) Meta-Regulation and Self-Regulation. In eds. M. Cave, R. Baldwin, and M. Lodge, *The Oxford Handbook on Regulation*. Oxford: Oxford University Press.

Federal Communications Commission (FCC). (2010) *Connecting America: The National Broadband Plan*, Washington, DC: Federal Communications Commission.

International Telecommunication Union (ITU). (2005) The Internet of Things. In *7th ITU Internet Report*. Geneva, Switzerland: International Telecommunication Union.

Isenberg, D. (1997), "Rise of the Stupid Network." Available at http://www.rageboy .com/stupidnet.html.

Jianli, P., S. Paul, and R. Jain. 2011. A Survey of the Research on Future Internet Architectures. *Communications Magazine, IEEE* 49 (7): 26–36.

Labovitz, C., S. Lekel-Johnson, D. McPherson, F. Jahanian, J. Oberheide, and M. Karir. (2009) "Atlas Internet Observatory Report (Arbor Networks, University of Michigan, and Merit 2-Year Internet Traffic Study)," North American Network Operators Group Meeting 47 (NANOG47), October 2009. Available at http://www .nanog.org/meetings/nanog47/abstracts.php?pt=MTQ1MyZuYW5vZzQ3&nm=nan og47.

Lehr, W. (2012), "Measuring the Internet: The data challenge," Organisation for Economic Cooperation and Development (OECD) Digital Economy Working Paper 184, ISSN 2071–6826, April. Available at http://www.oecd-ilibrary.org/science-and -technology/measuring-the-internet_5k9bhk5fzvzx-en/

Lehr, W., S. Bauer, and D. Clark. (2012), "Measuring Broadband Performance When Broadband Is the New PSTN," MITAS Working Paper, May 2012.

Lehr, W., S. Bauer, M. Heikkinen, and D. Clark. (2011) "Assessing Broadband Reliability: Measurement and Policy Challenges," 39th Research Conference on Communications, Information, and Internet Policy (www.tprcweb.com), Alexandria, VA, September 2011.

Lehr, W., D. Clark, P. Faratin, R. Sami, and J. Wroclawksi (2006). Overlay Networks and Future of the Internet. *Communications and Strategies* 63 (3rd Quarter 2006): 1–21.

Leibenstein, H. (1966). Allocative Efficiency vs. X-Inefficiency. *American Economic Review* 56 (June): 392–415.

Lucky, R. 1997. When Is Dumb Smart? *IEE Spectrum* 34 (11): 21.

Mell, P., and T. Grance. (2009) "The NIST Definition of Cloud Computing." http:// www.nist.gov/itl/cloud/upload/cloud-def-v15.pdf.

Odlyzko, A. 1998. "Smart" and "Stupid" Networks: Why the Internet Is Like Microsoft. *netWorker* 2 (5): 38–46.

Rimal, B., E. Choi and I. Lumb (2010). "A Taxonomy, Survey, and Issues of Cloud Computing Ecosystems Cloud Computing." In N. Antonopoulos and L.

Gillam, eds., *Cloud Computing: Principles, Systems, and Applications,* London: Springer.

Smith, J., R. Broberg, A. Agapi, K. Birman, D. Comer, C. Cotton, T. Kielmann, W. Lehr, R. VanRenesse, and R. Surton. (2011) "Clouds, Cable, and Connectivity: Future Internets And Router Requirements," Proceedings of 2011 Cable Connection Spring Technical Conference, June 14–16, Chicago.

Taleb, N. 2007. *The Black Swan: The Impact of Highly Improbable Events.* New York: Random House.

Thierer, A. 2006. Are "Dumb Pipe" Mandates Smart Public Policy? Vertical Integration, Net Neutrality, and the Network Layers Model. In *Net Neutrality or Net Neutering: Should Broadband Internet Services Be Regulated?* ed. T. M. Lenard and R. J. May, 73–108. New York: Springer.

Varian, H. (2004), System Reliability and Free Riding." In *Economics of Information Security,* ed. L. J. Camp and S. Lewis, 1–15. New York: Kluwer.

Zhu, J. 2010. Cloud Computing Technologies and Applications. In *Handbook of Cloud Computing,* eds. B. Furht and A. Escalante, 21–45. New York: Springer.

4 Cloud Computing, Contractibility, and Network Architecture

Christopher S. Yoo

One of the fundamental changes effected by the emergence of cloud computing is to take functions previously performed by resources contained within a user's personal computer or laptop and transfer them to servers located in a distant data center. For users running virtual desktops, every single keystroke must pass through the network and be remotely registered by a virtual machine.

Such a drastic rearrangement of where particular tasks are performed creates pressure for the architecture to evolve to meet these new demands. For example, the fact that data that previously did not need to leave the personal computer sitting on the user's desk must now pass through a transmission network may lead to increased demand for bandwidth and decreased tolerance for latency. Moreover, because the path over which the data may travel may not be secure and the legal requirements of various jurisdictions may be diverse, cloud computing may lead users to demand the ability to verify the source of a packet and to exercise a greater degree of control over the path over which their data will travel and the locations where their data will be hosted.

In short, the advent of cloud computing is placing new demands on the Internet and other communications networks that users are employing to access cloud-based services and resources. Unfortunately, the services that the Internet is designed to provide are rather limited in both number and scope. Moreover, the types of services being provided over the cloud are constantly changing. Any attempt to modify the Internet to incorporate a discrete set of new services risks being rendered obsolete by the next wave of innovation.

Rather than try to restructure the network to provide a particular set of services needed by the current iteration of the cloud, an alternative approach would seek to reengineer the architecture to provide the necessary primitives sufficient to enable present and future cloud service providers to support a wide range of policies. If properly designed, these primitives should allow both users and providers to create and monitor the services that they need by contract. Basic principles of contract theory have revealed two prerequisites that must be satisfied if contracts are to be effective. First, the information that is subject to the contract must be *observable*, in that both parties can perceive the relevant states of the world with respect to that information. Second, the relevant information must be *verifiable*, in that the parties must be able to prove after the fact in a court of law or to some other third party that the relevant state of the world did or did not occur (see, e.g., Hölmstrom 1979; Hart and Moore 1988). A classic example of a matter that is observable but not verifiable is effort exercised by an employee in the context of an employment contract. Both the employer and the employee may be well aware of the employee's level of effort or lack thereof, but it may be unable to be prove in a court of law.

If the architecture is to allow private actors to contract for certain levels of quality of service or data security, the minimum information needed for parties to be able to enforce their bargains must be observable and verifiable by the parties. The logical solution is to locate the primitives to make Internet transactions contractible in the network layer, which is the spanning layer visible to all network participants. The problem is that the Internet's current architecture does not satisfy either criterion. Users can observe or verify neither the source of data nor the precise path that a given transmission will take through the network. Moreover, the network layer of the Internet, which consists of the Internet Protocol (IP), is notoriously difficult to change.

Ongoing research sponsored by the National Science Foundation (NSF) and the Institute of Electrical and Electronics Engineers (IEEE) is exploring ways to redesign the architecture to provide the primitives necessary to make the network services demanded by cloud computing contractible. Such a revision would enable network providers and users to make their own arrangements regarding new network services required by the cloud, which would be more consistent with the Internet's traditional approach of relying on decentralized decision making and would preserve the flexibility to adapt to new developments and increases in scale.

The Cloud's Need for New Network Services

As noted previously, cloud computing takes functions that used to involve the interaction of physical resources connected directly to a personal computer or a laptop and distributes them to a remote data center. This reconfiguration will place new demands on the access network in terms of bandwidth, ubiquity, reliability, latency, and route control. The access networks' ability to meet these demands will go a long way toward determining cloud computing's attractiveness as an option.

Bandwidth

Cloud computing is likely to increase the demands that are placed on the local access network. As an initial matter, new cloud computing customers must have some means for uploading their data to the data centers when setting up new applications. At this point, however, the access network does not have sufficient bandwidth to support this level of utilization. Because data sets in the terabyte range would take weeks to upload, cloud computing providers currently recommend that customers download their data onto a physical storage medium and send it via an overnight mail service (Brodkin 2010). Eventually, the hope is that network capacity will increase to the point where large data sets can be provisioned through the network itself.

Even after data has been provisioned to a new cloud computing facility, the fact that processing that used to occur locally is now being performed in the data center typically means that a greater volume of traffic must pass to and from the client that the user is operating. Cloud computing may thus cause an increase in the total bandwidth required from the network on a day-to-day basis as well.

Ubiquity

Cloud computing requires a higher degree of ubiquity than traditional computing solutions. When the software and the data needed to run a particular application reside on the users' hard disk, the unavailability of a network connection may inconvenience them and reduce the application's functionality, but it does not necessarily stop them from being productive in any way. When the software and data reside in the cloud, however, the absence of a network connection has more serious consequences, effectively preventing them from running the application at all. As a result, cloud computing customers regard ubiquitous access to network connections as critical.

Reliability

A related concern is access network reliability. The availability of an access network connection is meaningless if it is not functioning properly. Even when the application and the data reside on a user's hard disk, the failure of a network connection can severely limit the user's ability to perform productive work. Network failure becomes an even more serious obstacle when these elements are hosted in the cloud. Indeed, Gmail, Salesforce.com, and Amazon's Simple Storage Service (S3) and Elastic Compute Cloud (EC2) have suffered from well-publicized service outages that imposed severe difficulties on their customers. These higher stakes mean that some customers are likely to demand that access networks offer higher levels of guaranteed uptime.

Quality of Service

Users' willingness to offload services that used to be provided locally into the cloud depends in no small part on how quickly the cloud is able to perform those functions. Aside from bandwidth, the most frequently discussed aspect of quality of service is latency, which is the delay that an application takes to register a change. Someone typing on a virtual desktop is likely to insist on latencies that are no more than a few hundred milliseconds. Other relevant aspects of quality of service include reliability (measured in terms of the accuracy of records) and jitter (measured in terms of variations in the spacing between packets). Different applications have different tolerances for each aspect of quality of service. As a result, cloud computing customers are likely to insist on service level agreements (SLAs) that guarantee them certain minimum levels of quality of service on those dimensions that matter most to them. These demands will likely vary in different cases. For example, financial services companies typically require perfect transactions, with latency guarantees measured in microseconds. In addition, these companies require the cloud provider to audit the accuracy and delivery time of every transaction after the fact.

Cloud computing is likely to require sophisticated network management techniques to provide minimum levels of quality of service. One way that cloud computing systems can improve the quality of service of network services is by taking advantage of the presence of multiple connections between two points. The Internet currently relies on protocols such as the Border Gateway Protocol (BGP) to determine the route that any particular stream of packets may take between domains. BGP is limited in its ability to manage multiple paths, routing all traffic along a single route instead of balancing traffic across multiple paths. BGP, moreover, is controlled by the core routers rather than by users. A new architecture for cloud computing could improve network performance by providing greater ability to allocate traffic across multiple paths and to allow faster recovery from congestion and network failure. It could also increase functionality by giving users control over the particular routes taken by their traffic.

Control Over Routing

Cloud computing necessarily requires large amounts of data that previously did not leave a company's computer or internal network to be transported via a series of networks to a data center. The fact that this data must pass outside the company's firewall and through the access network renders it vulnerable to attack vectors that are different from those that plague corporate campuses.

As a result, cloud-based solutions must be able to assure these institutions that their data are being handled in a way that preserves confidentiality by giving users greater ability to control which networks their traffic passes through. Because cloud computing requires that sensitive information must pass over a network connection, users may demand the ability to verify a packet's source, as well as the means to ensure that their data will pass only over networks they deem trustworthy.

Moreover, the ability to shift data from one data center to another potentially makes that data subject to another country's privacy laws. Current data protection requirements vary widely across jurisdictions. For example, US law holds all institutions that maintain health or educational records responsible for maintaining their privacy. The fact that such records are now housed in the cloud does not obviate those responsibilities. However, in the European Union, the law requires that data be retained only for limited purposes and for limited times. Because customers are ultimately responsible for any such violations, they are likely to insist on a significant degree of control over where their data reside at any particular moment. In addition, cloud computing may require an architecture that permits the exact routes that particular traffic takes to be auditable and verifiable after the fact.

The emergence of the cloud is thus causing users to place a different set of demands on the network. Moreover, not all cloud users will need the same combination of services. Word processing does not require significant bandwidth, but it is extremely sensitive to latency. Users who use the cloud to store video or music can tolerate the latency needed to buffer streaming media, but they demand significantly more bandwidth.

This heterogeneity has led many commentators to recognize that it is not appropriate to fold cloud computing into the conceptual framework traditionally applied to public utilities (Brynjolfsson, Hoffman, and Jordan 2010, Kushida, Murray, and Zysman 2011, Bayrak, Conley, and Wilkie

2011; also see chapter 3, "Reliability and the Internet Cloud," in this volume). History has shown that public utility regulation is ill suited to technologies where the product attributes are complex and where the production technology varies and is undergoing rapid technological change (Yoo 2013b). It comes as no surprise, then, that early commentators who first conceived the computing utility typically acknowledged that it did not fit within the classic conception of public utilities (see, e.g., Irwin 1966, Parkhill 1966, Baran 1967, Barnett et al. 1967, President's Task Force on Communications Policy 1968, Smith 1969).

Limits of the Current Architecture

Cloud computing may demand quality of service guarantees, as well as the ability to control the routes that particular data will pass through the network. The existing architecture does provide some tools to facilitate the provision of these services. For example, the engineering community has devised a wide range of protocols to help provide defined levels of quality of service. Indeed, the inclusion of a type-of-service field in the original Internet Protocol version 4 (IPv4) header reveals that quality of service through prioritization was part of the Internet's original design. Subsequently, the Internet community has developed a wide array of protocols to promote quality of service, including Integrated Services (IntServ), Differentiated Services (DiffServ), and MultiProtocol Label Switching (MPLS). More recent efforts include virtual circuit services such as Internet2's Interoperable On-demand Network (ION) and deprioritization regimes such as the Low Extra Delay Batch Transport (LEDBAT) from the Internet Engineering Task Force (IETF), both of which represent fairly substantial deviations from the principles around which the current Internet is organized (Yoo 2011a). The problem is that to date, none has attained sufficiently broad acceptance to support cloud services. The retention of the type-of-service field (renamed "Traffic Class") in Internet Protocol version 6 (IPv6) underscores the continuing importance of quality of service.

Regarding routing, the original IPv4 header includes an optional field to allow the source to determine the route that packets will take. This option is not mandatory and has largely been ignored. In addition, the BGP-based system responsible for routing traffic on the current Internet employs an algorithm that allows each router to make independent decisions about the path that particular packets will take through the network. In general, BGP by default simply sends traffic along the path that transverses the fewest autonomous systems. Although BGP is intended to permit networks to implement routing policies, these policies tend to be implemented by altering the routing table by hand by increasing the apparent length of a path in an effort to make certain routes unattractive. The fact that each firm makes such individualized adjustments on a distributed basis can lead to interactions that make such policies difficult to implement and even harder to guarantee.

Cloud computing providers and users wishing to exercise greater control over the paths that are taken by traffic that passes between data centers may rely on MPLS or some other protocol to exercise control over the precise paths that are taken by particular traffic. In fact, IPv6 added a "Flow Label" field to incorporate this functionality into the network layer itself. Such control mechanisms are essential to ensuring that flows between data centers maintain the required levels of quality of service, protect network security, and maintain the privacy of users' data. As of today, such services are provided as overlays rather than being designed into the network itself.

Most important in terms of contractibility, even if labels allow users to specify paths taken through the Internet, the Internet's architecture does not provide any basis for verifying a packet's source or the path that it traversed. Nor is there any basis for verifying whether any particular prioritization regime was followed. Stated in terms of contract theory, the information needed to make quality of service and route control contractible is neither observable nor verifiable.

In addition, with the Internet's current architecture, the information needed to make Internet privacy contractible is not observable or verifiable either. First, consider information about the source of Internet transmissions. One of the foundational principles on which the Internet is based is that every administrative domain connected to the Internet exchange packets through a single, uniform spanning layer, represented by the IP, in which each machine is identified by a unique address that is visible to every other machine connected to the network (Cerf and Kahn 1974). One problem is that the source address included in the IP header is insecure and can be misrepresented (spoofed), making it impossible to verify the source of any communication under the network's basic design. Although additional features, such as Internet Protocol Security (IPSec), have subsequently been developed that can support source authentication, they are not mandatory and are not widely deployed in IPv4. Although the specification for Internet Protocol version 6 (IPv6) makes IPSec mandatory, not all IPv6 implementations support IPSec.

Another core principle of the Internet is that routers operating in the network's core operate on a store-and-forward basis, with each router making its own independent decision about the path that any particular packet should take. As a result, users typically cannot specify the path that a particular packet should take through the network, as the source routing option included in the Internet's original design is not mandatory and remains nearly universally unused. Even if users were able to do this, the localized nature of information on the Internet makes path information difficult to observe and verify. Any component network of the Internet can only observe the identity of the network residing immediately upstream and downstream of its location. The store-and-forward nature of the Internet's architecture provides no mechanism through which the user can observe the path actually taken through the network. Thus, even if an user enters into an SLA with its Internet service provider (ISP) specifying the paths that its traffic must traverse, it has no reliable way to determine whether the ISP actually honored the terms of the SLA with respect to a specific transaction. Even if all of the relevant parties were able to observe the relevant information, the absence of any authoritative record of the path traversed by any particular packet makes this information difficult, if not impossible, to verify in a court of law.

Finally, the architecture restricts the configuration of economic relationships on the Internet. Money enters the network from the edge, typically as a payment to a last-mile network provider, but the network architecture provides no flow-based mechanism to allocate it among the different entities involved in providing service. Simply put, the Internet's design does not place the information needed to allocate value in the network layer which, as noted previously, is the spanning layer visible to all network actors. Restated in terms of contractibility theory, the economic information needed to support complex contracts is not observable, let alone verifiable. Or, as MIT computer scientist and former DARPA chief protocol architect David Clark is reported to have quipped, "We never learned how to route money" (McTaggart 2006).

The absence of any mechanism within the architecture itself for accounting for and distributing value among different actors forces money to flow through mechanisms that exist outside the network. Constraining value to flow exclusively through contracts between ISPs makes ISPs the irreducible unit of economic analysis and reinforces the current hierarchy of transit providers. Turning ISPs into indivisible artifacts for economic purposes also severely limits the flexibility with which services can be provided and contracted. Early proposals to create smart markets that would have permitted the money flow to follow the traffic flow were never adopted (Mackie-Mason and Varian 1995).

Contractibility as a Potential Nonregulatory Solution

The current network architecture thus restricts the services that the network can provide, as well as the flexibility with which economic relationships among different network elements can be configured. The emergence of new phenomena such as the cloud has prompted a wide range of new research initiatives designed to make the Internet more contractible.

NEBULA

The need to explore ways that the Internet may need to evolve to respond to new use cases has led the NSF to launch its Future Internet Architecture (FIA) project. One new architecture known as NEBULA is specifically designed to support the new demands placed on the network by cloud computing (Anderson et al. 2013, 2014). The challenge is to strike a balance between flexibility and efficiency by creating a minimal spanning set of features that can support an arbitrarily broad set of transit policies. The aspects of the NEBULA design that make the services on which cloud computing depends contractible are a control plane, known as the NEBULA Virtual and Extensible Networking Techniques (NVENT), and the NEBULA Data Plane (NDP), which is being adapted from a technology known as ICING (Naous et al. 2011).

A communication begins when the sending network places a request for a path to NVENT. NVENT envisions that each administrative domain comprising the Internet will maintain a policy engine that reciprocally exchanges information with other policy engines about the available services, resources, and paths. The policy engine identifies paths to reach requested destinations in ways that comply with any preferred transit policies governing the entities permitted to constitute the path, bandwidth, latency, reliability, and other considerations. The path or paths and the associated policies are then embodied in a token in a manner similar to MPLS. Any noncompliant paths are considered rejected by default. Once a path has been discovered, NVENT consults a consent engine maintained by each administrative domain and collects cryptographic proofs of consent from each of the administrative domains comprising the path. The fact that the policy and consent engines are distributed across the administrative domains comprising the network facilitates this system's flexibility and extensibility. It also provides flexibility in the specific policies being implemented.

The proofs of consent are then inserted into the NDP, which in effect replaces IP with a new spanning layer that supports source and path

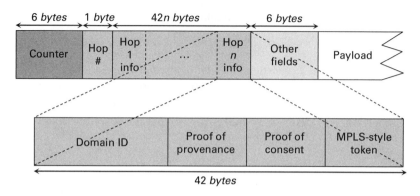

Figure 4.1
NDP packet format. Image by the author.

authentication. NDP reserves 42 bytes in its header (depicted in figure 4.1) for four elements with respect to each administrative domain contained in the path constructed by NVENT: (1) the domain identifier; (2) a cryptographic proof that the domain has authorized being included in the path, called the *proof of consent* (*PoC*); (3) a cryptographic proof that the packet has actually followed that path, called the *proof of provenance* (*PoP*); and (4) the MPLS-style token associated with this path.

These four elements are sufficient to allow networked entities to both express and enforce a broad range of policies about packet carriage. Decisions about policies are relegated to the control plane (NVENT), which remains distributed and flexible. Once those policies are embodied in the MPLS-style token, the four features embedded in the data plane (NDP) described previously are sufficient to allow these policies to be enforced. When a packet arrives at an administrative domain, that domain can check the PoC to verify that the packet was authorized by the policy. As the packet traverses the domain, the domain attaches its PoP to verify to all other network participants that it actually traversed that domain. The fact that both the PoC and PoP are cryptographically protected using public-key encryption allows every entity to authenticate the accuracy of the information contained therein. An added feature of NDP is that the key for decrypting the PoC and PoP is the domain identifier, which obviates the need to manage keys or maintain certificate authorities.

The four basic primitives contained in NDP are sufficient to encompass the functions enabled by a wide range of other efforts to make networks more secure. Specifically, NDP can determine that all communications traverse an assured path, prevent the entry of unauthorized communications, support the establishment of multiple paths to ensure availability and reliability, permit each administrative domain to exercise autonomous control, and enhance privacy by ensuring that communications only traverse trusted providers. In so doing, they provide a parsimonious set of information that provides the same functions as a wide range of more complex designs already appearing in the literature. Preliminary experiments and prototypes indicate that the architecture is feasible (Naous et al. 2010, 2011).

The cryptographically protected PoCs permit each administrative domain to authenticate that the particular transaction has been authorized ex ante. At the same time, the cryptographically protected PoPs permit each administrative domain to authenticate ex post that the approved path was followed.

These innovations have a dramatic impact on contractibility. By making the specific administrative domains traversed and the policies being applied visible, NEBULA renders the information needed to enforce privacy observable. In addition, the application of cryptographic signatures as each packet crosses an administrative domain makes any agreements as to paths to be used and policies to be honored verifiable.

Like any architecture, NEBULA is not without its potential concerns. As an initial matter, NDP requires the incurrence of significant overhead. For example, the inclusion in the network layer of the additional information associated with the four elements described here in the network layer header makes packets roughly 20 percent larger. Because NDP's functions are parallelizable, it appears that NDP can operate at backbone speeds. NDP-enabled routers would cost roughly 90 percent more than a bare-bones IP router but slightly less than a commercial IP router (Naous et al. 2010, 2011). These initial efforts are simply to provide proof of the concept. As was the case with the Internet itself, additional improvements on operating efficiency are likely to be realized once the network is refined and deployed. NDP is by no means the only approach to enhancing contractibility. In fact, NEBULA explored approaches based around alternative technologies (Anderson et al. 2013).

Although NDP enhances observability and verifiability, a trusted entity may nonetheless evade its limitations by subcontracting responsibility for transmission to another, unapproved entity or using tunneling to allow the communication to use unapproved routes. Moreover, although the information contained in the NDP header is designed to verify the path, it is less effective at revealing whether other policies were honored. NDP thus may require additional enforcement mechanisms outside its current design. Because contracting entities may not be in privity with these other parties, full enforcement may require recognizing a property interest in private information that is good against enforceable against all parties regardless of whether they have a contractual relationship.

The preliminary nature of the NEBULA project suggests that it is too soon to expect definitive answers to each of these issues. All of these considerations are the subject of future research. Any evaluation of its potential must bear in mind that it is the first implementation of such an architecture and is put forward as a proof of concept, not as an operational business model. One can reasonably expect performance improvements should the architecture be fully deployed.

IEEE Intercloud

Another research project that would provide the primitives needed to make cloud connectivity contractible is the IEEE's Intercloud working group (IEEE 2012, 2013). The primary goal of the Intercloud initiative is to standardize cloud services. Not only would this make them more portable; it would allow providers to combine cloud services offered by different providers and dynamically integrate them into a single offering.

The basic architecture of the Intercloud is modeled on the Internet. The architecture centers on community-governed Intercloud root providers that serve as the naming authority for the Intercloud in much the same manner as the domain name system does for the Internet. The Intercloud root providers also serve as the trust authority for the public key infrastructure (PKI) used to authenticate each entity. Presumably, the Intercloud root would not be a single entity. Instead, there would be multiple Intercloud roots that would host the cloud computing resource catalog in a federated manner.

In addition to performing these functions, the Intercloud root providers offer other services needed to support contracts for cloud services. Most important, they maintain cloud computing resource catalogs that make visible the available cloud resources. These advertisements are made using uniform semantics that describe not only physical resources, such as servers, disks, and connectivity, but also other less tangible attributes, including SLAs, pricing policies, and security and compliance policies. It thus provides visibility and access to the information needed to form contracts through the Intercloud (Bernstein and Vij 2010).

The architecture also envisions the Intercloud exchanges that provide locations where multiple cloud providers can interoperate in a manner similar to the role currently served by Internet exchanges for the Internet.

These exchanges draw on the catalog information hosted by the root providers to broker cloud transactions with users.

The typical transaction falls into the following pattern: Cloud 1 uses its Intercloud gateway to query the cloud computing resources catalog maintained by the Intercloud root server to determine if the resources needed to support a particular cloud service are available. If Cloud 1 finds out from the catalog that the resources needed to meet its requirements and constraints are available from Cloud 2, the Intercloud exchange brokers an agreement between the two clouds. If an agreement is successfully reached, the clouds bilaterally establish the web sockets and other protocols needed for Cloud 2 to provide services to Cloud 1. Cloud 1 then uses Cloud 2's resources as part of its federated architecture, while Cloud 2 meters resource usage and compliance with the terms of the SLA.

Once this happens, most of the primitives needed for contractibility will be met. The cloud computing resource catalog makes the necessary resources observable to others prior to performance. Importantly, this includes not just the physical elements of the cloud, but also the SLAs, pricing, and other terms needed for contacts to operate. Each cloud conducts its own metering.

The only thing missing is ex post auditability. The Intercloud's architects recognize that an audit trail constitutes an essential part of the architecture. These responsibilities are supposed to be borne by the Intercloud root servers, although the necessary implementations have not been designed yet. Deployment of this auditing capability would make these transactions observable and verifiable during and after performance.

eXpressive Internet Architecture

Other NSF-sponsored FIA projects are pursuing architectures that enhance contractibility in different ways. For example, the eXpressive Internet Architecture (XIA) project has developed an architecture known as Scalability, Control, and Isolation On Next-generation networks (SCION) that relies more on trust than explicit enforcement (Zhang et al. 2011; Naylor et al. 2014).

SCION envisions that each autonomous system (AS) joins with other ASes to form a trusted domain (TD) that separates trusted from distrusted entities. Each TD designates an AS to represent the TD in the TD core, which initiates path construction, disseminates policy-complaint paths, allows destinations to choose their preferred paths, and uses cryptographic methods to ensure the authenticity of end-to-end paths.

Once the route has been joined, the source domain embeds "opaque fields" into each packet that encode the path information. Because SCION does not require each domain to cryptographically sign each packet as it traverses the domain, this solution does not fully support verifiability. Instead, SCION relies on trust or some other mechanism outside the information contained in each packet to authenticate the source and to determine whether the domains actually honored the selected path.

ChoiceNet

The research program that most explicitly attempts to make Internet-based transactions contractible is ChoiceNet, which was also funded by the NSF's FIA program (Wolf et al. 2014). The current architecture imposes a number of constraints on the network. Money enters the network only through its edges and flows outside the network architecture. Moreover, traffic is constrained to move through the network in accordance with the economic relationships between network providers implicitly reflected in BGP routing policies. The result is that both users and content providers have little control over how their traffic is handled within networks.

ChoiceNet is designed to create an "economy plane" that enables actors to create contracts that dynamically integrate the offerings of multiple providers of network components into a single service offering. The goal is to allow the money flow to follow the traffic flow instead of vice versa. The resulting flexibility in configuring services from different providers should enable new entities to combine the underlying network elements in new ways, which can promote innovation and competition.

ChoiceNet provides a uniform address architecture and a minimal set of service semantics sufficient to permit network providers to advertise the nature of the services they are offering. The semantics must cover not only the physical services being provided, but also other contractual terms such as quality of service and price. ChoiceNet entities then act as intermediaries to combine and bundle these services into end-to-end offerings. ChoiceNet then provides a marketplace where customers can shop for different end-to-end service offerings that the intermediaries have created. The semantics of the marketplace advertisements must be general enough to be searchable, yet specific enough to specify the necessary dimensions of performance. Finally, ChoiceNet envisions a verification process through which customers can determine whether actual performance lived up to the contract specifications. While ChoiceNet's designers are rather vague about the details of how to implement this function, suggesting that it might be fulfilled by third-party measurement providers or by the exchange of measurement data within the research community, they have acknowledged that verification plays an indispensable role in their scheme.

A ChoiceNet transaction can be envisioned as a five-step process. In the *advertisement* step, the intermediary advertises in the marketplace the end-to-end offering that it has created. In the *planning* step, prospective customers use algorithms to search the marketplace and explore the bundles of services created by the intermediaries. In the *provisioning* step, the customers and intermediaries establish contracts, exchange consideration, commit the resources to provide the agreed-upon service, and generate tokens that serve as credentials to obtain access to the contracted-for resources and to prove policy compliance. In the *usage* step, each resource examines the token to verify that usage has been authorized in the economy plane. In the *verification* step, the customer employs a verification service to confirm that it received the promised level of performance.

ChoiceNet was not designed specifically for the cloud, although cloud computing would be able to employ its architecture to the same extent as other Internet-based applications. Admittedly, the ChoiceNet architecture is not yet well developed. But the basic approach is fully consistent with the concerns raised in this chapter. The ChoiceNet architecture is designed to provide the elements needed for contractibility. Creating semantics and loci for sharing information about service attributes makes the necessary information observable prior to performance. The envisioned verification mechanism would make the actual performance both observable and verifiable.

At this early stage, one must be careful not to become overly distracted by debates over the relative merits of any particular proposal. The principle of making Internet transmissions contractible by making key information both observable and verifiable is ultimately more important than the details of how that is done in any particular implementation.

Conclusion

Cloud computing is creating new demands for network services that the current architecture was not designed to support. The increasing diversity of new technologies and applications and the accelerating rate of innovation suggest that direct regulation will continue to lag behind the current environment and will struggle to scale as use cases continue to proliferate.

A more fruitful approach may be to focus instead on supporting more contract-oriented governance by making Internet transactions more contractible. Rather than envisioning any particular type of contractual relationship, this approach revises the network layer visible to all Internet-connected actors to provide sufficient primitives to permit individual actors to construct a wide range of interconnection relationships. The resulting ability to authenticate the source of packets as well as the path they used to traverse the network should greatly enhance Internet privacy.

Clean-slate redesigns of network architecture are notoriously difficult to implement. The presence of a large installed base creates significant inertia behind the existing architecture. Such inertia can be overcome if the new architecture provides sufficient value. Even so, such transitions are likely to pose significant multilayer coordination problems (Yoo 2013a). The details of the specific implementation are less important than the need to refocus the privacy debate away from command-and-control regulation in favor of a more flexible, decentralized, and evolvable regime that is more consistent with the Internet philosophy and relies primarily on private ordering.

Acknowledgments

I would like to thank Bill Boebel, Daniel Burton, Robert Krauss, Bill Lehr, Antonio Nicolosi, Don Norbeck, Todd Proebsting, Jonathan Smith, Jeff Vagle, Michael Walfish, and Joe Weinman, as well as participants in the conference on "Cloud Computing: Economic and Regulatory Implications" held at the University of Pennsylvania Law School on February 24, 2011, and the Research Roundtable and Public Policy Conference on "The Law and Economics of Privacy and Data Security" held at George Mason University School of Law on December 12–13, 2012, and June 19, 2013, for input on earlier drafts. This work is partially supported by National Science Foundation Grant CNS-10–40672. It explores solutions to problems identified in Yoo (2010, pp. 83–87) and Yoo (2011b).

References

Anderson, Tom, Ken Birman, Robert Broberg, Matthew Caesar, Douglas Comer, Chase Cotton, Michael Freedman, 2013. The NEBULA Future Internet Architecture: A Mid-Course Report. In *The Future Internet—Future Internet Assembly 2013: Validated Results and New Directions*, ed. Alex Galls and Anastasius Gavras, 16–26. New York: Springer.

Anderson, Tom, Ken Birman, Robert Broberg, Matthew Caesar, Douglas Comer, Chase Cotton, Michael J. Freedman, 2014. A Brief Overview of the NEBULA Future Internet Architecture. *Computer Communication Review* 44 (3): 81–86. .10.1145/ 2656877.2656889

Baran, Paul. 1967. The Future Computer Utility. *Public Interest* 8 (June): 75–87.

Barnett, C. C., Jr., B. R. Anderson, W. N. Bancroft, R. T. Brady, D. L. Hansen, H. Simmons, D. C. Snyder, D. Wechsler, and J. L. Wilcox. 1967. *The Future of the Computer Utility.* New York: American Management Association.

Bayrak, Ergin, John P. Conley, and Simon Wilkie. 2011. The Economics of Cloud Computing. *Korean Economic Review* 27 (2): 203–230.

Bernstein, David, and Deepak Vij. 2010. "Using Semantic Web Ontology for Inter-cloud Directories and Exchanges." 2010 International Conference on Internet Computing (ICOMP), Las Vegas, NV. Available at http://www.intercloudtestbed .org/uploads/2/1/3/9/21396364/using_semantic_web_ontology_for_intercloud _directories_and_exchanges.pdf.

Brodkin, Jon. 2010. "Amazon Cloud Uses FedEx Instead of the Internet to Ship Data," *Network World*, June 10. Available at http://www.networkworld.com/news/ 2010/061010-amazon-cloud-fedex.html.

Brynjolfsson, Erik, Paul Hoffman, and John Jordan. 2010. Cloud Computing and Electricity: Beyond the Utility Model. *Communications of the ACM* 53 (5): 32–34. .10.1145/1735223.1735234

Cerf, Vinton G., and Robert Kahn. 1974. A Protocol for Packet Network Intercon-nection. *IEEE Transactions on Communications* 22 (5): 637–648. .10.1109/TCOM. 1974.1092259

Hart, Oliver, and John Moore. 1988. Incomplete Contracts and Renegotiation. *Econometrica* 56 (4): 755–785. .10.2307/1912698

Hölmstrom, Bengt. 1979. Moral Hazard and Observability. *Bell Journal of Economics* 10 (1): 74–91. .10.2307/3003320

Institute of Electrical and Electronics Engineers (IEEE). 2012. "IEEE P2302/D0.2: Draft Standard for Intercloud Interoperability and Federation (SIIF)." Available at http://www.intercloudtestbed.org/uploads/2/1/3/9/21396364/intercloud _p2302_draft_0.2.pdf.

Institute of Electrical and Electronics Engineers (IEEE). 2013. "IEEE Intercloud TestBed: Technical Overview and Engineering Plan." Available at http://www .intercloudtestbed.org/uploads/2/1/3/9/21396364/ieee_intercloud_testbed _technical_overview_engineering_plan_v6.pdf.

Irwin, Manley R. 1966. The Computer Utility. *Datamation* 12 (11): 22–27.

Kushida, Kenji E., Jonathan Murray, and John Zysman. 2011. Diffusing the Cloud: Cloud Computing and Implications for Public Policy. *Journal of Industry, Competition, and Trade* 11 (3): 209–237. doi:10.1007/s10842-011-0106-5

Mackie-Mason, Jeffrey K., and Hal R. Varian. 1995. Pricing the Internet. In *Public Access to the Internet*, ed. Brian Kahin and James Keller, 269–314. Cambridge, MA: MIT Press.

McTaggart, Craig. 2006. "Was the Internet Ever Neutral?" Paper presented at the 34th TPRC, Arlington, VA. Available at http://ssrn.com/abstract=2117601.

Naous, Jad, Arun Seehra, Michael Walfish, David Mazières, Antonio Nicolosi, and Scott Shenker. 2010. "Defining and Enforcing Transit Policies in a Future Internet." University of Texas at Austin Department of Computer Sciences Technical Report TR-10–07. Available at www.cs.utexas.edu/~mwalfish/icing_tr_1007.pdf.

Naous, Jad, Michael Walfish, Antonio Nicolosi, David Mazières, Michael Miller, and Arun Seehra. 2011. "Verifying and enforcing network paths with ICING." *Proceedings of the 7th International Conference on emerging Networking Experiments and Technologies (CoNEXT)*, art. 30. doi:. Available at http://dl.acm.org/ft_gateway.cfm?id=2079326&ftid=1066769&dwn=1&CFID=543066384&CFTOKEN=90992542.10.1145/2079296.2079326

Naylor, David, Matthew K. Mukerjee, Patrick Agyapong, Robert Grandi, Ruogo Kang, and Michel Machado. 2014. XIA: Architecting A More Trustworthy and Evolvable Internet. *Computer Communication Review* 44 (3): 50–57. doi:10.1145/2656877.2656885

Parkhill, Douglas F. 1966. *The Challenge of the Computer Utility*. Reading, MA: Addison-Wesley.

President's Task Force on Communications Policy. 1968. *Final Report*. Washington, D.C.: Government Printing Office.

Smith, Delbert D. 1969. The Interdependence of Computer and Communications Services and Facilities: A Question of Federal Regulation. *University of Pennsylvania Law Review* 117 (6): 829–859. doi:10.2307/3310940

Wolf, Tilman, Jim Griffioen, Ken Calvert, Rudra Dutta, George Rouskas, Ilya Baldin, and Anna Nugurney. 2014. ChoiceNet: Toward an Economy Plane for the Internet. *Computer Communication Review* 44 (3): 58–65. doi:10.1145/2656877.2656886

Yoo, Christopher S. 2010. The changing patterns of Internet usage. *Federal Communications Law Journal* 63 (1): 67–89.

Yoo, Christopher S. 2011a. Rough consensus and running code: Integrating engineering principles into Internet policy debates. *Federal Communications Law Journal* 63 (2): 341–356.

Yoo, Christopher S. 2011b. Cloud computing: Architectural and policy implications. *Review of Industrial Organization* 38 (4): 405–421. doi:10.1007/s11151-011-9295-7

Yoo, Christopher S. 2013a. Protocol layering and Internet policy. *University of Pennsylvania Law Review* 161 (6): 1707–1771.

Yoo, Christopher S. 2013b. Is there a role for common carriage in an Internet-based world? *Houston Law Review* 50 (2): 545–608.

Zhang, Xin, Hsu-Chun Hsiao, Geoffrey Hasker, Haowen Chan, Adrian Perrig, and David G. Anderson. 2011. "SCION: Scalability, control and isolation on next-generation networks." Paper presented at the TRUST Autumn 2011 Conference, Washington, DC. Available at http://sparrow.ece.cmu.edu/group/pub/SCION.pdf.

5   Cloud Privacy Law in the United States and the European Union

Andrea Renda

The legal approach to privacy and data protection has always been very different in the United States versus the European Union (Schwartz and Solove 2013). First, the United States has traditionally relied on piecemeal, sectoral regulation and private regulation to address privacy issues. The European Union, in contrast, enacted the first horizontal, omnibus data protection laws in the 1970s, followed by the adoption of the Convention for the Protection of Individuals with Regard to Automatic Processing of Personal Data in 1981, and the enactment of the EU Data Protection Directive 95/46 (DPD 95/46) in 1995.

Moreover, in Europe, privacy is explicitly considered as a fundamental right, whereas the US Constitution contains no explicit reference to privacy.[1] Many prominent US scholars consider privacy as amounting to a property right—that is, an alienable commodity that can be traded in exchange for customized service. Finally, in the United States, privacy legislation and case law traditionally focused on the protection of the citizen against violations and misbehavior of public authorities (also due to the scope of the Fourth Amendment), whereas in the European Union the focus is rather on the private sector. In a widely cited article published on the *Yale Law Journal,* James Whitman (2004) interpreted the fundamental divergence between the legal approaches to privacy in the United States and in the European Union as rooted in a cultural difference between privacy as an aspect of liberty and privacy as an aspect of dignity.[2]

Against this background, the emergence of cloud computing creates significant legal challenges in addition to the undoubted potential benefits. The features of cloud computing technology permit a degree of flexibility, which makes it increasingly difficult to identify who is responsible for data handling, who should be held accountable vis à vis cloud customers for the handling and processing of personal data, and the legal regime of data transfers outside the US and EU jurisdictions (Hon et al. 2011a, 2011b, 2012; Schwartz 2013; Schwartz and Solove 2013). A recent document authored by the Article 29 Working Party (WP29) (2012) summarizes the data protection risks of cloud computing as follows:

- *Lack of control.* Because cloud clients commit personal data to systems managed by cloud providers, which in turn could rely on subcontractors to deliver their services, cloud clients may no longer be in exclusive control of the data and may not be able to deploy the technical and organizational measures necessary to ensure the availability, integrity, confidentiality, transparency, isolation, intervenability, and portability of the data. This can lead to problems such as lack of interoperability ("vendor lock-in"); lack of integrity caused by the sharing of resources; lack of confidentiality in terms of law enforcement requests made directly to a cloud provider; lack of intervenability due to the complexity and dynamics of the outsourcing chain or to the fact that the cloud provider does not provide sufficient assistance to the data controller; and lack of isolation, especially when cloud providers use their physical control over data from different clients to link personal data and provide broad administrator privileges to too many individuals.

- *Lack of transparency.* This can occur especially when data processors (the cloud providers) do not share enough information with their counterparts (the cloud clients). Specific cases include when chain processing involves multiple processors and subcontractors and when personal data are processed in different geographic locations, some of which do not provide an adequate level of data protection.

This chapter describes the existing legislation on privacy in the United States and the European Union, its applicability to the cloud computing environment, and the extent to which current rules are able to address the problems outlined here. The first section, "Privacy Legislation in the United States," introduces the main privacy laws (along with case law and enforcement practice) in the United States, whereas the second section, "The EU Legal Framework for Data Protection," describes the legal regime in the European Union, paying specific attention to cloud computing and taking stock of transatlantic issues such as the Safe Harbor regime, the Binding Corporate Rules (BCRs), and the current tensions that emerged after the Datagate scandal. The final section presents a brief conclusion to the chapter.

Privacy Legislation in the United States

In the United States, the "right to privacy" is historically and legally rooted in the Fourth Amendment, which provides, "The right of the people to be secure in their persons, houses, papers, and effects against unreasonable searches and seizures, shall not be violated, and no Warrants shall issue, but upon probable cause, supported by Oath or affirmation, and particularly describing the place to be searched, and the persons or things to be seized." The Supreme Court has framed such a right since 1878 with respect to the confidentiality of personal postal correspondence such as letters and sealed packages.[3]

Likewise, the academic debate in the United States date back to the late nineteenth century, and particularly to Samuel Warren and Louis Brandeis's article "The Right to Privacy," published in the *Harvard Law Review* in 1890. But while Warren and Brandeis supported the idea of applying the common law of torts to protect a right to privacy, which they famously summarized as a "right to be let alone," their work did not spur major developments in courts, and privacy remained a matter related to government intrusion into the private sphere of the individual, also in the 1960s and 1970s.[4] When Congress adopted the Privacy Act in 1974, this vision of privacy was entered into statutory law: the act applies to records of personal information held by federal agencies and stipulates that the government create no secret files and provide the public with a right to access and copy their own files. Agencies were obliged to keep reasonably accurate records when "relevant and necessary," and to seek the individual's consent before disclosing any content (except within the agency, for "routine use" or for law enforcement).[5]

Over the past few decades, various scholarly approaches to privacy have emerged, mostly viewing privacy as control over data and framing it as a "commodity" rather than a fundamental right, with important consequences in terms of its alienability (Solove 2006).

Statutory Law

Concerning statutory law, early attempts to regulate privacy include the Fair Credit Reporting Act (FCRA) of 1970 and the Family Educational Rights and Privacy Act (FERPA) of 1974. Other federal statutes addressing specific privacy issues include the Children's Online Privacy Protection Act (COPPA), the Health Information Portability and Accessibility Act (HIPAA), the Electronic Communications Privacy Act (ECPA), and the Gramm-Leach-Bliley Act (GLBA). Several of these federal statutes focused on the presence of "personally identifiable information," while others focus on transparency and access to information, on protecting consumers from inappropriate use of their personal data, or on imposing duties of confidentiality. Next, we discuss in more detail the legislation that is most relevant for cloud computing [i.e., the ECPA, and in particular, its Title II, the Stored Communications Act (SCA); the USA PATRIOT Act; and the Foreign Intelligence Surveillance Amendments Act (FISAA)].

ECPA and the Stored Communications Act ECPA was adopted in 1986, reportedly in response to concerns that the protections for email were "weak, ambiguous, or nonexistent" (Office of Technology Assessment 1985). It consists of three federal statutes: the Stored Communications Act (SCA), the Pen Register statute, and the Wiretap Act. Its protections supplement those of the Fourth Amendment, and as such, essentially focus on the relationship between individuals and government authorities.[6] Title II of ECPA, the SCA, was designed to regulate the access and dissemination of electronic communications stored on computers. It essentially addresses two points: (1) the procedures that the government must follow to compel disclosure of stored communications; and (2) the situations in which a service provider may voluntarily share a customer's communications. Here are more details on the law:

- § 2702 of the SCA establishes when a service provider may voluntarily disclose the content of communications and customer information to another entity. This section applies only to service providers to the "public"; thus, nonpublic providers can turn over these documents without any specific procedural requirements.
- § 2703 of the SCA addresses how the government can compel a provider to produce stored information.

Notably, there are numerous exceptions to the principles established by these two sections.[7] These include cases in which the customer consents to disclosure (but then the definition of consent is not clear); cases of disclosure to persons who provide the service, which (as also confirmed by the Wiretap Act) allow service providers to monitor activities on their networks in real time; and cases of private employers that want to share internally information about the online activities of employees when the employer provides these services in house.[8]

The SCA introduces a distinction between electronic communication services (ECS), such as handling data transmissions and electronic mail, and remote computing services (RCS), such as providing outsourced computer processing and data storage).[9] Importantly, the protection afforded to RCS is generally lower than the protection afforded to the ECS. However, case law has revealed a great deal of uncertainty regarding the boundaries between RCS and ECS, and technological progress seems to be exacerbating this fundamental problem of classification.[10]

Regarding voluntary disclosure (§ 2702), ECS providers are prohibited from disclosing communication contents that they hold in "electronic storage," whereas RCS providers are prohibited from disclosing communication contents that they maintain for the sole purpose of providing the subscriber or customer with "storage or computer processing services."

Relative to the process required for government to obtain information (§ 2702), this also varies based on the type of information sought. The SCA foresees three different methods for compelling information: warrants, special court orders, and subpoenas. Warrants are needed in case governments seek access to the content of a communication from an ECS provider that has been in "electronic storage" for 180 days or less. Communications stored for more than 180 days from an ECS provider or from an RCS provider require prior notice to the customer and a subpoena or a court order under § 2703(d).[11] Only a subpoena is needed to compel ECS or RCS providers to disclose noncontent, basic subscriber information, with no prior notice to the customer.[12]

Thompson (2013) and Kesan et al. (2013) discuss the applicability of the SCA to cloud computing and more specific services such as email, social networks, and YouTube videos. What emerges is the following:

- Government access to the content of unopened emails stored for 180 days or less by an electronic communication service requires a warrant. Government access to opened or unopened emails stored for more than 180 days may be accessed with a subpoena or a § 2703(d) order, so long as the government provides notice to the subscriber.[13]
- However, the degree of privacy in an email crucially depends on whether it is stored on a hard drive or in the cloud. Emails downloaded from a service provider are easily covered by the requirement in the SCA that requires a warrant to obtain unopened emails less than 180 days old, but it is unclear whether a webmail provider would be considered an ECS or an RCS. In *Theofel v. Farey-Jones* (2004) and *United States v. Weaver* (2009), the cloud-based email provider (NetGate and Microsoft, respectively) were considered to be RCS providers, not ECS providers. Thus, the emails were subject only to the subpoena requirement, not the warrant requirement.

- Some question whether the SCA would protect "free" cloud services at all. Ryan (2014) observes that advertising-supported business models often give the providers access to communication contents for targeted advertising purposes. This may prevent these services from being considered RCS providers because the provider is allowed to access communication content for purposes other than rendering storage and computer processing services. Notably, the mere fact that a terms of service (TOS) agreement or a privacy policy (PP) give the provider explicit authority to access content can exclude that the cloud provider is considered an RCS provider.
- Also social networks and video streaming sites have been affected by the vague language of the SCA. In *Crispin v. Christian Audigier* (2010), which involved private messages sent on social networking sites, the US District Court for the Central District of California relied on precedents such as *Weaver* and *Theofel* to hold that when messages are opened and retained on the site, social networking sites such as Facebook and MySpace operate as RCS providers, and thus the messages are subject only to the subpoena requirement. Also, in *Viacom Intern. Inc. v. YouTube Inc.* (2008), the US District Court for the Southern District of New York concluded that Google was an RCS provider under the SCA and added that the SCA did not permit Viacom access to those videos that had been marked private by the user who posted them.

As a result, as observed in Thompson (2013), "the few courts that applied the SCA to e-mail and other Internet communications seem to have created a dividing line between traditional forms of Internet computing and cloud-based computing." While traditional email services are covered under the SCA's more stringent warrant requirement, cloud-based emails seem to be subject to the lesser subpoena requirement.

This discrepancy is only one example of a more general criticism often leveled at the ECPA and particularly the SCA: that these laws have been largely outpaced by technological developments and are too rigid to accommodate the emergence of paradigmatic changes such as that of cloud computing (Kerr 2004). This applies in particular to the distinction between RCS and ECS. Fischer and Moloney Figliola (2013) conclude, "It is extremely difficult to interpret or predict the privacy protections available under ECPA for the wide range of cloud computing activities."

The USA PATRIOT Act and the FISAA   Applicable laws on privacy in the United States also include exceptional measures taken in the name of security and the fight against terrorism. This is certainly the case of the USA PATRIOT Act and the FISAA, which we describe next.

Adopted in the aftermath of the 9/11 attacks, the Uniting and Strengthening America Provide Appropriate Tools Required to Intercept and Obstruct Terrorism (PATRIOT) Act of 2001 amended a number of existing laws, including the three titles of ECPA. As a result, companies can be forced to turn over data to the US government even without notice to the affected customers. Data stored outside US borders, if held in servers owned by a US company, are potentially covered by this provision. Even contract provisions specifying that data will be governed by foreign law can be ignored by the US government.[14]

After widespread allegations of "warrantless wiretapping" of US citizens after the attacks of 9/11, Congress enacted the Foreign Intelligence Surveillance Amendment Act (FISAA), which amended the 1978 Foreign Intelligence Surveillance Act (FISA). FISAA departs from the taxonomy of the ECPA and defines ECS as also including RCS (thus covering cloud computing). Section 1881a introduces the possibility that the US government can monitor foreign communications and access data of foreign citizens located outside the United States without a warrant (a requirement that, by virtue of the Fourth Amendment, would apply only to US citizens). A recent report for the European Parliament (Bigo et al. 2012) observed that while "there has been a lot of concern at the international level over the PATRIOT Act, there has been virtually no discussion of the implications of … § 1881a of FISAA," which "for the first time created a power of mass-surveillance specifically targeted at the data of non-US persons located outside the US, which applies to cloud computing."

The Fourth Amendment and the Cloud

Supreme Court jurisprudence on the Fourth Amendment in the area of privacy follows the landmark ruling in *Katz v. United States* (1967). In *Katz*, the Court recognized that people have a "reasonable expectation of privacy" (REOP) when two conditions are met: "First that a person have exhibited an actual (subjective) expectation of privacy and, second, that the expectation be one that society is prepared to recognize as 'reasonable.'" What is reasonable in a given case, of course, can depend greatly on the facts of the case.

In analyzing relevant Fourth Amendment jurisprudence, a few elements bear mentioning:

- The Fourth Amendment applies only to state searches; as such, it does not protect individual privacy from intrusion by private cloud providers.
- The case law establishes an important distinction between "content" and "non-content" information, with the latter category including things

like addresses on the outside of an envelope and phone numbers dialed on a phone. In the cloud context, a person is likely to not have a REOP in subscriber information provided to an Internet service provider (ISP). Other noncontent information, like email addresses in the "To" field of an email or Internet Protocol (IP) addresses of visited websites, are unlikely to fall under the Fourth Amendment.

- The third-party doctrine of Fourth Amendment jurisprudence prevents a REOP from being found in papers and effects turned over to a third party (*United States v. Miller,* 1976; *Couch v. United States,* 1973). Scholars often argue that this third-party doctrine prevents Fourth Amendment protections from applying in the cloud because users must inherently reveal their information to third parties for it to be transmitted or processed.[15]

As already mentioned, the primary purpose of the Fourth Amendment is to protect the privacy of the citizenry and to prevent arbitrary government intrusion into their lives. The Fourth Amendment does not limit what information the government may collect, but it does limit the means by which that information may be collected, making information collectors accountable to the judiciary.

Contract Law, Tort Law, and State Law

As already mentioned, most US statutes and case law on cloud privacy focus on public interference with privately stored information. For the relationship between customers or subscribers and their cloud providers, contract and tort laws apply, together with consumer protection enforcement by the Federal Trade Commission (FTC), as discussed in the next section.

With respect to contract law, user privacy becomes relevant, especially with respect to documents such as the service level agreement (SLA), acceptable use policy, TOS, and PP, which often leave a great degree of discretion to the provider for handling consumer data and contains terms that most often are not subject to negotiation. TOS agreements vary significantly: in *United States v. Warshak* (2010), the US Court of Appeals for the Sixth Circuit ruled that excessively permissive TOS agreements may deprive a customer of a REOP in contents stored or transmitted using a service, so the validity of these contracts has implications for privacy law. The Court held that government agents violated the Fourth Amendment when they compelled an ISP to turn over the defendant's emails without first obtaining a search warrant based on probable cause. Most notably, the court further declared the SCA unconstitutional to the extent that it allows the government to obtain emails without a warrant.

In contract law, it is important to recall that TOS agreements and similar documents can be held void if they are "unconscionable," and some courts have reportedly invalidated excessively one-sided TOS agreements on unconscionability grounds. Typically, this requires a finding of both procedural and substantive unconscionability.[16]

In the area of tort law, one area that has seen significant case law developments over the past few years is that of security breaches, which are inevitably relevant to privacy and are normally dealt with through a negligence standard. One good example is *Wong v. Dropbox, Inc.* (2011), a class-action related to an update to the Dropbox software that inadvertently allowed anyone to log into any account using any password for approximately four hours.

The FTC as Data Privacy and Security Enforcer

An increasingly important player in the privacy domain is the FTC in its role of consumer protection enforcer. Hartzog and Solove (2014) report:

[F]or more than 15 years, the FTC has regulated data security through its authority to regulate unfair and deceptive trade practices. In the late 1990s, the first complaints were brought under a theory of deception based upon a company's failure to honor its own promises of data security, usually made as part of a privacy policy. About a decade ago, the FTC also began to allege that inadequate data security was an unfair trade practice regardless of whether good data security was promised.

The number of investigations and sanctions accumulated by the FTC over the past few years is remarkable (Cline 2014). To be sure, the FTC has filled an important gap in US privacy law by protecting customers against privacy- and security-reducing practices adopted by their providers.

All entities that store consumer information on the cloud face the threat of FTC enforcement if the way they store and secure information does not match their declarations to their customers. This unfair behavior amounts to a deceptive or unfair practice under Section 5 of the FTC Act. In addition, the FTC enforces a handful of sector-specific privacy laws, including COPPA, GLBA, FCRA, Telephone Consumer Protection Act (TCPA), and the Telecommunications Act, as well as the EU-US Safe Harbor.

Under Section 5, a trade practice is characterized as follows:

- Deceptive, if it involves a "material representation, omission, or practice that is likely to mislead a consumer acting reasonably in the circumstances, to the consumer's detriment."

- Unfair, if it "causes or is likely to cause substantial injury to consumers which is not reasonably avoidable by consumers themselves and is not outweighed by countervailing benefits to consumers or competition" [the so-called three-part test of Section 5(n) of the FTC Act].

Based on current practice, it would seem that a cloud client that hires a cloud provider without exercising due diligence might be challenged under Section 5. At the same time, designing a mobile system such that one application that has permission to access sensitive information allows another application that has not been given the same level of permission to access that information (i.e., permission re-delegation) might be considered unfair under Section 5. A material retroactive change to the privacy policy without seeking consumers' express opt-in consent might also fall under this category.

The expansion of FTC authority over privacy issues was recently challenged when Wyndham Worldwide Corp. refused to settle with FTC and challenged the complaint in federal court, arguing that the FTC lacked authority to regulate data security and that it failed to provide fair notice of what constitutes actionable data security practices. The court however rejected Wyndham's argument and concluded that the FTC has broad power under Section 5 to support its exercise of authority (Hartzog and Solove 2014).

Concluding Remarks

Our survey of the US legal approach to privacy, specifically as applied to cloud computing, portrays a patchwork of rules with very different scopes. In addition, three main phenomena can be highlighted: the strong and almost exclusive focus of the Fourth Amendment and related statutory law (ECPA/SCA, USA PATRIOT Act, FISAA, etc.) on government seizure of personal communications; the emergence of the FTC as the real regulator of privacy issues between private parties, including in the cloud; and the growing gap between practices covered by the law and the evolution of information technology (IT) services such as cloud computing.

More specifically, the SCA is considered to be at once too vague in its definitions and obsolete in its distinction between RCS and ECS providers. In the case law, significant uncertainty also remains because the Supreme Court has thus far refrained from clarifying if and when individuals have a reasonable expectation of privacy in digital communications.[17]

Finally, the role and powers of the FTC appear to be still evolving and in search of a more systematic definition. The FTC acts mostly on the basis of consumer injury, and it seems to have filled, through Section 5 of the FTC Act, an undeniable gap in US privacy law. However, there seems to be significant space for a clarification of the FTC powers, as well as of the criteria and definitions used by the FTC in enforcing legislation to protect consumer privacy and data security.

The EU Legal Framework for Data Protection

The first European data protection laws were enacted in the 1970s, followed by the adoption of the Convention for the Protection of Individuals with regard to Automatic Processing of Personal Data in 1981. At the EU level, the right to privacy has been so far regulated by Directive 95/46 (1995), which, however, does not cover judicial and police cooperation. Such areas are currently covered by the Council of the European Union's 2008 Framework Decision on the protection of personal data processed in the framework of police and judicial cooperation in criminal matters. Other relevant legislation in force are the 2002 and 2009 e-Privacy Directives, and the Data Retention Directive, which has however been declared invalid by the European Court of Justice in a recent decision (see the section "The Data Retention Directive," later in this chapter, for more information).

More specifically, the DPD applies in every case where personal data are being processed as a result of the use of cloud computing services. On the other hand, the e-Privacy Directive applies to the processing of personal data in connection with the provision of publicly available electronic communications services in public communications networks (telecom operators), and thus it is relevant only if such services are provided by means of a cloud solution.

The EU DPD
The EU DPD applies to data held both by the public sector and by the private sector. There are, however, important exemptions that give government the ability to access and process data for tax and criminal law purposes. As a result, it is fair to state that, contrary to what occurs under US statutory law, the main EU DPD applies far more stringently to the private sector than to the public sector.

In terms of scope, the DPD focuses on the protection of "personal data," which it defines as "information relating to an identified or identifiable natural person." No data protection rules will apply at all where data is not "personal" but is instead "anonymous"; i.e., "data rendered anonymous in such a way that the data subject is no longer identifiable" (Recital 26). Conversely, where data is "personal," the whole regime regarding personal data applies regardless of context or degree of risk, with additional specific rules applying where personal data belong to so-called special categories of personal data.[18] Moreover, the DPD applies to data controllers that use "equipment" within the European Union for the processing of personal data: however, it must be considered that this term has been interpreted very broadly and applies also to intangible items, like cookies and JavaScript (Kuner 2010).

The DPD identifies three main classes of persons to whom EU data protection law applies:

- *Data controllers*, who are those persons who determine the purposes for which and the means whereby personal data are collected and processed.
- *Data processors*, who act under the instruction of controllers and do not themselves decide the processing purposes.
- *Data subjects*, the individuals whose personal data is being processed.

The DPD directed the EU member states to impose legal obligations on controllers to protect personal data by complying with certain principles when processing personal data. These principles, in brief, require the following (again, subject to various exceptions):

- Processing of personal data must be fair and lawful.
- Personal data must be collected for specified lawful purposes only and be adequate, relevant, and not excessive for those purposes.
- Personal data must be accurate and kept updated as necessary, not be kept for longer than required for the purpose, processed in accordance with certain data subject rights, and not transferred to a country outside the European Union that does not ensure an adequate level of protection.

In order to meet the fair and lawful processing requirement, controllers must give individuals notice of the processing and meet one of the conditions required to render the processing lawful.[19] A controller may engage a "processor" to process personal data for it, but it must choose a processor providing "sufficient guarantees" with respect to the technical security measures and organizational measures governing the processing to be carried out, and the controller must ensure compliance with those measures. Furthermore, the controller's contract with the processor must be in writing and must require the processor to act only on instructions from the cloud client.

Roles and Responsibilities in the Cloud Environment   The authoritative WP29 pointed out in its January 2010 opinion on the concepts of "controller" and "processor" that "the first and foremost role of the concept of controller is to determine who shall be responsible for compliance with data protection rules, and how data subjects can exercise the rights in practice. In other words: to allocate responsibility."[20] As a matter of fact, most EU member states impose data protection obligations only on controllers (e.g., to ensure that their contracts with processors meet the requirements). Because few member states impose data protection obligations directly on processors, processors in most member states are accountable only to controllers under the controller-processor contract.

Against this background, the European Commission recently observed that "cloud providers usually consider themselves as data processors; however, whether the cloud provider is to be regarded as a controller or processor depends on the circumstances" (European Commission 2012a). The WP29 also confirmed in a recent opinion that "any contractual designation of the parties' status, e.g., that the provider is only a processor, is relevant but not determinative of the legal status of the provider, because factual circumstances are important in attributing the roles above" (Article 29 Working Party 2012). Cloud providers would normally be regarded as "processors" because even passive, temporary storage of personal data is considered "processing," regardless of whether the provider knows that stored data is personal data. Data transmission or disclosure also constitutes "processing." A provider may be considered as a controller if it uses personal data stored by a cloud user for its own purposes or discloses such data to third parties without the controller's authority.

In their role of processors, cloud providers have a duty to ensure confidentiality. The DPD states in Article 16, "Any persons acting under the authority of the controller or of the processor, including the processors themselves, who have access to personal data must not process them except on instructions from the controller, unless he is required to do so by law." Processors must take into account the type of cloud in question, whether it be public, private, community, or hybrid, infrastructure as a service (IaaS), software as a service (SaaS), or platform as a service (PaaS); and the type of service contracted by the client. They are responsible for adopting security measures in line with those in EU legislation as applied in the controller's and the processor's jurisdictions. Processors must also support and assist the controller in complying with exercised data subjects' rights.

The Client-Provider Relationship: Main Requirements   The basic principles that should be respected by data controllers under the DPD in their relationship with data subjects are the following:

- *Transparency*. The controller must provide data subjects detailed information on the identity of those that will collect the subject's personal data, and for what purpose; in addition, the client should also provide any further information on the recipients or categories of recipients of the data, which can also include processors and subprocessors insofar as such information is necessary to guarantee fair processing in respect of the data subject (cf. Article 10 of the DPD). Transparency obligations also arise between controllers and processors (and their subcontractors). The controller should carefully check the cloud provider's terms and conditions and assess them from a data protection point of view (including the location of the data centers in which data will be stored). If the provision of the service requires the installation of software on the cloud client's systems (e.g., browser plug-ins), the cloud provider should as a matter of good practice inform the client about this circumstance, particularly about its implications from a data protection and data security point of view. Conversely, the controller should raise this matter ex ante if it is not addressed sufficiently by the processor.
- *Purpose specification and limitation*. This principle requires that personal data must be collected for specified, explicit, and legitimate purposes and not further processed in a way incompatible with those purposes [Article 6(b) of the DPD]. Controllers must determine the purpose of the processing prior to the collection of personal data from the data subject and inform the data subject. Moreover, controllers must ensure that personal data are not illegally processed for further purposes by the cloud provider or one of its subcontractors.[21]
- *Erasure*. According to Article 6(e) of the DPD, personal data must be kept in a form that permits the identification of data subjects for no longer than necessary for the purposes for which the data was collected or for which it is further processed. Controllers must ensure that personal data that is not necessary any more are erased or truly anonymized. If this is impossible due to legal retention rules (e.g., tax regulations), access to this personal data should be blocked. Notably, the principle of erasure applies regardless of whether personal data is stored on hard drives or on other storage media. Data controllers have a duty to ensure that processors and their subcontractors adopt all necessary measures to ensure secure erasure, and that their contract with the processors

and the client contains clear provision for the erasure of personal data. The same holds true for contracts between cloud providers and subcontractors.

Key Content of the Client-Provider Contract   Controllers that decide to contract for cloud computing services are subject to stringent duties to ensure that the contractor respects technical security standards and good organization of the processing activity; and that a written contract is signed (Article 17(3) DPD), with explicit description of applicable and measurable SLAs and related penalties. As clarified in a dedicated WP29 opinion, the contract should be very detailed in terms of the following:

•In the event of infringement by the controller, any person suffering damages as a result of unlawful processing shall have the right to receive compensation from the controller for the damages caused. Should the processors use the data for any other purpose, or communicate or use it in a way that breaches the contract, they shall also be considered to be controllers and shall be held liable for the infringements in which they were personally involved.

Key Conditions of Service   As clarified by the WP29, Article 17(2) of the DPD places full responsibility on cloud clients (acting as data controllers) to choose providers that implement adequate technical and organizational security measures to protect personal data and to be able to demonstrate accountability. The security conditions that should apply are:

- *Availability,* i.e., timely and reliable access to personal data. Severe threats to availability in the cloud include accidental loss of network connectivity between the client and the provider or of server performance caused by malicious actions such as distributed denial of service (DDoS) attacks. Other availability risks include accidental hardware failures (both on the network and in the cloud processing and data storage systems), power failures, and other infrastructure problems.
- *Integrity,* i.e., the property that data is authentic and has not been maliciously or accidentally altered during processing, storage, or transmission. Interference with the integrity of IT systems in the cloud can be prevented or detected by means of intrusion detection systems/intrusion prevention systems (IPS/IDS). This is particularly important in the type of open network environments in which clouds usually operate.
- *Encryption of personal data,* which should be used in all cases when "in transit" and when available to data "at rest." In some cases (e.g., an IaaS

storage service), a cloud client may not rely on an encryption solution offered by the cloud provider, but it may choose to encrypt personal data prior to sending them to the cloud. Communications between cloud provider and client, as well as between data centers, should be encrypted. Remote administration of the cloud platform should take place only via a secure communication channel. If a client plans to not only store, but also further process personal data in the cloud (e.g., searching databases for records), it must bear in mind that encryption cannot be maintained during processing of the data (except of very specific computations).

- *Isolation* (purpose limitation), i.e., data shall not be used beyond its initial purpose (Article 6(b) of the DPD). The implementation of roles with excessive privileges should be avoided (e.g., no user or administrator should be authorized to access the entire cloud). More generally, administrators and users must be able to access only the information that is necessary for their legitimate purposes (i.e., the least privilege principle). Isolation also depends on technical measures, such as the hardening of hypervisors and proper management of shared resources if virtual machines are used to share physical resources between different cloud customers.
- *Intervenability*, whereby the data subject has the rights of access, rectification, erasure, blocking, and objection (cf. Articles 12 and 14 of the DPD). The controller must verify and ensure (also contractually) that the processor does not impose technical and organizational obstacles to these requirements.
- *Portability*, i.e., the cloud client should check whether and how the provider guarantees the portability of data and services prior to ordering a cloud service.
- *Accountability*, i.e., the ability to establish what an entity did at a certain point in time in the past and how. In the field of data protection, it often takes a broader meaning and describes the ability of parties to demonstrate that they took appropriate steps to ensure that data protection principles have been implemented.

Other Applicable Legislation

The e-Privacy Directive   The Directive 2002/58/EC of the European Parliament and of the Council of 12 July 2002 concerning the processing of personal data and the protection of privacy in the electronic communications sector, often referred to as the ePrivacy Directive (as amended in 2009), being part of the regulatory framework for electronic communications, introduces obligations of security and confidentiality for providers of e-communications only. It deals with a number of important issues, such as confidentiality of information, treatment of traffic data, spam, and cookies. The security of services concept includes the duty to inform subscribers whenever there is a particular risk, such as a virus or other malware attack. Confidentiality obligations are addressed by member states, which should prohibit listening, tapping, storage, or other kinds of interception or surveillance of communication and "related traffic" unless the users have given their consent or the conditions of Article 15(1) have been fulfilled.

The applicability of the e-Privacy Directive to cloud computing is disputed for two reasons. First, not all cloud services can be qualified as e-communications services under the EU regulatory framework. Second, not all cloud services are publicly available services. Private and community cloud services do not belong to this category, and as such are not subject to the e-Privacy Directive. In conclusion, only public cloud services that fall within the scope of the e-communications regulatory framework are subject to the directive.

The Data Retention Directive   The Data Retention Directive (2006/24/EC) was adopted to amend the e-Privacy Directive to provide a more effective response to the terrorist attacks in New York in 2001 and Madrid in 2004. It focused on the regulation of data retention to enable the access of law enforcement authorities for a certain period if necessary as a means of preventing, investigating, and prosecuting serious crime as defined by each of the member states in its national law. In April 2014, a judgment of the European Court of Justice held the directive invalid as it "interferes in a particularly serious manner with the fundamental rights to respect for private life and to the protection of personal data." Hence, "by adopting the Data Retention Directive, the EU legislature has exceeded the limits imposed by compliance with the principle of proportionality" (*Judgment in Joined Cases C-293/12 and C-594/12* 2014).

The Proposed New EU Data Protection Regulation
The European Commission, in evaluating the DPD and related legislation, acknowledged that new challenges to the protection of personal data have emerged compared to when the DPD was adopted, mostly due to technological developments and globalization. At the same time, there are wide divergences in the way member states have transposed and enforced the directive, so in reality, the protection of personal data across the European Union cannot be considered as equivalent today. Moreover, the application

of the EU data protection *acquis communautaire* in the area of police cooperation and judicial cooperation in criminal matters, in particular the 2008
Framework Decision, resulted in gaps and inconsistencies (European Commission 2012a).

Accordingly, the commission proposed a strong and consistent legislative reform, which consists of a regulation (replacing Directive 95/46/
EC) setting out a general EU framework for data protection[22] and a directive replacing the 2008 Framework Decision, setting out rules on the
protection of personal data processed for the purposes of prevention,
detection, investigation, or prosecution of criminal offenses and related
judicial activities.

The new proposed rules pursue the following effects:

- *Improve individuals' ability to control their data*, by ensuring that when
  their consent is required, it is given explicitly, meaning that it is based
  either on a statement or on a clear affirmative action by the person
  concerned and is freely given; by equipping Internet users with an effective "right to be forgotten" in the online environment[23]; by guaranteeing
  easy access to one's own data and a right to data portability; and by
  reinforcing the right to information so that individuals fully understand
  how their personal data is handled, particularly when the processing
  activities concern children.
- *Improve the means for individuals to exercise their rights*, by strengthening
  national data protection authorities' independence and powers and
  enhancing administrative and judicial remedies when data protection
  rights are violated. In particular, qualified associations will be able to
  bring actions to court on behalf of the individual.
- *Reinforce data security*, by encouraging the use of privacy-enhancing technologies, privacy-friendly default settings, and privacy certification
  schemes; and introducing a general obligation for data controllers to
  notify data breaches without undue delay to both data protection
  authorities and the individuals concerned.
- *Enhance the accountability of those processing data*, in particular by requiring data controllers to designate a Data Protection Officer in companies
  with more than 250 employees and in firms that are involved in processing operations which, by virtue of their nature, their scope, or their
  purposes, present specific risks to the rights and freedoms of individuals
  ("risky processing").

Harsh sanctions are foreseen for noncomplying companies, including a
warning in writing in cases of first and nonintentional noncompliance,

regular periodic data protection audits, and fines of up to 100 million euros or up to 5 percent of the annual worldwide turnover in the case of an enterprise (whichever is greater).

In a recent commentary, Berkeley professor Paul Schwartz (2013) observed that the proposed new rules would significantly affect US companies in their daily practice of communicating the use of personal information through simple "notice and consent." As mentioned, the proposed regulation lists "consent" as one of the legal justifications for the processing of personal data, but it requires that written consent for personal information processing be presented in a form "distinguishable" from any other matter. More important, Article 7 of the proposed text places the "burden of proof" of demonstrating consent on the "controller"; this requirement "heightens the risk that a user's consent will not stand up if a data protection commissioner or the user herself challenges the assent after the fact."

Finally, and most problematically, the proposed regulation rules out the possibility of seeking consent for many situations involving the cloud, since it states that consent "shall not provide a legal basis for the processing" when "there is a significant imbalance between the position" of the controller and the party to whom the data refers. Thus, cloud companies would not be able to justify processing by a party's consent if they offered take-it-or-leave-it terms for the processing of personal data, or provided cloud services for employees or other parties that lack effective bargaining power. As a consequence, Schwartz concludes that US cloud companies cannot rely on one-sided, click-through agreements.

In terms of jurisdiction, Schwartz also observes that, given that it applies to "processing activities" that are related to "the offering of goods or services" to individuals within the European Union or "the monitoring of their behavior," the proposed regulation potentially subjects all cloud services to EU privacy law. Also the fact that the regulation seems to equate "monitoring" with "profiling" potentially subjects the new provisions to many kinds of value-added services. Moreover, the regulation seems disproportionate, as it subjects several transactions to stringent legal constraints in which no EU citizen is involved, but companies are. Finally, problems for the cloud industry would emerge if the European Union does not preserve in the regulation the provision contained in the DPD, which withheld jurisdiction if "equipment is used only for purposes of transit through the territory of the Community." As observed by Schwartz, certain cloud services, such as the provision of IaaS, would fit within this exemption.

In May 2014, the European Court of Justice ruled against Google in *Google Spain SL, Google Inc. v Agencia Española de Protección de Datos, Mario Costeja González*, a case brought by a Spanish individual who requested the removal of a link to a digitized 1998 article in the newspaper *La Vanguardia* about an auction for his foreclosed home for a debt that he subsequently paid. He initially attempted to have the article removed by complaining to the Spanish Data Protection Agency, which rejected the claim on the grounds that it was lawful and accurate, but accepted a complaint against Google and asked Google to remove the results. Google sued in the Spanish *Audiencia Nacional*, which referred a series of questions to the European Court of Justice. The court ruled in *Costeja* that search engines are "data controllers" and, as such, are responsible for the content they point to. Thus, Google was required to comply with EU data privacy laws.

In ruling, the Court also clarified the following issues:

- Even if the physical server of a company processing data is located outside Europe, EU rules apply to search engine operators if they have a branch or a subsidiary in a member state that promotes the selling of advertising space offered by the search engine.
- Search engines are controllers of personal data. Therefore, Google cannot escape its responsibilities before European law when handling personal data by arguing that it is a search engine. EU data protection law applies, as does the right to be forgotten.
- Individuals have the right—under certain conditions—to ask search engines to remove links with personal information about them. This applies where the information is inaccurate, inadequate, or excessive, and it is subject to a "balancing test" with other fundamental rights, such as freedom of expression. Such a test is the responsibility of the data controller in the first place.

EU-Level Work on Contract Terms   The European Commission and the European Data Protection Supervisor have also emphasized the need for improvement and standardization of the contract terms of cloud service providers. Following the European Commission communication "Unleashing the Potential of Cloud Computing in Europe" (European Commission 2012b), a recent document by the Commission announced that a working group was established in the context of the Cloud Select Industry Group with the objective to deliver a Data Protection Code of Conduct for cloud service providers to support a uniform application of data protection rules and to build trust and confidence in the field of cloud computing. In

February 2014, the Code of Conduct was submitted to the WP29 for its opinion in order to ensure legal certainty and coherence between the Code of Conduct and EU law. The opinion from the WP29, as well as the establishment of a governance framework for the code, is expected by early 2015.

Cross-Border Data Flows: What Is the Future of the EU Safe Harbor?

A very important feature of cloud computing is the possibility that data processors can offer their services from remote locations. This, in turn, also means that data stored in the cloud might flow across borders, with consequent problems in terms of jurisdiction and applicable law. The DPD also governs data transfers, permitting them only to other countries with an "adequate" level of protection. The United States is not included in the list of countries with "adequate" protection; however, the Safe Harbor agreement developed by the US Department of Commerce in consultation with the European Union and designed to prevent accidental information disclosure or loss ensures that US companies can transfer data to the United States if the company handling the transfer essentially complies with the DPD in handling and processing the data.[24]

However, after the recent revelations by National Security Agency (NSA) whistleblower Edward Snowden, the European Commission, and later the European Parliament, called for a suspension and a thorough revision of the Safe Harbor agreement. Meanwhile, on the basis of a thorough analysis and consultations with companies, the European Commission made thirteen recommendations to improve the functioning of the scheme. The commission called on US authorities to identify remedies by summer 2014. The commission would then review the functioning of the Safe Harbor scheme based on the implementation of these recommendations.

Transatlantic data transfers can also be significantly facilitated by reliance on Binding Corporate Rules (BCRs). These are rules developed by the WP29 to allow multinational corporations, international organizations, and groups of companies to make intraorganizational transfers of personal data across borders in compliance with the EU DPD, and they were developed as an alternative to the Safe Harbor. BCRs must be approved by the data protection authority in each EU member state in which the organization will rely on the BCRs. BCRs by themselves do not automatically allow transfers for all EU member states: in most states, a formal "transfer notification" is needed.

The WP29 has observed that BCRs can be adapted to provide adequate safeguards for EU data exported into the cloud. The proposed new data protection regulation normalizes the procedure of BCRs for data processors, as the latter are no longer regarded technically as a "derogation." However for the same reasons, Bigo et al. (2012) observe that since "Safe-Harbour-for-processors is a problematic concept … BCRs-for-processors's role should also be questioned. All they can do is pledge to maintain the Cloud datacentres. They can say nothing about the meaning of the data, or the substantive functions at the software level of personal data processing."

Also, it must be recalled that the negotiations to arrive at a so-called umbrella agreement governing data transfers for the purposes of law enforcement and national security have stalled since the United States has rejected the idea to apply the agreement to data transferred from private parties in the European Union to private parties in the United States.

Conclusion

In the age of convergence, globalization, and the data-driven economy, the United States and the European Union do not seem to be converging in their approach to data protection. First, existing legislation confirms the main approach followed by the two legal systems, with a clear focus on government intrusion into the private sphere in the United States, and significant emphasis on the relationship between data controllers and data subjects in the European Union. In a second, related point, while privacy law in the United States focuses on redressing consumer harm and balancing privacy with efficient commercial transactions, privacy in the European Union is considered as a fundamental right that prevails over competing interests (Hartzog and Solove 2014). Third, privacy protection is essentially triggered by the existence of personal data or personally identifiable information (PII); however, the definition of PII on the two sides of the Atlantic significantly diverges, with the United States featuring a patchwork or partly inconsistent definitions, and the European Union relying on a single definition that broadly defines PII to encompass all the information that is identifiable to a person.[25] Fourth, coverage of personal *identified* and *identifiable* information seems to be more consistent in Europe than in the United States: however, the European Union seems too expansionist in its coverage of PII, whereas the United States might err in the opposite extreme.

In addition, frictions between the United States and European Union authorities have mounted in the months following Snowden's revelations, such that even established cooperation and recognition frameworks such as Safe Harbor regime are now being reconsidered. Calls for a European cloud, or even clouds limited to national territory (e.g., in Germany alone) have become common in the debate over cloud privacy and security. The European Parliament has expressed its intention to reconsider the Safe Harbor, as well as the Data Protection Umbrella Agreement, which has been under discussion between the two parties since 2011. In terms of law enforcement and the mutual protection of citizens, Viviane Reding, former EU vice president for justice, fundamental rights, and citizenship, observed that "when Americans come to Europe and they think the authorities have not handled their case correctly, they can go to a European court. However an EU citizen cannot do the same in the U.S. and go to an American court. There is no reciprocity; we do not have the basis for judicial redress ... The U.S. has recognised the importance of this request on several occasions—but they need to have a law. I have not yet seen it."

Needless to say, this persisting divergence can become an obstacle (or, at minimum, a source of unnecessary compliance burdens) for companies wishing to operate across the Atlantic to provide cloud services. This is especially the case for world-leading, US-based cloud providers, which might enormously profit from a streamlining, update, and harmonization of the definition of PII and, more generally, the rules that apply to data protection in the cloud.

Apart from this widening transatlantic divergence, this chapter has highlighted a number of existing problems related to the application of privacy legislation to cloud computing in both the United States and the European Union. More specifically:

- In the United States, the existing statutory legislation and case law are in need of an update and are largely focused on government seizure cases. Distinctions such as the ECS/RCS taxonomy of the SCA seem hardly suited to the emerging world of cloud aggregators. The growing role of the FTC in protecting privacy and data security is not accompanied by an adequate effort to clarify duties and responsibilities of cloud providers and clients. In addition, legislation such as the USA PATRIOT Act and— even more—the FISAA allow public authorities to largely overcome the right to privacy, particularly when it comes to non-US citizens.
- In the European Union, the work of the definition of model contracts, as well as the reform of the legislative framework, seems to be more advanced. However, new proposed legislation seems to introduce a number of rigidities that could negatively affect the development of innovative business models and a thriving cloud sector. The new rules

should be revised in a way that does not jeopardize the viability of cloud models, such as removing the current equation between monitoring and profiling, restoring legal certainty as to the possibility of securing individual consent, and withholding jurisdiction if equipment is used only for purposes of transit through the territory of the European Union.

To be sure, the cloud is challenging both legal regimes in a way that might end up requiring a thorough reform process. As of now, what seems likely is that the United States will keep underprotecting privacy in the name of efficient commercial transactions (with a great responsibility being placed on the FTC to monitor abuses of bargaining power and other deceptive or otherwise abusive practices), whereas in the European Union, cloud services might end up caught in the net of an overformal, overcomprehensive legal framework that leaves little room for trade-offs between privacy and welfare-enhancing customized service for data subjects.

Notes

1. The word *privacy* does not appear explicitly in either the US Constitution or the Bill of Rights. However, the US Supreme Court has ruled in favor of various privacy interests, deriving a right to privacy from the First, Third, Fourth, Fifth, Ninth, and Fourteenth Amendments to the Constitution.

2. See Whitman (2004, 161), quoting Post (2001) and arguing that "Continental privacy protections are, at their core, a form of protection of a right to respect and personal dignity … By contrast, America, in this as in so many things, is much more oriented toward values of liberty, and especially liberty against the state."

3. See *Ex parte Jackson* (1878), in which the Supreme Court ruled that "[t]he constitutional guaranty of the right of the people to be secure in their papers against unreasonable searches and seizures extends to their papers, thus closed against inspection, wherever they may be … No law of Congress can place in the hands of officials connected with the postal service any authority to invade the secrecy of letters and such sealed packages in the mail; and all regulations adopted as to mail matter of this kind must be in subordination to the great principle embodied in the fourth amendment of the Constitution."

4. This was due in part to public concern with surveillance of war protestors during the Vietnam War and by abuses of wiretapping powers and seizure of tax, bank, and telephone records during the Watergate scandal. In 1966, the Supreme Court famously stated in *Hoffa v. United States* (1966) that when an individual "puts something in his filing cabinet, in his desk drawer, or in his pocket, he has the right to know it will be secure from an unreasonable search or an unreasonable seizure." In *Nixon v. Administration of General Services* (1977), the Court upheld the federal

statute that required national archivists to examine written and recorded information accumulated by the president. The Court ruled that while "the appellant has a legitimate expectation of privacy in his personal communications," that right must be weighed against the important public interest in the preservation of materials. The Court did not believe that the appellant's privacy interest was a match for the competing public interest.

5. Records from the Central Intelligence Agency (CIA) and other law enforcement officers are exempt from the right of access and correction. Other exemptions cover materials prepared in anticipation of litigation.

6. The Wiretap Act covers the interception of wire, oral, and electronic communications. Under the Wiretap Act, obtaining email contents in real time requires a Title III order to be issued with Department of Justice approval and a grant by a federal judge, and the order must be renewed every thirty days. Under the Pen Register statute, obtaining real-time subscriber data requires an *ex parte* pen register order. Stored electronic information and the requirements for obtaining each type are addressed under the SCA.

7. Exceptions in § 2702(b) include having the consent of one of the parties to the communication; being as a necessary incident to the rendition of services; being in connection with a missing child; having been inadvertently obtained and pertaining to the commission of a crime; or if there is imminent risk of death or serious physical injury to any person. A public provider may release customers' records or other non-content information if it meets one of the six exceptions provided in § 2702(c), which include consent of the subscriber; as a necessary incident to the rendition of services; and in connection with a missing child.

8. It is unclear whether employers will lose the right to monitor their employees' online activities if they outsource IT to a cloud service provider (Kesan et al. 2013).

9. An ECS is defined as "any service which provides to users thereof the ability to send or receive wire or electronic communications," while an RCS is defined as a "provision to the public of computer storage or processing services by means of an electronic communications system."

10. In *Theofel v. Farey-Jones* (2004), the boundary between RCS and ECS appears essentially arbitrary, holding that even indefinite email backup storage constitutes an ECS service provision.

11. To obtain a court order, the governmental entity must show "specific and articulable facts" establishing "reasonable grounds" to believe that the information sought is "relevant and material to an ongoing criminal investigation." A warrant must satisfy a more stringent "probable cause" standard, whereas a "reasonable relevance" standard applies to the subpoena.

12. Basic noncontent information includes the customer's name, address, phone records (including session times and durations), length and type of service, phone number, and how the customer pays for the service.

13. However, there is a split in the courts as to whether an opened email stored 180 days or less is in "electronic storage" under the SCA.

14. Specifically, section 215 of the PATRIOT Act allows the Federal Bureau of Investigation (FBI) to access data related to investigations in an *ex parte* proceeding with the requirement that "no person shall disclose to any other person ... that the [FBI] has sought or obtained things under this section."

15. However, in *United States v. Warshak* (2010), the Court distinguished email interception from other third-party doctrine cases by holding that the email provider was an intermediary in the communication, not a recipient. The *Warshak* decision also noted that if an agreement with a service provider gave the service provider the authority to "audit, inspect, and monitor" the emails of its subscribers, that might cause the subscriber to lose a REOP in those emails. See also *State v. Bellar* (2009), as described by Pinguelo and Muller (2011).

16. Procedural unconscionability is seen as the disadvantage suffered by a weaker party in negotiations, whereas substantive unconscionability is the unfairness of terms or outcomes. For example, see *Bragg v. Linden Research, Inc.* (2007), in which procedural and substantive unconscionability were found to be sufficient to invalidate an arbitration clause included in a TOS; and *People v. Network Associates, Inc.* (2003), in which the court declared the unfairness and the consequent unenforceability of some terms of a software license.

17. *City of Ontario v. Quon* (2010) held that the presence of a clause allowing the employer to monitor activity eliminated the need for Fourth Amendment analysis. A number of lower courts have considered this issue, however, and held that a reasonable expectation of privacy exists even for nonlocal data (*State v. Bellar* 2009), holding that neither storing data on a hard drive or storing that data in secure medium owned by a third party destroyed the privacy interest; *Crispin v. Christian Audigier, Inc.* (2010) (holding that Media Temple, Facebook, and MySpace are generally ECS providers); *In re United States' Application for a Search Warrant to Seize and Search Electronic Devices from Edward Cunnius* (2011). ("[T]he sheer volume of ESI involved distinguishes a digital search from the search of, for example, a file cabinet.")

18. More specifically, rules are made stricter for companies that want to use data in direct marketing or to transfer the data for other companies to use in direct marketing; and also in case the data contains sensitive information relating to racial and ethnic background, political affiliation, or religious or philosophical beliefs, trade-union membership, sexual preferences, and health. To collect this information, the data subject must give explicit consent. The definition of "personal data" has caused practical concerns given the increasing ease of identifying individuals from supposedly anonymous data, anonymization, and pseudonymization.

19. These include data subject consent, where the processing is necessary to perform a contract to which the data subject is party, to comply with a legal obligation, or for the purposes of the legitimate interests of the controller or the third party or parties to whom the data are disclosed.

20. The WP29 is an advisory body made of a representative from the data protection authority of each EU member state, the European Data Protection Supervisor, and

the European Commission. It was created by the DPD with three main missions: (1) give expert advices to the member states regarding data protection; (2) promote the same application of the DPD in all EU members, as well as Norway, Liechtenstein, and Iceland; and (3) give to the commission an opinion on community laws (first pillar) affecting the right to protection of personal data.

21. The WP29 observes, "As a typical cloud scenario may easily involve a larger number of subcontractors, the risk of processing of personal data for further, incompatible purposes must therefore be assessed as being quite high. To minimize this risk, the contract between cloud provider and cloud client should include technical and organizational measures to mitigate this risk and provide assurances for the logging and auditing of relevant processing operations on personal data that are performed by employees of the cloud provider or the subcontractors" (Article 29 Data Protection Working Party 2012).

22. It should be noted that the choice of a regulation replacing the DPD implies much less discretion in the implementation of the text at the national level, as the regulation is directly applicable and requires no transposition measure by EU member states.

23. The right to be forgotten is described as users' right to have their data deleted if they withdraw their consent and if there are no other legitimate grounds for retaining the data. See European Commission (2012a).

24. Safe Harbor principles include the following points:

• Notice—Individuals must be informed that their data is being collected and about how it will be used.

• Choice—Individuals must have the option to opt out of the collection and forward transfer of the data to third parties.

• Onward transfer—Transfers of data to third parties may only occur to other organizations that follow adequate data protection principles.

• Security—Reasonable efforts must be made to prevent loss of collected information.

• Data integrity—Data must be relevant and reliable for the purpose it was collected for.

• Access—Individuals must be able to access information held about them and correct or delete it if it is inaccurate.

• Enforcement—There must be effective means of enforcing these rules.

25. Hartzog and Solove (2014, 888) explain that there are three predominant approaches to defining personal information in the United States: (1) the "tautological" approach, (2) the "nonpublic" approach, and (3) the "specific-types" approach.

References

Article 29 Working Party. 2012. Opinion 05/2012 on Cloud Computing, 01037/12/ EN, WP 196, (July 1, 2012). Available at http://ec.europa.eu/justice/data-protection/ article-29/documentation/opinion-recommendation/files/2012/wp196_en.pdf.

Bigo, Didier, Sergio Carrera, Nicholas Hernanz, Julien Jeandesboz, Joanna Parkin, Francesco Ragazzi, and Amandine Scherrer. 2012. *Fighting Cyber Crime and Protecting Privacy in the Cloud*. Brussels: European Parliament.

Bragg v. Linden Research, Inc., 487 F. Supp. 2d 593 (E.D. Pa. 2007).

City of Ontario v. Quon, 560 U.S. 746 (2010).

Cline, Jay. 2014. U.S. Takes the Gold in Doling out Privacy Fines. *Computerworld* 17 (February 17). Available at http://www.computerworld.com/s/article/9246393/ Jay_Cline_U.S._takes_the_gold_in_doling_out_privacy_fines?taxonomyId=84&page Number=3.

Convention for the Protection of Individuals with Regard to Automatic Processing of Personal Data, Council of Europe. 1981, European Treaty Series No. 108.

Couch v. United States, 409 U.S. 322 (1973).

Council of the European Union Framework Decision 2008/977/JHA of 27 November 2008 on the Protection of Personal Data Processed in the Framework of Police and Judicial Cooperation in Criminal Matters. 2008 *Official Journal* (L 350) 60.

Crispin v. Christian Audigier, Inc., 717 F. Supp. 2d 965 (C.D. Cal. 2010).

Directive 95/46/EC of the European Parliament and of the Council of 24 October 1995 on the Protection of Individuals with Regard to the Processing of Personal Data and on the Free Movement of Such Data. 1995 *Official Journal* (L 281) 31.

Directive 2002/58/EC of the European Parliament and of the Council of 12 July 2002 Concerning the Processing of Personal Data and the Protection of Privacy in the Electronic Communications Sector (Directive on Privacy and Electronic Communications). 2002 *Official Journal* (L 201) 37.

Directive 2006/24/EC of the European Parliament and of the Council of 15 March 2006 on the Retention of Data Generated or Processed in Connection with the Provision of Publicly Available Electronic Communications Services or of Public Communications Networks and Amending Directive 2002/58/EC. 2006 *Official Journal* (L 105) 54.

Directive 2009/136/EC of the European Parliament and of the Council of 25 November 2009 Amending Directive 2002/58/EC Concerning the Processing of Personal Data and the Protection of Privacy in the Electronic Communications Sector. 2009 official Jounal (L 337) 11.

European Commission. 2012a. *Commission Staff Working Paper, Impact Assessment*, SEC (2012) 72 final (January 25, 2012).

European Commission. 2012b. *Communication from the Commission to the European Parliament, the Council, the European Economic and Social Committee, and the Committee of the Regions—Unleashing the Potential of Cloud Computing in Europe*, COM(2012) 529 final (September 27, 2012).

Ex parte Jackson, 96 U.S. 727 (1878).

Fischer, Eric A., and Patricia Moloney Figliola. 2013. *Overview and Issues for Implementation of the Federal Cloud Computing Initiative: Implications for Federal Information Technology Reform Management. CRS 7–5700.* Washington, DC: Congressional Research Service.

Google Spain SL, Google Inc. v Agencia Española de Protección de Datos, Mario Costeja González (Case C- 131/12, 13 May 2014).

Hartzog, Woodrow, and Daniel J. Solove. 2014. The FTC as data security regulator: *FTC v. Wyndham* and its implications. *Bloomberg BNA Privacy and Security Law Report* 13 (xx): 621-xx.

Hoffa v. United States, 385 U.S. 293 (1966).

Hon, W. Kuan, Julia Hörnle, and Christopher Millard. 2011a. The Problem of "Personal Data" in Cloud Computing: What Information Is Regulated?—The Cloud of Unknowing. *International Data Privacy Law* 1 (4): 211–228.

Hon, W. Kuan, Julia Hörnle, and Christopher Millard. 2011b. Who Is Responsible for "Personal Data" in Cloud Computing? *International Data Privacy Law* 2 (1): 3–18.

Hon, W. Kuan, Julia Hörnle, and Christopher Millard. 2012. Data Protection Jurisdiction and Cloud Computing—When Are Cloud Users and Providers Subject to EU Data Protection Law? The Cloud of Unknowing. *International Review of Law Computers & Technology* 26 (2–3): 129–164.

In re United States' Application for a Search Warrant to Seize and Search Electronic Devices from Edward Cunnius, 770 F. Supp. 2d. 1138 (W.D. Wash. 2011).

Judgment in Joined Cases C-293/12 and C-594/12: Digital Rights Ireland and Seitlinger and Others (Court of Justice of the European Union April 8, 2014). Available at http://curia.europa.eu/juris/document/document.jsf?docid=150642&doclang=EN.

Katz v. United States, 389 U.S. 347 (1967).

Kerr, Orin S. 2004. A User's Guide to the Stored Communications Act, and a Legislator's Guide to Amending It. *George Washington Law Review* 72 (x): 1208–1243.

Kesan, Jay P., Carol M. Hayes, and Masooda N. Bashir. 2013. Information Privacy and Data Control in Cloud Computing: Consumers, Privacy Preferences, and Market Efficiency. *Washington and Lee Law Review* 70 (1): 341–472.

Kuner, Christopher. 2010. Data Protection Law and International Jurisdiction on the Internet (Part 2). *International Journal of Law & Information Technology* 18 (3): 227–247.

Nixon v. Administrator of General Services, 433 U.S 425 (1977).

People v. Network Assocs., Inc., 758 N.Y.S.2d 466 (N.Y. Sup. Ct. 2003).

Office of Technology Assessment. U.S. Congress. 1985. Federal Government Information Technology: Electronic Surveillance and Civil Liberties. Washington, DC: U.S. Congress. Available at http://www.fas.org/ota/reports/8509.pdf.

Pinguelo, Fernando M., and Bradford W. Muller. 2011. Avoid the Rainy Day: Survey of U.S. Cloud Computing Caselaw. *Boston College Intellectual Property & Technology Forum* 1.

Post, Robert C. 2001. Three Concepts of Privacy. *Georgetown Law Journal* 89 (6): 2087–2098.

Robison, William J. 2010. Note, Free at What Cost?: Cloud Computing Privacy Under the Store Communications Act, 98 GEO. L.J. 1195.

Schwartz, Paul M. 2013. EU Privacy and the Cloud: Consent and Jurisdiction under the Proposed Regulation. *BNA Privacy and Security Law Report* 12 (April 29): 1–3.

Schwartz, Paul M., and Daniel J. Solove. 2011. The PII Problem: Privacy and a New Concept of Personally Identifiable Information. *New York University Law Review* 86 (6): 1814–1894.

Schwartz, Paul M., and Daniel J. Solove. 2013. Reconciling Personal Information in the United States and European Union. UC Berkeley Public Law Research Paper No. 2271442.

Solove, Daniel J. 2006. A Taxonomy of Privacy. *University of Pennsylvania Law Review* 154 (3): 477–560.

State v. Bellar, 217 P.3d 1094 (Or. App. 2009).

Theofel v. Farey-Jones, 359 F.3d 1066 (9th Cir. 2004).

Thompson, Richard M, II. 2013. *Cloud Computing: Constitutional and Statutory Privacy Protections. CRS R43015*. Washington, DC: Congressional Research Service.

United States v. Miller, 425 U.S. 435 (1976).

United States v. Warshak, 631 F.3d 266 (6th Cir. 2010).

United States v. Weaver, 636 F. Supp. 2d 769 (C.D. Ill. 2009).

Viacom Intern. Inc. v. YouTube Inc., 253 F.R.D. 256 (S.D.N.Y. 2008).

Warren, Samuel D., and Louis D. Brandeis. 1890. The Right to Privacy. *Harvard Law Review* 4 (5): 193–220.

Whitman, James Q. 2004. The Two Western Cultures of Privacy: Dignity Versus Liberty. *Yale Law Journal* 113 (6): 1151–1221.

Wong v. DropBox, Inc., Case No. CV-11–3092 (N.D. Cal., filed June 22, 2011). Available at http://www.courthousenews.com/2011/06/24/Dropbox%2016.pdf.

6 Understanding Regulatory and Consumer Interest in the Cloud

Jonathan Cave, Neil Robinson, Svitlana Kobzar, and Helen Rebecca Schindler[1]

Introduction

The blurring of traditional differentiated models of information and communications technology (ICT) service provision under various cloud computing offerings—specifically infrastructure as a service (IaaS) and hardware as a service (HaaS) models as specified by the National Institutes of Standards and Technology (NIST) definition of cloud computing—have attracted the regulatory interest of a number of bodies in the European Union across a range of topics. Neelie Kroes, then–Commissioner for Digital Agenda for Europe (an organization with the task of addressing a variety of policy concerns germane to cloud computing, including network and information security, electronic privacy, and telecommunications) noted in a 2012 speech that the policy perspective toward cloud computing in Europe needed to address a variety of issues, including the security of networks, the safety and security of data in the cloud, legal certainty about enforcement of cloud contracts, and competition to facilitate consumer choice and encourage innovation (Kroes 2012).

This chapter analyzes a list of cloud-related issues and concerns mentioned in the literature against a stylized framework for classifying areas of concern to telecommunications regulators. These (intentionally) reflect a mixed bag of topics to consider. Some can easily be identified with very specific consumer and/or citizen harms, so they qualify for consideration because they appear to fall within current regulatory remits or to impinge directly on existing areas of regulatory intervention. Other implementation-level concerns are more diffuse, comprising aspects of the cloud that affect the severity or tractability of existing issues, indicate new challenges or opportunities in addressing them, or overlap with—but go significantly beyond—regulators' current remits and jurisdictions. Citizen and consumer harm issues include the following:

- *Consumer switching and mobility:* Consumers may be locked into cloud service providers by limited portability of their data and applications, restricted interoperability, and lack of information.
- *Copyright and IPR:* (1) liability of Cloud Service Providers for actions of users and hosted service providers; (2) ownership of user-generated content; (3) content-matching and legitimization; etc.
- *Unfair and potentially anticompetitive contract terms:* Standard form SLAs are efficient for large numbers of consumers but prevent bargaining. This raises switching costs and can lead to lock-in, damage competition, and reduced efficiency. More serious for cloud because providers "have" user data.
- *Security, reliability, resilience capacity:* Concerns: (1) transparency of cloud providers' practices; (2) security and reliability of services; (3) data loss and unauthorized release—even when not illegal, this can create significant harm, especially when data owners are not aware; (4) data security includes e.g. infrastructure resilience (continuity), authentication.
- *Crime:* Range of criminal threats: (1) identity theft; (2) data theft; (3) fraud; (4) malicious system, processing, or data interference; (5) data loss or unauthorized release.
- *Privacy and data protection:* Privacy may be weakened by indirect relationships, limited visibility, mismatch with legal roles, and privacy-invasive technologies and business models.
- *CaaS:* Integrated or converged video, voice, and data communications and associated services that overlap with existing regulated communications but are not limited to communications service providers.
- *Cloud as a utility (including risk of foreclosure):* Aspects of cloud computing share some technical, economic and societal features with other utilities (e.g. economies of scale and potential for universal service).
- *Advertising and marketing:* Consumers may not be fully informed; may see repeat of problems with broadband or mobile (for example). Providers may be unable to certify, deliver, or even inform consumers about the services they expect and those they receive.

Implementation and related issues include:

- *Location and jurisdiction:* Locations are hard to verify and constantly changing; this raises consumer protection and jurisdictional issues.
- *Consumer information, transparency of CSP practices:* Linked to mobility, but important in other areas where interests depend on consumer choice (e.g. identity management), which is central to consumer choice and protection; if individuals cannot know or verify the identities of those with whom they transact, it may be hard to enforce rights.

- *Locus of control:* Difficult to identify points of leverage for effective intervention; existing regulation could be undermined by cloud-hosted alternatives. Also, control is different in different architectures and deployment models.
- *Complexity of the cloud:* The cloud's inherent complexity and adaptability challenges conventional regulation.
- *Certification and other self- and co-regulation:* Market-provided solution for a range of concerns; may require national monitoring and/or enforcement and be multiple, inconsistent, ineffective, costly, unmanageable, or anticompetitive.
- *Cloud neutrality:* Cloud should be OS, hardware, software neutral; but this may be restricted to support discrimination.
- *Consumer/SME similarities, regulatory heritage, and convergence:* In the cloud, both SMEs and users are potential CHS providers; consumer harms thus occur in both B2B and B2C. A related issue is the fit of communications, privacy, and regulation with the cloud environment.
- *Trust:* Security (especially for firms, including SMEs) and privacy issues may reduce trust in cloud-hosted services, affecting their uptake or leading to "privacy/security as a service" innovations.

These issues are briefly summarized in tables 6.1 and 6.2 and are discussed in more detail later in this chapter. These tables list the issues and indicate (in the final column) their association with common communications regulator responsibilities: D ("direct") cloud issues that affect the communications value chain; I ("indirect") issues beyond the communications sector affected by regulated communications services; and E ("extended") areas affecting regulatory objectives but requiring an extension of authority. These are prioritized according to potential severity, immediacy, relevance, and necessity of intervention. Because it is difficult quantitatively to measure or weigh these factors, we rank them as high (dark shading), medium (light shading), or low (unshaded) priority. The following discussion differentiates standard models of cloud service and deployment (following the NIST schema) and divides relevant cloud-related services into three layers:

- *Cloud services* include services used to provide access to computing resources and the computing services themselves (e.g., storage or processing as technical capabilities). They tend to be provided by communications service companies and other firms that maintain and operate data centers and other physical assets used to meet cloud users' service needs.

Table 6.1

Citizen and Consumer Harm Issues

Issues	Access	Participation	Citizen Protection	Competition	Consumer Protection	Consumer Empowerment	Existing Regulation	Market Solution?	Remit
Consumer switching and mobility				Ability to switch		Information on competing services	Telecommunications and broadband switching	N	I
Copyright and IPR	Access to knowledge		Ownership of user-generated IP	Supply of content, (vertical) lock-in of IPR	Threats from pirated content		Antipiracy	N	I
Unfair and potentially anticompetitive contract terms				Reduced scope for competition, possible market segmentation	May not protect niche interests	Consumer bargaining power eliminated by "take-it-or-leave-it" contracts, too much or too little choice	Unfair Terms in Consumer Contracts Regulations 1999	Not so far	D

Issue							
Security, reliability, resilience capacity	Continuity of critical infrastructures and services, security of critical data		Risk allocation	Scope to negotiate security	?	?	E
Crime	Vulnerability of cloud	Depend on cloud for security, safety	ID theft, data loss, fraud.	Identifying trustworthy services	Legal proscriptions may not bind cloud (hosted) services	N	E
Privacy and data protection	Data protection	Indirect monetization of personal data	Privacy rights; data release may damage interests	Lack of necessary information	DPA, breach notification	? (Privacy by design, certify)	I
CaaS			Potential unfair competition		Bypass	?	D
Cloud as a utility (including risk of foreclosure)	Universal service	Economies of scale, interoperability		QoS		N	E
Advertising and marketing			Misleading advertisements, unreliable QoS		Possibly BPRs (2008), CPRs (2008)	N	I

Table 6.2
Implementation and Related Issues

Issues	Citizen-Related	Competition	Consumer Protection	Consumer Empowerment	Existing Regulation	Market Solution?	Remit
Location and jurisdiction	Location changes may shut down essential services	Ability to switch locations may provide cost advantages	Data loss in unprotected locales	Cannot know where data reside	Not harmonized	?(Certified location)	i
Consumer information, transparency of CSP practices	Authentication	Limits consumer sovereignty, function of reputations, accountability			For electronic communications service providers	?	I
Locus of control	Lack of direct accountability	Interplatform competition	Migration from SaaS to PaaS; liability failures	Hard to negotiate with cloud-hosted service providers	May need to regulate cloud providers; change regulation of communications providers	?	D, I, and E

Complexity of the cloud	Consumers may not understand choices				May miss self-organisation, difficulty of decisions	D
Certification and other self- and co-regulation		Potential harm to competition	Lay involvement	Can support search	Varies	Co-reg.	I
Cloud neutrality		Vertical restraint, walled gardens			Bypass	N	I
Consumer/SME similarities, regulatory heritage, and convergence		Potentially applies across the board					D
Trust	Untrusted services not used	Does market treat trust failures efficiently?	Reliance on cloud services			N	E

- *Cloud-hosted services* (sometimes called *cloud-based*) are applications made available to cloud services' users. They overlap to a degree with cloud services—for example, data storage services can be provided in ways that more closely resemble a hard drive or a database application. They are often provided by entities that contract with cloud platform providers to meet users' needs.
- *Cloud-enhanced services* are those provided by users of cloud-hosted services, such as retailers that use cloud-hosted data services to manage their operations.

Following the discussion of each potential regulatory issue, we briefly recap its cloud specificity, the likelihood that the market will resolve the issue on its own, and any details affecting the implementation of regulatory solutions.

Regulatory Scope of Telecommunications

It is useful to think of regulating the cloud through the prism of telecommunications regulation for three main reasons. First, in the absence of a general ombudsman for "information society" services, telecommunications regulators represent the closest authority with regulatory purchase upon the broadest set of abstract challenges raised by cloud computing. The debate around Federal Communications Commission (FCC) involvement in net neutrality demonstrates how contemporary policy challenges undermine the separation between content and communications, which previously provided a degree of clarity regarding which areas would be outside the scope of such authorities.

Second, such regulatory bodies possess a broad range of tools and duties that *could* uniquely fit them to tackle these challenges. Telecommunications regulatory bodies like the Office of Communications (Ofcom) in the United Kingdom (UK) have a wide range of statutory duties covering technical efficiency/resilience, spectrum allocation, citizen safety (including emergency communications and aspects of cybersecurity), consumer protection, and other areas. Furthermore, such regulators might have at their disposal a number of tools useful in tackling the cloud computing concerns identified in this chapter. These include controls over spectrum allocation, telecom and related services pricing, universal service obligations, "must carry" regulatory requirements, and even investment approval.

Finally, telecommunication regulators have been around for a relatively long period of time (by Internet standards) and thus possess a degree of institutional knowledge in understanding the complexities of policy intervention in matters relating to electronic communications and consultative, legislative, and judicial procedures for adjusting regulations to changing circumstances.

Citizen and Consumer Harm Issues

This section discusses issues of potential citizen and consumer harm (in the priority order in table 6.1) arising from or exacerbated by the cloud and potentially lying within a telecommunications regulator's authority. Each issue is briefly explained, after which we indicate the extent to which this issue is specific to the cloud, the extent to which the market or other parties are likely to address the issue, and any "intervention issues" that might complicate regulatory action.

Limits to Consumer Switching and Mobility

The current lack of agreed-upon cloud service standards, limited interoperability, and cloud service provider policies could restrict consumers' ability to mix and match data and services hosted on different clouds. This may be more serious than being locked in to a telephone or Internet service provider (ISP); switching customers need to maintain access to stored data and may need to link data and applications from multiple providers. This tendency to favor closed models and neglect transparency is a natural development because many cloud service and cloud-hosted-service business models started with large firms outsourcing services that were formerly shared within their organizations and supply chains. Therefore, although cloud computing itself is based on the mobility of data and applications *within* the facilities offered by a single provider,[2] mobility *between* providers remains problematic. This limits competition between the platforms offered by different providers and potentially makes cloud users more vulnerable to the consequences of cloud business failure. Conversely, switching between cloud-hosted services on a given cloud provider's platform[3] may be too easy, resulting in inefficient churn and volatility; services may even change without consumers' knowledge or consent (Zittrain 2008). In principle, markets might eventually resolve the problem.

Switching cloud platforms may be facilitated by virtualization. This makes users less dependent on their current cloud service providers' specific hardware, software, and operating systems; moreover, it is often easy to relocate from one data center to another, taking advantage of flexibility and scalability. The success of this solution depends on interoperability and standardization, but the legacy of most cloud service providers limits mobility. Transparency and self-regulatory standards may thus create semi-isolated interoperability clusters rather than open competition. In other words, if competition can be restricted using interoperability as a way to coordinate the activities of providers on a single platform, the range of choice and pricing may be restricted for consumers, who are thus locked in. This happens because intensive competition (on the platform) is suppressed and only extensive competition (between platforms and the applications they provide) is available, which increases the disruption involved in switching applications (e.g., Cave et al. 2009). Conversely, if users can change cloud-hosted services quickly (or are unaware of such changes), the power of the platform provider is enhanced in much the same way as a provider of a shared retail space gains extra traction with consumers who prefer a range of choice without the costs involved in exploring other locations. If consumers do not know (or notice) when the providers of cloud-hosted services change, they cannot express their preferences effectively. As a result the incentives of providers of cloud-hosted services to invest in meeting users' longer-term needs are weakened (Zittrain 2008).

Cloud specificity: Consumer switching is an issue across communications and content services but is sharpened by cloud providers' control of subscribers' data, programs, and activity logs; limited contractual protection; and the complexity of choices available to consumers for all but the most basic or intermediated services.

Prospects for market solution: Very limited, especially for business-to-consumer (B2C) providers. The problem has been commented on for many years, and yet impediments remain, not least because it is not currently in providers' interests to enhance mobility.

Intervention issues: Lack of regulatory traction with cloud service providers; lack of the legal basis to enforce open platforms.

Copyright and Intellectual Property Rights

Cloud storage may make it hard to comply with or enforce copyright and other Internet Protocol (IP) protections. Some aspects of these compliance and enforcement difficulties are common to many environments in which hosted content is made available to others (e.g., Internet web hosting) but are trickier in the cloud, where content location may be unknown to those who provide or use access and may change in response to cloud providers' management of traffic and data. At the same time, cloud providers may not be able to verify the legal status of specific stored or hosted data, or they may find that legal certainty of data location conflicts with the technical and economic drivers of cloud provision. There have been many proposals to extend third-party liability for copyright violation to online access providers based on a least-cost-avoider argument, for example. Thus far, these have been primarily directed at ISPs, but they also may be applied to cloud providers. Recent examples include the Stop Online Piracy (SOPA) and Protect Intellectual Property (PIPA) acts, two pieces of legislation in the United States that are currently postponed amid considerable protest.[4] While PIPA in particular concentrated on websites in general, the use of third-party liability highlights both the potential of uncontrolled clouds to disseminate pirated material and the risk that cloud platforms will be targeted by government authorities from other countries. The threat or certainty of legal action may cause cloud providers and cloud users thoroughly to vet providers of online data storage, backup,[5] and information hosting to ensure that users' critical data and platform providers' business continuity will not be damaged. Indeed, given the location independence (see section titled "Location and Jurisdiction" below) of many of these services, US regulators may not provide the necessary deterrent.

Other aspects are unique to the cloud, such as content matching services like the Apple iTunes Match service provided with the iCloud.[6] These arrangements may help enable the legitimization of pirated content and lets those rights holders who have licensing arrangements with the cloud service provider recover some payment that would otherwise be lost; on the other hand, it gives dominant providers of matching services a particular advantage in negotiating licensing deals, increases their vertical market power over their subscribers by locking in illegitimate content along with their legitimate content, and may crowd out efforts to enforce copyright directly by appearing to provide a "light-touch" alternative that content owners can sign up with. This is reflected in recent market and legal developments suggesting that copyright per se does not seem to be a major concern for users but is featured more strongly in licensing arrangements between cloud service providers and license owners.[7] These challenges have arisen from the market; there is no a priori reason to believe that they will not ultimately be met by the market; however, if the market solution has serious adverse consequences for competition in the cloud services market or departs significantly from the approach being adopted for other web-hosted content, intervention may be necessary.

Cloud-specificity: Not unique to cloud markets, but nontransparency of elements such as location makes this issue harder to deal with in the cloud, and some troubling developments (e.g., iTunes Match) are cloud-specific.

Prospects for market solution: Limited and dependent on general changes in intellectual property rights (IPR) protection law and implementation.
Intervention issues: Global scope of the problem; conflation of IPR and competition issues.

Unfair and Potentially Anticompetitive Contract Terms

Cloud services offered to consumers tend to be governed by standard form "take it or leave it" service level agreements (SLAs). This is an efficient way of serving many small users, but the unequal bargaining power (lack of opportunity to bargain) between provider and consumer creates a risk of unfair and potentially anticompetitive terms. In the United Kingdom, this is potentially covered by the Unfair Terms in Consumer Contracts Regulations 1999; other jurisdictions have similar laws. The economic problem is that such terms raise switching costs; if the costs are unreasonable, the result can be harmful (for consumers and for competition) lock-in. This is potentially more serious in cloud environments where providers also control consumers' data (and programs). At a minimum, telecoms (and competition) authorities should keep a watching brief to see how easily consumers can switch their provider, how much switching costs, how quickly provider changes are completed, whether their data are safely returned or removed, and whether this is appropriately reflected in contract provisions. More generally, regulators may wish to monitor the way the industry manages this issue to see whether regulatory intervention is required. Related issues arise regarding other contract terms (i.e., aside from contract termination): for instance, when can providers change contract terms, what rights do users have in such cases, and how are complaints dealt with?

Although the quality, price, and functionality of cloud services are typically governed by SLAs, payments—except in free or freemium models—are controlled by subscription contracts that incorporate SLAs. Despite the wide range of user characteristics, consumer concerns, and cloud (and cloud-hosted) services, the limited range of highly standardized SLAs available is regarded as providing insufficient flexibility, an inefficient allocation of responsibility, and an excessive assignment of risk to subscribers (Bradshaw et al. 2011). This threatens consumer empowerment and dampens the signals that should encourage innovation, and limits the extent to which pricing for subscription can be used to infer the value of alternative service levels and quality of service provisions. By the same token, payment terms currently favor static and easy-to-understand pricing models such as pay-as-you-go or subscription, but they do not generally provide dynamic pricing—for example, prices that vary with congestion, or tariffs for storage and other services that change automatically in response to changing usage patterns. Taken together, these can reduce consumer surplus, facilitate anticompetitive market segmentation, promote lock-in and reduce efficiency.

Cloud specificity: SLAs are particularly important with the cloud, where users' vulnerability and lack of information are greater than with other Internet services.

Prospects for market solution: Limited, as it is not in the interest of providers.

Intervention issues: Need to reconcile with competition, commercial law, and unfair practices regulations; possibly outside telecommunication regulators' authority.

Security, Reliability, and Resilience

There is a direct citizen interest in the functioning of critical infrastructures, which may well come to include the cloud. The US Department of Homeland Security defines critical national infrastructures as "systems and assets, whether physical or virtual, so vital to the United States that the incapacity or destruction of such systems and assets would have a debilitating impact on security, national economic security, national public health or safety, or any combination of those matters." The threat can be indirect, as the functioning of other critical infrastructures comes increasingly to depend on the cloud.[8] A current project sponsored by the United Kingdom's Technology Strategy Board[9] recognizes these dependencies as follows[10]:

Our critical national infrastructure is increasingly dependent on information systems and the services they support. Cloud computing ecosystems of service providers and consumers including individuals, charitable and public bodies, SMEs [small and medium-sized enterprises], large enterprises, and governments will become a significant part of the way these services are provided, allowing more agile coalitions, cost savings and improved service delivery.

Such indirect dependency is enhanced by the movement of increasing proportions of critical (business and government) information assets and functions to the cloud. More directly, the cloud itself plays a central role in critical information infrastructure, as recognized by organizations such as the Centre for the Protection of National Infrastructure (Deloitte 2010; Cornish et al. 2011).

An issue related to both personal and societal security concerns the availability of cloud-hosted data and cloud activity logs for forensic and law enforcement purposes; this arises with respect to other Internet activity, but the cloud represents a much larger scale and greater practical difficulties of obtaining access, as well as possibly interfering with the data subjects right to the protection of their personal data (see section titled "Cloud Neutrality" below).

There is a corresponding consumer interest in the continuity and quality of purchased services. This is not limited to personal users; it extends to those who sell services over cloud platforms or use cloud-hosted services to deliver ICT-intensive services to others. Enterprises are particularly concerned about privacy of stored data (including activity logs), compromised virtual machines, data access, and service continuity. Lack of transparency of cloud providers' practices currently prevents service users from being sure that they are meeting security and accountability obligations. In addition, the structure of the cloud may create a unique environment for hosting cyberattacks, propagating compromised virtual machines and other malware, and (more positively) for identifying and containing malicious traffic.

Beyond the specific consumer interests lies a general economic issue: information security (i.e., data access and integrity, and prevention of unauthorized access to information) is among the most frequently cited concerns for current and potential cloud users and an important impediment to the development of the sector (e.g., Chow et al. 2009). These concerns go well beyond the protection of personal or proprietary data to include infrastructure resilience (continuity) and authentication, among other examples. This gives security a stronger consumer orientation. Potential market solutions may be associated with market dominance, which would create additional consumer harm. In addition, some of these information security issues may arise from the interest of providers or third parties in exploiting consumers' information or from the potential liabilities associated with leaks of information. Here, we distinguish the costs imposed on information controllers, information processors, or cloud platform providers in the value chain from the costs to data subjects and other cloud users of information security breaches. We also note that these adverse impacts may arise from loss of trust and the insufficient, excessive, or inappropriate use of different cloud platforms and services as a result of the fear of information security breaches or as a result of precautions taken to manage these potential adverse effects.

Cloud specificity: Information security issues may be more important or different in the cloud due to information asymmetries, increased dependence, and novel threats (e.g., compromised virtual machines). As a consequence, approaches and solutions developed for other contexts may not work as planned.

Prospects for market solution: This issue may be resolved by self-regulation, increased transparency, or both.

Intervention issues: There is a need to take account of or balance a wide range of business and consumer interests and overlaps with critical infrastructure protections.

Crime

Cloud services can be used for a range of criminal activities (in addition to IPR theft, as discussed previously). While none of these are specific to the cloud, they may take different forms in this complex and nontransparent environment. This may be a matter of regulatory interest because communications services are essential to the delivery of cloud services and may play a vital role in detection and evidence gathering. Collectively, such criminal activities may threaten citizen access to vital services and general societal protection interests by increasing the vulnerability of the cloud infrastructure, especially as cloud-hosted services become more important in enhancing citizen security and safety.

Among the illegal activities that can adversely affect consumer interests are the following:

- *Theft, alteration, or denial of access to identity and other data.* Individuals whose cloud-hosted identifying information and records are usurped, corrupted, or blocked may be unable to use the Internet for a whole range of activities and may suffer financial loss as a result. This is not unique to the cloud, as stated before, but with the migration of an increasing range of activity, combined with the indirect and variable contact between users and cloud-hosted providers of data storage, transaction processing may exacerbate problems found on the Internet, where users and service providers typically have more direct contracts or at least higher visibility than in the cloud. In much the same way, small firms using the cloud for primary storage or backup of sensitive data may find their resilience and security threatened. As a result, their competitive position will be weakened vis-à-vis rivals who do not suffer such losses or who are able to use private clouds.
- *Fraud.* As the scope of cloud services expands, the potential for fraudulent use also increases. This is fairly obvious with regard to services intended to collect and resell personal information, but it is increasingly

raised as a possible risk in relation to cloud-hosted financial services and financial advice (e.g., providing access to sophisticated financial models hosted in the cloud).[11] Although fraud is certainly present in the real world, it may be more severe in the cloud due to the aforementioned lack of transparency and the wider availability of highly sophisticated computation intensive tools for implementing such frauds.

• *Malicious system processing or data interference.* These are known and increasing sources of citizen and consumer harm. They may be more difficult to detect, prove, or prevent in the cloud because of its complexity, the flexibility of arrangements for storage and exchange, continual changes in computing and application environments, and other factors that make it hard to assemble and interpret evidence. In addition, legal traction may be limited: existing criminal sanctions against hacking or interference with networks or data stored in computer systems (to cite just two examples) provide only limited scope for cloud service providers or users to take action against cybercriminals; cloud providers could play a vital role in detecting infringements and gathering evidence by applying to their management and activity logs the emerging tools of "big data" (NetworkComputing 2012; Storm 2012);

• *Data loss or unauthorized release.* This is a potent source of potential consumer harm, especially when data subjects are unaware of the breach. The enormous scale, flexible location, and other attributes of consumer data holdings of large storage providers make them attractive targets, but SLAs and criminal sanctions designed to improve their performance may be difficult to enforce. The standard approach (breach notification) has had only limited efficacy in the Internet in general (Cavoukian 2009; Dresner and Norcup 2009); it may be even weaker in the cloud, especially if reversibility (i.e., ability to leave the cloud) is limited. In any case, notification requirements currently apply only to electronic communication service providers (a definition that does not include most cloud service or cloud-hosted service providers). There are further potential citizen harms associated with attempted or successful data breaches that lead to loss of service continuity or network integrity.

Cloud specificity: This is useful to distinguish two types of criminal activity—the targeting of clouds by criminals and the use of cloud infrastructure by criminal elements. The former may essentially be an extension of current issues with the attractiveness of large databases to hacking and data exfiltration. The latter is much more cloud-specific, as it concerns the way in which cloud-hosted services can be used to enable a criminal digital underworld.

Prospects for market solution: Given the poor record of crime-proofing many technologies, targeted regulatory intervention and improvements in law enforcement capabilities would seem necessary. However, regulatory intervention will need to address the root of the problem (e.g., vulnerabilities that give rise to exploitation by criminals) and not the symptoms (e.g., by disseminating information about the poor performance of cloud service providers and leaving the rest to the market).

Intervention issues: Telecommunications regulators with competition powers clearly have a role in receiving breach notification reports (as under the current arrangements of Article 13a of the European Telecommunications Package)[12] and they could also indirectly support measures to help improve the transparency of security levels in cloud service providers.

Privacy and Data Protection

Cloud services may intrude on personal data privacy because the user of cloud-hosted services typically does not have a direct relationship with the provider of the service and may not have a relationship with the cloud service provider either, which limits the accountability of those who hold data and the visibility of their practices to data subjects and regulators alike. Existing protections rest on a legal distinction between data controllers and data processors that may be inadequate in cloud environments (Cave et al. 2011 and Ismail 2011), where the roles overlap.

Another area of great concern is the extent to which consumers will be unable to exercise their rights in the face of large cloud service providers. This may grow in importance along with the expansion of freemium (especially B2C) cloud services provided in exchange for personal information, or advertising-supported models in which users' bargaining power is weakened by lack of direct payment.

Existing legal frameworks protect the privacy of communications to a degree but may be less effective with regard to stored information or activity logs showing users' access and processing activity and may do little to ensure the accountability of those processing data in the cloud (Robinson et al. 2011). However, the telecommunications regulator's interest may be limited; other authorities (e.g., data protection or privacy authorities[13] for *inter alia* data privacy in the cloud) have primary responsibility for privacy per se, and there may be market solutions in the form of privacy-by-design, cloud-specific privacy-enhancing technologies, or the provision of privacy as a service in cloud environments (Kroes 2012; Pearson 2009).

Cloud-specificity: Issues of accountability and visibility of relationships, who does what with data subjects' personal data, and the roles played by data controllers and data processors are unique to cloud computing because of the dynamic and autonomic properties of cloud service provision.

Prospects for market solutions: Market-based solutions may exist as noted previously. However, policy intervention might be required to kick-start take-up or, in the case of insurance against liability from losses of personal data, perhaps even act as an insurer of last resort, and also to manage potential lock-in and other distortions resulting from such market-generated "default" roles.

Intervention issues: Any policy intervention would need to be undertaken in close cooperation with privacy/data protection authorities and take into account recent proposals at the European level that may reduce national freedom of maneuver to craft more specific interpretations of EU law in the realms of privacy and data protection (European Commission Directorate-General Justice 2012).

Communications as a Service (CaaS)

Communication as a service (CaaS) involves integrated or converged video, voice and data communications, and associated services such as voice over IP (VOIP), instant messaging, videoconferencing, call recording, and message routing available from multiple devices and offered to small and medium-sized enterprises (SMEs) and to a certain extent consumers (e.g., Skype offering voicemail and a variety of other communications services). It is a matter of regulatory interest because CaaS services, which overlap strongly with regulated electronic communications services, are provided by currently unregulated cloud service providers. This raises consumer and small business concerns associated with potential regulatory bypass[14] and with the ability of CaaS providers credibly to deliver communication capability in the cloud that is service-oriented, configurable, schedulable, predictable, and reliable. Cloud delivery also meets such other consumer or user requirements as network security, dynamic provisioning of virtual overlays (to isolate traffic or provide dedicated bandwidth), guaranteed message delay, communication encryption, and network monitoring that other forms of communications service may struggle to provide.

Cloud-specificity: These issues appear to be specific to the cloud since they conflate some legacy aspects of the provision of a simple pipe with services that are more focused upon managing different types of traffic (video, voice, and data) with the associated quality of service (QoS) issues. Furthermore, CaaS, with its need to leverage presence-sensing technology—for example, identifying whether recipients are online or offline and whether they wish to receive Short Message Service (SMS), video, or voice communication—has the potential to affect other issues (e.g., privacy).

Prospects for market solution: It is not clear how markets might respond to the consumer issues that arise if CaaS providers are seen to bypass regulatory regimes. The result may be increasing fragmentation, as different CaaS providers target distinct customer segments interested in specific requirements such as security or QoS.

Intervention issues: Addressing these concerns would appear to lie directly within many telecommunications regulators' duties; it might even require extension of regulatory mandate over CaaS providers.

Cloud as a Utility, Including Risk of Market Foreclosure

While some layers of the cloud computing system are potentially competitive, others have strong natural monopoly characteristics, including economies of scale and scope in the operation of data centers.[15] As a result, there is a need to ensure that these resources are not used to foreclose the market vertically, while at the same time meeting the costs of the demand for bandwidth and communications services caused by cloud usage—the connection being that the parts of the value chain providing network bandwidth and communications services will assert that the rents that they derive from restricted competition are needed to provide the networks and other facilities, especially those needed for the maintenance and upgrade of the network infrastructure. This is the argument most often made against net neutrality rules, for example.

The incentives to foreclose are magnified by the Bring Your Own Device (BYOD) openness of user interfaces because this increases the costs of provisioning (in order to accommodate arbitrary devices) and reduces the extent to which such costs can be recovered through hardware acquisition charges. The potential costs of meeting demand are magnified by high-bandwidth advanced cloud services, remote storage, and retrieval and content-streaming applications. However, on average, telecommunications service providers are able to capture less average revenue per user (ARPU) due to the ubiquity and low cost of alternative "added value" services, as has been seen with the impact of VOIP on voice telephony revenues.[16] This may lead to other structural changes in the form of mergers between dominant telecommunications service providers and cloud providers (e.g., Verizon-Terremark).[17] This vertical integration will try to internalize the externalities between the cloud providers and the telecommunications networks on which they run, but it may not alleviate deadweight loss or increase consumer choice.

There may be additional citizen interests if cloud computing becomes a dominant mode of delivery for critical services[18] and the informational resources necessary for social participation; in the future, there may be a case for governments to consider expanding the Universal Service Obligations to encompass the Internet access offered by cloud-hosted services as the objective of an expanded definition of Universal Services. However, it does not obviously follow from this that telecommunications regulators must be centrally involved. In some countries (e.g., Germany), regulation converges around networked industries and utilities; in others (e.g., the United Kingdom), communications regulation is unified; access to the cloud flows through the communications network, but processing and storage are not communication in the strict sense. Even if they were included, would the regulatory control extend beyond platforms to hosted services, and beyond pricing and availability to security or reliability?[19]

Cloud specificity: The provision of cloud as a utility increases the cloud specificity of the other issues discussed.

Prospects for market solution: To the extent that cloud computing becomes a public good, the prospects for market solution might depend on the basis for potential intervention (e.g., minimizing foreclosure per se and protecting internal subsidies to deliver widespread coverage or essential infrastructure). Unlike with broadband, where delivery to remote regions required investments that the market would simply not supply, the main fixed capital investment requirements with cloud computing take the form of data centers (which need not be publicly provided) and enhancements to existing infrastructure capacity.

Intervention issues: The inclusion of cloud computing as part of a new Universal Service obligation would undoubtedly fall to telecommunications regulators (at least in the European Union) as the main regulatory actors in this domain.

Advertising and Marketing Practices

Cloud computing is still in its infancy, so there are both risks and opportunities for the industry in relation to advertising and marketing. In the cloud, it is particularly important for providers to earn or capture users' trust; this would be undermined if providers engaged in the practices used in other parts of the communications and ICT industries (which many regulators have been active to try to prevent). At a minimum, subscribers should be fully and effectively informed of what they are signing up for. This may not be a problem if the combination of a higher premium on trust and the lessons of experience allow the industry effectively to self-regulate. On the other hand, the complexities of the cloud may leave some providers unable to certify, deliver, or even inform consumers about the cloud-hosted services they receive.

Cloud specificity: These issues are specific to the cloud. However, the complexity of the relationships and interactions among cloud service providers makes trust even more difficult to encourage.

Prospects for market solution: There is a scarcity of empirical data on the extent to which markets might exist for services to protect or manage online persons to keep them from seeing advertising. This makes it hard to predict whether such a market might emerge to resolve these issues. Furthermore, economic interests representing advertisers who benefit from the broad use of ad supported models for delivering B2C cloud services may outweigh any latent demand for commercial cloud opt-out or "Robinson lists."

Intervention issues: As with advertising in other areas, we may see policy intervention (more squarely within regulators' mandates) to curb the excess of advertising. Ironically, this may result from improved privacy protections since by knowing less about individuals, there is more chance that inappropriate (and not just undesired) advertising material is offered, which will actively motivate consumers to want to avoid it.

Issues with Policy and Regulatory Interventions

In this section, we discuss some issues that are more strongly linked to potential solutions to cloud-related problems or to general issues of regulation, as opposed to unique or direct harmful consequences of the cloud that telecommunications regulators can and should consider.

Location and Jurisdiction

Cloud and cloud-hosted service locations are hard to pin down (especially for users) and constantly changing. Location-based law and jurisdiction are important for consumer and data protection, competition law (establishing market boundaries), and copyright licensing. In other situations, the law attempts to force even foreign providers of services to European citizens to offer equivalent protection[20]; this may be problematic or unfeasible in the cloud environment. More specifically, issues such as data privacy and freedom from unfair contract terms may be effectively managed in the UK context, but the cloud operates across borders. Managing these issues will require stronger international cooperation to protect consumers and industry from unscrupulous market elements. When cross-jurisdictional enforcement is possible, it is important to ensure that it is efficient and effective. In general, providers offering services to UK consumers should obey UK consumer protection laws, but this may be difficult to enforce across borders, and enforcement across the borders of EU members may differ from enforcement against non-EU providers. A related issue is whether such laws can be enforced uniformly or consistently against providers of cloud services, cloud-hosted services, or cloud-enhanced services.

In some situations (e.g., data protection), proposals have been made to ensure that rights are protected by requiring providers to hold data in a specific location.[21] However, by restricting the ability of cloud providers to shift data in response to load and other factors, this may reduce efficiency of the service and reduce competition among providers. However, the macroeconomic returns of attracting data centers are substantial and could deter nations from regulating against consumer harm in return for tax revenues and national employment. Therefore, location is a horizontal issue that affects all aspects of cloud-hosted activity whose regulation varies from country to country. There is a further direct source of consumer harm, if data are held in locations with inherently greater risk of loss or criminal attack.

One aspect is well known from the Internet in general: the contrast between regional telecommunications and the often globalized nature of Internet services. For pragmatic and legal reasons, extending ISP obligations—for example with respect to content piracy—to cloud providers may be problematic.

Other aspects are unique to the cloud, such as the mobility of data among data centers in different locations (for traffic and quality of service management) and the fact that the locations of cloud-hosted service providers may not be known by any of the parties involved. As noted previously for data protection, this could be addressed by legal requirements for location specificity or disclosure of location information, but this may well impair economic and technical efficiency of the cloud model and the costs and benefits are not known. A market-based alternative is the provision of locational certification (or its legal equivalent) by cloud service providers; but monitoring and enforcement of this tactic may be difficult.

Consumer Information and Transparency of CSP Practices

The mobility issue (see the section on "Location and Jurisdiction") turns on consumer information, but so does the loss of privity of contract (see the section on "Complexity of the Cloud") and the potential for market-based, consumer-driven solutions to privacy (see the section on "Cloud Neutrality") and security (see the section on "Security, Reliability, and Resilience") concerns. Therefore, there may be a basis for mandated disclosure of a specific set of data on price, quality of service, security, and location.

Locus of Control
It may be difficult to identify points of leverage for effective intervention; moreover (e.g., applying rules for telephone service providers such as those of the UK's General Authorisation Regime to VoIP-based communications or CaaS), existing regulation could be undermined by cloud-hosted alternatives. In addition, consumer protection and control are different in SaaS, IaaS, and platform as a service (PaaS) architectures; informed consent is different in private versus public clouds. This also creates an issue of continuity of consumer protection as B2C cloud users migrate from SaaS to PaaS (where their influence and scope for direct involvement are greater).

Complexity of the Cloud
Cloud services are delivered through extended pathways; the user of cloud-hosted services typically does not have a direct relationship with the provider of the service and may not have a relationship with the cloud service provider. The cloud value chain contains a number of potentially distinct markets that appear to present different competition and consumer protection concerns. Weyl (2010) identifies five separate layers[22] and notes the strongly different prospects for workable competition across them. Telecommunications authorities' regulatory traction is stronger in the access market than in the hypervisor market, for instance, although it is their combined operation that affects consumer interests.

This view may conform to a multilayered version of two-sided models of platform competition, where the geometry of the layers between the ends of the market (i.e., cloud-hosted service providers and cloud users) is constantly changing. Moreover, the ends may themselves overlap and change as new services are developed. Therefore, regulation based on fixed roles may be inappropriate.

A more direct consequence that affects the viability of market-generated solutions to consumer issues is the reduction of direct contact and visibility between the ends that hinders their efforts to internalize or contract around issues of mutual concern—this is due in part to privity of contract, which prevents cloud users from binding those with whom they interact on the cloud, since the parties typically only have contracts with the cloud provider and not with each other. More generally, the complexity and adaptability of the cloud pose challenges to conventional forms of regulation and to the way that harms are measured and remedies crafted.

Certification and Other Forms of Self-Regulation or Coregulation

Certification by individual firms or self-regulatory bodies provides a market-based solution that potentially addresses a number of concerns, including privacy[23], security, resilience (Carvalho 2010), and QoS (Lachal 2010), especially for public clouds. Ideally, such arrangements should be international in scope. In order to be effective, they may require national regulatory monitoring, enforcement, or both. However, the market may produce multiple and inconsistent guidelines and certification regimes of doubtful efficacy, high cost, limited manageability, or potential to harm competition (Cave, Marsden and Simmons 2008). This issue is not specific to the cloud; the danger of lock-in by dominant platform providers may be greater. The potential for certification to produce suboptimal or harmful results may be greater in the cloud, especially in public clouds, where the demand for assurance by customers is highest and where recognition (or coregulatory enforcement[24]) by government can increase the leverage of a particular standard or create a form of "Potemkin regulation," which is more apparent than real. On the other hand, self-regulation and coregulation do have advantages over formal regulation in being better informed about changing market and technical conditions, having lower cost, and (under some conditions) being more effective (Cave, Marsden, and Simmons 2008).

Cloud Neutrality

The relationships among cloud-hosted service providers, cloud platform providers, and cloud users create a two-sided market. While users may expect to use hosted services independent of their own hardware, software, and operating system, the hosting of these services on a particular platform may be highly restricted and can provide an additional basis for the kinds of discrimination cited in the net neutrality debate (Marcus et al. 2011). In that setting, pricing and quality of service discrimination by type of content were seen as potential sources of competitive harm and consumer disempowerment; this danger would seem to be greater when discrimination can be backed up by technological and interoperability restrictions. The market can generally solve the problem of unjustified price discrimination by consumer sovereignty (switching and bargaining power) and by arbitrage—in this case resale of cloud services. This is far harder if artificially high "technical" barriers[25] can be used to exclude rivals, favor affiliated service providers, and restrict consumer sovereignty and mobility.

Therefore, there may be a basis for requiring cloud service providers (and the electronic communications service providers who support them, if different) to price their services on a strictly accountable cost basis, without discriminating between different uses or services hosted on the cloud, offering hosting on a fair, reasonable, and non-discriminatory (FRAND) basis, including charges, quality of service and visibility. This would also have to consider whether cloud service providers could implement throttling, as some multinational organizations are doing with data plans, in anticompetitive ways (though we are unaware of any evidence on this point).

Consumer/SME Similarities, Regulatory Heritage, and Convergence

Both SMEs and personal users are potential providers of cloud-hosted services, and are therefore affected by issues at both ends of the cloud value chain. In addition, despite the apparent differences between business-to-business (B2B) and B2C cloud services[26], including in SMEs, both types of user are vulnerable to the same privacy, security, and consumer protection risks; consumer harms can thus occur in both B2B and B2C cloud services. As a result, it may be desirable to take steps to ensure consistency of approach as the two markets develop. A related issue is the extent to which legacy forms of regulation of communications privacy (especially for individuals) and security (for a range of businesses, including SMEs) work together in the cloud environment.[27]

Trust

Finally, cloud-hosted services (especially storage and processing) are attracting the interest of regulators from the perspective of trust (Robinson et al. 2011, Rittinghouse and Ransome 2009 and Global Access Partners 2011) because they establish additional perceptual distance between the data subject and data, which renders consumers even more powerless in the face of broad-scale service offerings designed to meet mass demand. In particular, the one-size-fits-all service models of many cloud providers are seen as a key indicator of the loss of consumer power to cloud service providers.

Conclusions

In this chapter, we have presented two frameworks that serve to frame analytical considerations regarding cloud computing from the perspective of telecommunications regulators. In the first, we considered issues relating to specific consumer or citizen harms that stay within the regulatory frameworks of telecommunications regulators or impinge directly upon existing areas of intervention. These include concerns relating to consumer switching and mobility; copyright and intellectual property rights; unfair and potentially anticompetitive contract terms; security, reliability, and resilience capacity; crime; privacy and data protection; CaaS; the cloud as a utility, and finally advertising and marketing. The second framework is a more diffuse set of concerns that relate to implementation-level challenges, including location and jurisdiction, consumer information and transparency, locus of control; complexity of the cloud, certification and other self-regulation and coregulatory models, cloud neutrality, consumer SME similarities, and finally trust. These latter issues go beyond the current authority and jurisdiction of telecommunications regulation. We believe that it is useful to try and place these issues (which often come across as a jumbled list of pressing concerns) into a comparative framework that facilitates evidence-based robust comparison. Such comparisons are not just academic; they permit better identification of those issues that are of a high priority for policy makers.

We further believe that these issues and this framework should be used as the starting point for a future-oriented examination by means of scenario development, exploration, and gaming. Clouds change more rapidly than regulation, so leading the target is essential. On the other hand, the underlying issue linkages and uncertainties are so profound that prediction in the strict sense is a fool's errand. The original paper on which this chapter was based developed a scenario framework and explored the prospects for these issues and for interventions to tackle them in three scenarios. These are necessarily products of their time; readers are encouraged to develop and maintain their own and use them as a platform for engagement with others.

Notes

1. This chapter is based on material from a longer paper given at the 2012 Telecommunications Policy Research Conference (Cave et al. 2012).
2. This involves using virtualization and data sharing to provide agile and efficient load balancing.
3. Although the analogy is not exact, the market for apps provides a useful point of reference. Between the two dominant platforms (iOS and Android), there is almost no direct mobility, but each hosts a vast number of potentially competing apps (500,000 for iOS, 350,000 for Android) offered by a very large number of suppliers (the average number of apps per supplier is around 3), according to

data from the European Commission's Joint Research Centre (JRC) Institute for Prospective Technological Studies (IPTS).

4. Both bills were suspended following the "Internet blackout," an offline and online demonstration against the legislation on January 18, 2012, which included a number of websites being taken down deliberately. SOPA would have increased the power of US law enforcement authorities to combat web-based trafficking in counterfeit products and intellectual property; PIPA would have created powers to restrict the activities of websites involved with such activity. One such website that was successfully taken down was Megaupload; the indictment identified the site as hosting user-created clouds for the storage and sharing of content. Similar concerns have been raised in relation to Wikipedia and Craigslist.

5. In the case of consumers, this may come via user ratings.

6. This service allows users access—for a fixed price—to licensed copies of any content that they place in the cloud and for which the cloud provider has a licensing agreement with the rights holder. Because this access does not depend on the legitimacy of the users' original content, it provides an alternative (and less expensive) access to this content; this strikes a balance between legitimizing violations of IPR and partially monetizing content that would otherwise be pirated.

7. See, for example, Zimmerman (2011) or Wittow (2011) for legal analysis of the recent Mp3.com case; and for a broader discussion about liability and consumer protection, Wittow and Buller (2010).

8. An example is provided by the IBM/Cable & Wireless project; see IBM (2011).

9. UK Technology Strategy Board Project Database listing for Cloud Stewardship Economics (#400091), https://connect.innovateuk.org/publicdata.

10. A workshop held under the HP Cloud Stewardship Economics Project, sponsored by the UK Technology Strategy Board, Hewlett-Packard and Research Councils UK, discussed cloud stewardship in the context of the prospects for cloud computing to become part of the critical national infrastructure: See the workshop summary at: https://chapters.cloudsecurityalliance.org/uk/2012/10/24/cloud-stewardship -economics-workshop-organised-by-hp-labs and a summary of the project itself at: http://gtr.rcuk.ac.uk/project/FB57FE55-0A81-46C4-974A-88B44E3F2C18.

11. Resale of financial modeling and machine-trading services to private equity firms is already widespread and is expected to expand into retail investment markets in the near future. Such models are inherently hard to audit and control and existing financial consumer protection rules may struggle to cope with cloud-hosted (and the delocalized) services of this nature.

12. Council Directive (EC) 2009/140/EC, amending Directives 2002/21/EC on a common regulatory framework for electronic communications networks and services; 2002/19/EC, on access to, and interconnection of, electronic communications networks and associated facilities; and 2002/20/EC, on the authorization of electronic communications networks and services, [2013] OJL L 337/37.

13. The Information Commissioner's Office in the United Kingdom has issued guidelines on this topic at https://ico.org.uk/for-organisations/guide-to-data -protection.

14. This includes the possibility of using cloud capability to undermine competition in the communications market.

15. These include using large servers and high-performance computing to serve larger user pools, smoothing capacity utilization by clustering large and differentiated demands, and exploiting the physical colocation of commercial cloud users to underwrite the installation of dedicated high-speed lines.

16. A detailed analysis of the impact of VoIP on telephony is provided in Biggs (2009). In the case of mobile telephony, In-Stat (2009) projected that by 2013, mobile VoIP applications will generate annual revenues of $32.2 billion, driven by more than 278 million registered users worldwide. See http://rcs-volte.tmcnet.com/articles/66906-report-mobile-voip-growth-will-impact-operator-voice.htm.

17. This creates a practical issue of cloud market definition for telecom regulators with their own competition authority.

18. For example, power, traffic management, or emergency services. See Bhuvaneswari and Karpagam (2011).

19. For example, there is a current debate about '"breach notification reporting systems" since under current EU telecommunication rules, they apply only to providers of public e-communications networks.

20. European examples include the Data Protection, Services, and eCommerce Directives.

21. Such restrictions may be used to ensure compliance with data protection rules or to ensure government access to stored data for security or law enforcement purposes; in addition, as Rittinghouse and Ransome (2009) note, "some banking regulators require that customers' financial data remain in their home country."

22. These layers are data centers, hypervisors, operating systems, routers, and access. See Weyl (2010).

23. For example, TRUSTed Cloud Privacy Certification; see http://www.truste.com/business-products/trusted-cloud.

24. In the domain of privacy certification, the US Department of Commerce promises to enforce violations of the self-certified compliance of US firms with data protection principles. See Cave et al. (2011) for a discussion of the evidence concerning its effectiveness.

25. Cave et al. (2011).

26. Some see the distinction between B2B and B2C clouds as indicating an explicit and specific contract as opposed to a standard-form SLA; others see this as a distinction without a difference (Verstraete 2012).

27. This is addressed in the ICO Personal Data Guidelines (see note 13).

References

Bhuvaneswari, A., and G. Karpagam. 2011. Ontology-Based Emergency Management System in a Social Cloud. *International Journal on Cloud Computing: Services and Architecture* 1 (3): 15–29.

Biggs. P. 2009. "Voice over Internet Protocol: Enemy or Ally?" (ITU Global Symposium for Regulators, 2009). Available at http://www.itu.int/ITU-D/treg/Events/Seminars/GSR/GSR09/doc/GSR09_VoIP-Trends_Biggs.pdf.

Bradshaw, S., C. Millard, and I. Walden. 2011. Contracts for Clouds: Comparison and Analysis of the Terms and Conditions of Cloud Computing Services. *International Journal of Law and Information Technology* 19 (3): 187–223.

Carvalho, L. 2010. "What Are Cloud Certifications?" *Cloud Computing Journal* (May 3, 2010). Available at http://cloudcomputing.sys-con.com/node/1378183.

Cave, J., C. Marsden, and S. Simmons. 2008. "Options for and Effectiveness of Internet Self- and Co-Regulation." Technical Report TR566. Santa Monica, CA: RAND Corporation.

Cave, J., N. Robinson, H. R. Schindler, G. Bodea, L. Kool, and M. van Lieshout. 2011. *Does It Help or Hinder? Promotion of Innovation on the Internet and Citizens' Right to Privacy.* Report to European Parliament Committee on Industry, Research, and Energy. Available at http://www.europarl.europa.eu/document/activities/cont/2011 12/20111220ATT34644/20111220ATT34644EN.pdf.

Cave, J., C. van Oranje-Nassau, H. R. Schindler, A. Shehabi, P. Brutscher, and N. Robinson. 2009. "Trends in Connectivity Technologies and Their Socioeconomic Impacts. Final Report of the Study: Policy Options for the Ubiquitous Internet Society." Technical Report TR776. Santa Monica, CA: RAND Corporation.

Cave, J., N. Robinson, S. Kobzar, and R. Schindler. 2012. "Regulating the Cloud: More, Less, or Different Regulation and Competing Agendas." 2012 TRPC paper. Available at http://ssrn.com/abstract=2031695 or http://dx.doi.org/.10.2139/ssrn .2031695

Cavoukian, A. 2009. "Privacy Externalities, Security Breach Notification, and the Role of Independent Oversight." (Eighth Workshop on the Economics of Information Security, University College, London, November, 2009). Available at http://www.ipc.on.ca/images/Resources/privacy_externalities.pdf.

Chow, R., Golle, P., Jakobsson, M., Masuoka, R., Molina, J., Shi, E., and J. Staddon, J. 2009. "Controlling Data in the Cloud: Outsourcing Computation without Outsourcing Control." (Cloud Computing Security Workshop, Chicago, November 13, 2009).

Cornish, P., D. Livingstone, D. Clemente, and C. Yorke. 2011. *Cyber Security and the UK's Critical National Infrastructure.* Chatham House Report. Available at http://www.chathamhouse.org/sites/default/files/public/Research/ International%20Security/r0911cyber.pdf.

Deloitte 2010. *Information Security Briefing 01/2010: Cloud Computing.* Available at http://www.cpni.gov.uk/documents/publications/2010/2010007-isb _cloud_computing.pdf.

Dresner, S., and A. Norcup. 2009. "Data Breach Notification Laws in Europe." *Privacy Laws & Business.* Available at http://privacylaws.com/Documents/data_breach _conference.pdf.

European Commission Directorate-General Justice. 2012. "Commission Proposes a Comprehensive Reform of the Data Protection Rules," Data-Protection News-room, January 25, 2012. Available at http://ec.europa.eu/justice/newsroom/data -protection/news/120125_en.htm.

Global Access Partners (joint with Australian government's Department of Broad-band, Communications, and the Digital Economy). 2011. *Task Force on Cloud Computing.* Available at http://www.globalaccesspartners.org/Cloud-Computing -GAP-Task-Force-Report-May-2011.pdf.

IBM. "UK Smart Energy Cloud." 2011. http://www.ibm.com/smarterplanet/global/ files/uk__en_uk__smart_energy__ibm_smart_meters_feb_2011.pdf.

In-Stat 2009. "Mobile VoIP—Transforming the Future of Wireless Voice." Mobile Unified Communications. Available at http://www.tmcnet.com/channels/mobile -unified-communications/articles/66906-report-mobile-voip-growth-will-impact -operator-voice.htm.

Ismail, N. 2011. Cursing the Cloud (or) Controlling the Cloud? *Computer Law & Security Report* 27:250–257.

Kroes, N. 2012. "Cloud-Computing—Between Growth Opportunities and Privacy." Speech 12/490, A European Cloud Strategy Economic Council Symposium, Euro-pean Commission, Brussels, June 25, 2012.

Lachal, L. 2010. "Cloud-Computing Quality of Service in Perspective." OVUM Report at http://www.researchandmarkets.com/research/f4181e/cloudcomputing_qu.

Marcus, S., P. Nooren, J. Cave, and K. Carter. 2011. *Network Neutrality: Challenges and Responses in the EU and in the US.* Report to the European Parliament Committee on Internal Market and Consumer Protection. Available at http://www.europarl. europa.eu/document/activities/cont/201105/20110523ATT20073/20110523ATT200 73EN.pdf.

NetworkComputing. 2012. "Sourcefire Uses Big Data Analytics to Stop Malware," January 25, 2012. http://www.networkcomputing.com/cloud-infrastructure/ sourcefire-uses-big-data-analytics-to-stop-malware/d/d-id/1233346?

Pearson, S. 2009. "Taking Account of Privacy when Designing Cloud Comput-ing Services" HP Labs Working Paper. Available at http://www.hpl.hp.com/ techreports/2009/HPL-2009-54.pdf.

Rittinghouse, J., and J. Ransome. 2009. *Cloud Computing: Implementation, Manage-ment, and Security.* New York: Auerbach Publications.

Robinson, N., L. Valeri, J. Cave, T. Starkey, H. Graux, S. Creese, and P. Hopkins. 2011. "The Cloud: Understanding the Security, Privacy and Trust issues." Technical Report TR-933-EC Santa Monica, CA: RAND Corporation.

Storm, D. 2012. "Welcome to Minority Report IRL: Police Armed with Pre-crime Detection Tools." *Computerworld* (January 26, 2012). Available at http://blogs.computerworld.com/19644/welcome_to_minority_report_irl_police_armed _with_pre_crime_detection_tools?source=CTWNLE_nlt_emgtech_2012-02-01.

Verstraete, C. 2012. "B2B or B2C for Cloud Services? Does It Matter?" Enterprise CIO Forum (January 17, 2012). Available at http://m.enterprisecioforum.com/en/ blogs/christian/are-concepts-b2b-and-b2c-still-relevant?device=mobile.

Weyl, E. G. 2010. A Price Theory of Multi-Sided Platforms. *American Economic Review* 100 (4): 1642–1672.

Wittow, M. H. and D. J. Buller 2010. Cloud Computing: Emerging Legal Issues for Access to Data, Anywhere, Anytime. *Journal of Internet Law* 14 (1): 1–10.

Wittow, M. H. 2011. Cloud Computing: Recent Cases and Anticipating New Types of Claims. *Computer & Internet Lawyer* 28 (1): 18–24.

Zimmerman, M. 2011. MP3.com Redux? Music Venture's Model Survives Copyright Challenge, as S.D.N.Y. Provides Guidance for Cloud-Hosted Services. *Computer & Internet Lawyer* 28 (12): 1–4.

Zittrain, J. L. 2008. *The Future of the Internet and How to Stop It.* New Haven, CT: Yale University Press.

7 Digital Records and Archives in the Commercial Cloud

Luciana Duranti

Individuals and organizations are increasingly attracted to the lure of cloud computing for the many benefits it offers. Scalable, agile, efficient, and on-demand computing resources mean that email, photos, data, documents, and records can be easily stored and shared through a seemingly endless number of hosted web applications, and that sophisticated software, platforms, and infrastructure are available to the budget-conscious and technology-resource-limited consumer.

This chapter discusses the use of cloud computing for record creation, record keeping, and archival preservation in relation to the trustworthiness of records as evidence and of archives as the authentic memory of the past. It will do so with a particular focus on the commercial (or public) cloud because of its attractiveness to individuals, small businesses, and increasingly budget-stripped cultural organizations.

Commercial cloud architectures offer on-demand access to services across a network of standard Internet-accessible devices—mobile phones, tablets, laptops—and a vast array of other devices, such as game consoles, MP3 players, and e-business technologies. Resources are shared among users, and resource utilization is monitored and invoiced based on service usage. People use—and increasingly rely on—cloud services for communication, backup and storage, collaboration, distribution, record keeping, and preservation. While they engage in such use, though, these technologies and services change their behavior.

Records in the Cloud

Information Producers' Behavior

On a personal level, social networking and photo sharing websites encourage users to communicate online and give their contacts permission to add comments, notes, tags, images, and other elements to their materials, so the boundaries between content producers and users become blurred. The by-products of such interaction are no longer finite entities; rather, they are processes that are always changing, mediated by the technological platform that hosts them through metadata, protocols, and codes. On an organizational level, working practices tend to coalesce into one of two models: the first is a distributed workforce that connects to a shared space on a web platform from home or anywhere else outside the office, and carries out its activities by generating and contributing to coauthored and coowned documents and data sets; the second is the practice of bringing to the office one's own computer or mobile device and use it to perform the work processes and procedures of the organization.

The first model results in the concentration of all corporate digital information into a shared space, but a blurring of responsibilities for each piece of information, which is difficult to attribute to one author or owner due to the collaborative way in which people act. The second model, however, has more serious consequences. The Bring Your Own Device (BYOD) practice can create issues because corporate digital information is no longer captured or moved into a central record-keeping system, so records are rarely complete, as each employee has parts of them on his or her own device and the files are continuously updated as needed without saving the previous versions. As a result, the information is not clearly linked to one business process, action, or transaction. What makes the BYOD practice a serious concern in the context of the present discussion is that employees tend not to keep the information they produce, receive, or refer to in the memory of their own devices; rather, they create, use, and maintain it in several different commercial cloud environments. Thus, the corporate information controlled by each employee is stored in a widespread way, mostly related to applications (e.g., Dropbox or Google Docs) rather than to business functions, and de facto, the BYOD becomes a Bring Your Own Cloud (BYOC) practice.

The behavior induced by the use of cloud computing at both the individual and organizational level constitutes a problem for persons and organizations, as well as for society at large, because it has an impact on the existence of records and on their trustworthiness. A record is a document (i.e., recorded information) that is made or received by a physical or juridical person in the usual and ordinary course of activity as an instrument for or a by-product of such activity, and kept for further action or reference by that person or a legitimate successor. Records must have fixed form and stable content, a clear relationship to other records participating in the same activity, and a unique identity established by the sum of their attributes, such as date, names of author and other involved parties, the action in which they participate, and other elements.[1] Records have a special status in evidence law: in common law systems, they are considered an exception to the hearsay rule and only require relevance and authentication to be admitted as evidence, while in civil law systems, they are automatically admitted if relevant.[2] Furthermore, records are the primary means by which employees are held accountable for their actions. Of course, producing and keeping records of activities is not sufficient to provide evidence of them and ask people to respond for them. Records also must be trustworthy. This specific issue will be discussed later in this chapter.

Over time, the digital information produced using cloud services grows in volume, and, being spread across multiple online platforms, becomes unmanageable. As a result, its producers may simply choose to let it accumulate, given the availability of large amounts of free cloud storage. Thus, the problem of the absence of records that are usable as precedent or as evidence of actions and transactions is compounded by their uncontrolled abundance. Providers have offered a solution by enabling automatic deletion after a certain amount of time[3]—a time span usually based not on a plan for record retention and disposition approved by the employer, but on the intention of the person initiating the communication.[4] However, deletion often simply means removal by the relevant cloud provider search engine of links that allow the retrieval of the record by means of keywords, but the information remains where it is and can be found by other search engines and tools.[5] When these self-destruct tools are not used, data, documents, and records are simply left in the provider's servers in a state of "involuntary permanence" and may constitute a serious liability for the cloud user in case of legal discovery, and an infringement of privacy for individuals who want their data to be deleted.[6]

The characteristics of the digital information produced in the commercial cloud are quite clear: When it is traceable and has identifiable boundaries, it tends to be a coauthored entity (by persons and platforms, software codes, and protocols of the host applications), in continuous becoming, generated to serve multiple purposes in multiple contexts, composed of more than one medium, performed, rather than issued, and therefore ephemeral in nature, generally accessible by anyone who shares the same platform and/or belongs in the same circles, and unprotected by intellectual rights. This means that this information does not achieve the status of records, having no fixity, defined identity and relationships, and a clear connection to an activity and a functional context and to a record system.

How does this blurring of boundaries between public and private, organizational and personal, ephemeral and permanent, complete and in a state of becoming, platform-generated and user-generated, owned and open, recorded and performed, etc., meet the expectations of records and archives users, be they lawyers, administrators, researchers, citizens pursuing personal matters, or journalists? Has the way that they use such materials also changed with the availability of the commercial cloud?

Records and Archives Users' Behavior

The users of records and archives are also discovering new opportunities in the online environment. Administrators, professionals, and researchers who have always worked collaboratively in a physical location now expect to do so in a virtual environment; users of material in archival holdings expect that these materials will be made available through the Internet, possibly instantaneously and in the required and interoperable formats; citizens interested in the actions of government and corporations expect open access to the records of these actions over time; scientists who deal with data and statistics are interested in open data initiatives and expect to be able to trace such data to the records from which they were extracted; and more and more users from the private sector and academia are employing diverse sources of big data to create data mashups for a variety of purposes. While the records and archives profession has been aware of these users' behaviors and expectations for a long time, the most noticeable change has been a growing interest in data as opposed to records, and in large aggregations of research data, observational data, and government-collected data for supporting decision making—data that is expected to be both available and reusable in a cloud environment (mostly commercial).[7] The key consideration to make here, though, is that this interest in data comes with a strong interest in their accuracy, reliability, and traceability to an authentic source. This requirement of trustworthiness is becoming an explicit need for a documented chain of unbroken and responsible preservation: in other words, while traditionally people trusted source material (i.e., data, documents, records, and archives) implicitly if they trusted the custodian, now they increasingly require the custodian (i.e., records manager or archivist) evidence of uninterrupted custody and of proper activities of storage, migration, conversion, duplication, reduction, and so on.

How are archival institutions, organizations, units and programs addressing the opportunities and challenges posed by the pervasive use of the cloud by creators and users of records, and by their expectations? This question will be discussed next.

Archives in the Cloud

The focus of the archival profession on memory and evidence encourages the popular misperception of archives as being concerned only with records of the past (in any medium). But archivists have known for a long time that records generated in digital form[8] (i.e., born-digital records) will not remain usable and trustworthy if their preservation is not considered from the moment of their creation. While this is difficult enough for born-digital records that mirror traditional counterparts, such as correspondence, reports, contracts, or memoranda, it creates many new challenges for records created collaboratively, reproduced, reused, and modified in the cloud. Identifying issues of authorship, ownership, access, and intellectual rights would merely scratch the surface of the archival challenge. What are the responsibilities and strategies of the archival system that is asked to support a controlled creation of data, documents, and records that can demonstrate transparent processes of creation, maintenance, and use and a clear chain of custody or provenance, and whose accuracy, reliability, and authenticity can be guaranteed over time and across technology platforms? Do complexity of technologies; need for specialized and quickly upgradable professional knowledge; economies of space, technology, and human resources; the requirement for easy access from anywhere in the world; and particularly the fact that records are increasingly created in the commercial cloud compel archives to perform their preservation function in the cloud? If such a mandate exists, in addition to creating unprecedented challenges, will this change the nature of archives as social institutions?

Archives as a Place
In both Western and Eastern cultures, the concept of *place* lies at the core of the nature of archives as trusted custodians of documentary memory. For millennia, the place where this memory is kept has been as important to its permanence and quality as the knowledge of the professionals responsible for it (Duranti 1996). In the Justinian Code, which is the *summa* of all Roman law and jurisprudence, an archives is defined as *locus publicus in quo instrumenta deponuntur* (i.e., the public place where deeds are deposited), *quatenus incorrupta maneant* (i.e., so that they remain uncorrupted), *fidem faciant* (i.e., provide trustworthy evidence), and *perpetua rei*

memoria sit (i.e., and be continuing memory of that to which they attest) (Justinian n.d.). In the ancient world, an archives was a place of preservation under the jurisdiction of a public authority. This place, which was public as well, endowed the documents that passed its threshold with trustworthiness, thereby giving them the capacity of serving as evidence and continuing memory of facts and acts.

In 1664, though, a German jurist named Ahasver Fritsch specified that archival materials did not acquire trustworthiness simply by crossing the archival threshold, but because (1) the place to which they were destined belonged to a public sovereign authority, as opposed to its agents or delegates; (2) the officer forwarding them to such a place was a public officer; (3) the documents were placed both physically (i.e., by location) and intellectually (i.e., by description) among authentic documents; and (4) this association was not meant to be broken (Fritsch 1664). Over time, the "archival right" (i.e., the right to keep a place capable of conferring trustworthiness, and therefore authority, to the documentary by-products of activities—namely, records), was acquired by all those bodies to which sovereignty was delegated by the supreme secular and religious powers— among these, cities and churches. In medieval times, corporations of every kind, including universities, deposited the documents of their activities in the *camera actorum* (i.e., chamber of the acts) of the municipality with jurisdiction over them or in the archives chests of ecclesiastical institutions before they could acquire the right to "hold archives" (Lodolini 1991).

This remained the state of affairs until the French Revolution, when, with the decree of July 25, 1794, the records of defunct institutions and organizations, concentrated in the National Archives of France, were declared to be the patrimony of the nation and were made accessible to the public. By virtue of this declaration, the state recognized its duty to preserve them as historical memory for subsequent generations—that is, to ensure the records' physical and technological stability and protection of intellectual content.[9] Since then, the responsibility of archival institutions[10] as trusted custodians of the records destined to indefinite preservation has remained.

Given the centrality of place to the concept of archives, how can we reconcile archival preservation—encompassing the responsibilities derived by the archival right/duty, which remains by mandate and mission with the archival organization—with storage by a commercial cloud provider, which would not be accountable for the records themselves but only for respecting its own terms of service? The use of a commercial cloud to keep archives would imply that centralized legal custody of the records and responsibility for their intellectual control be left with the archival institution, while physical custody and technological access provisions be delegated to the cloud provider, which can be a pure commercial provider (public cloud), or a mix of public and private providers (hybrid cloud).

Similar circumstances in different contexts have been examined by several research projects in order to find usable models.[11] Maritime rules of shipping have been closely studied, as they center on the recognition of the authority of three separate states: the *port* state, the *flag* state, and the *coastal* state. Early international maritime agreements established that the nationality of the transport vessel (the flag state) would establish jurisdiction, and by extension, the laws that would be in effect. Following the abuse of such rule, the port state was given greater control to inspect vessels coming within its territorial waters by the Law of the Sea Convention in 1982. Similarly, coastal states, through whose waters the flagged vessels transit, were given authority over the safety and competence of the ship and its crews and allowed inspection and enforcement while the vessel is in the coastal state's waters, regardless of the flag of either the vessel (flag state) or its destination (port state). On the basis of these rules, an analogy can be made. An Australian university could place its archives in the care of a US cloud provider, which in turn maintains its data centers in India. The US company would be the flag state, that would be moving the "goods" through coastal states to their ultimate destination in the port state of India. This situation would be problematic, not only because the university owning the archives would have no jurisdiction, but also with regard to the rights of the coastal state, in that the "pipe" used to move the records can transit through several countries (coastal states) as they are routed along the way and, traditionally, "coastal states" have not been granted access to inspecting packets of records as they move along the Internet. The rules of conduct then become very difficult, if not impossible, to enforce by any of the parties involved.[12]

In addition to legislation addressing similar circumstances, these research projects have examined law harmonization instruments concerned with privacy protection, free flow of information, efficiency, international commerce, and cybercrime investigation. Among them, the most relevant to the jurisdictional issues linked to the concept of place is the Budapest Convention on Cybercrime, created in 2001 by the Council of Europe. Presently, a subgroup of the Cybercrime Convention Committee (T-CY) is working on additional instruments to address several issues regarding transborder access to data in the context of criminal procedures and investigations undertaken by member states, which have increased with the use of cloud computing technologies. Although the convention was a product of the Council of Europe, several non-European countries have adopted it (with or without reservations), and it is the key piece of legislation on cybercrime. At the time of writing, 39 countries have ratified the convention, and 21 have reservations (Council of Europe, 2004).

To address this jurisdictional problem linked to location, other alternatives have been considered with unsuccessful results: the *territoriality principle* is not applicable because it is not possible to know the location of the records at any given time; the *nationality principle* is not applicable because nationality is an attribute of persons, not things, and the principle cannot be used to connect persons to data or records; the *power of disposal* principle, which connects any data to the person or persons holding the right to alter, delete, suppress, or render them unusable, does not address the issue of the different jurisdictions of custodians and providers; and the *power of preservation principle,* which assigns jurisdiction to the institutions controlling the records as their trusted custodian and the place guaranteeing their authenticity, is not helpful because jurisdiction with responsibility, but not actual custody, does not address the identified issues.[13]

Thus, the issue of location independence remains open with respect to both current records and archives. The distinction between the entity responsible for records retention, preservation, and accessibility (creator and designated preserver) and the entity storing them (the cloud provider), as well as the possibility that the jurisdiction under which either entity exists is different from that in which the materials physically reside, are obstacles to the widespread adoption of commercial cloud providers. India has imposed a ban on the use of foreign cloud-based email services to send official communications. It prevents civil servants from using services such as Gmail, Yahoo!, or Outlook.com. Instead, they would be required to use a service provided by the country's own National Informatics Centre (NIC).[14] Also Brazil has confirmed plans to set up its own secure and encrypted email service and cloud services for all levels of administration, but this choice is not shared by the majority of countries, especially those with few resources.[15] Furthermore, it does not necessarily address the other key issue presented by the use of the cloud for records retention and archival preservation: trustworthiness.[16]

Archives and Trust

In fact, if one subtracts custody and provision of access to records from the functions and responsibilities of archival institutions by entrusting them to an overarching government cloud, it becomes impossible for archival institutions to protect the identity and integrity of the material for which they are accountable and through which the creating individuals, corporations, and governments are accountable. As a consequence, such material cannot serve as a trustworthy source and evidence of facts and actions. Archival preservation is controlled by very strict principles: the principle of *respect des fonds*, according to which data and records created by different bodies cannot be intermingled; the principle of *provenance* (i.e., original order), according to which archival materials must be kept in the same procedural order in which they had originally accumulated; and the principle of the *unbroken chain of legitimate custody*, according to which the custodial history of data and records must be demonstrable at any given time or else the material will not be considered authentic (Jenkinson 1968). Respecting these principles ensures the physical and moral defense of archives—that is, their enduring trustworthiness. Whereas archival institutions have evolved over millennia to be the ideal providers of a preservation that observes such principles, their work needs to be protected through security and continuity of storage, and verifiable through transparency and accessibility in context (Duranti 1996). There are concerns about the ability of commercial cloud providers to fulfill these requirements.

In archival science, trustworthiness comprises three concepts: reliability, accuracy, and authenticity. *Reliability* is the trustworthiness of content; that is, of records as statements of facts. It is assessed on the basis of the competence of the author or authors and the controls exercised on record creation. *Accuracy* is the correctness and precision of such content and is assessed with the same factors and controls exercised upon recording and transmission. *Authenticity* is the trustworthiness of records as records; they are what they purport to be, are uncorrupted and untampered with, and are assessed on their identity and integrity as shown by external attributes associated with them (e.g., date and office of receipt, and name of handling office). In the digital world, metadata is used to check these concepts. *Metadata* is information about records, regardless of medium, that is used to identify, describe, manage, authenticate, and access them. Metadata produced at the time of record creation (i.e., when a record is made or received and saved into an aggregation of records) is an integral part of a record, and it is called *identity metadata*. Additional metadata accumulates over the record's life cycle and its production and management form an integral part of record keeping: this is called *record-keeping metadata* (MacNeil 1995, 2000).[17] In a cloud environment, the identity metadata (e.g., names of author, addressee, and other recipients, name of action or matter, date of creation and receipt, classification code or registry number, documentary form, technological format, etc.) follows the document to which it relates since creation, as the document comes into being with it and collectively they constitute "the record." However, the record-keeping metadata, which relates to use and to actions carried out on the records through time, and to the consequent technological and structural transformation of the records as they move from creation, use, and maintenance to preservation (often through encryption, conversions, migrations, etc.), is added by the cloud provider storing the records.

Thus, the questions that need to be answered are: How does metadata follow or trace records in the cloud from the creator to the preserver? How is this metadata migrated as a preservation activity over time? Who owns the metadata created by the service providers related to their management of the records (i.e., record-keeping metadata)? Is metadata intellectual property? If yes, whose property is it? How can this metadata be accessed by the public, and what are the responsibilities of the provider toward users of records preserved over the long term for a community or the public at large?

Until such time when we will be able to unequivocally answer these questions, there will be no trustworthiness of records in the cloud because reliability cannot be inferred from known management processes; accuracy cannot be inferred from known transmission and protection processes; and authenticity cannot be inferred from documentary context and a known preservation process. Archives require that each record's context be defined and immutable, with all its relationships intact, and this is difficult to demonstrate in the dynamically provisioned environment of the cloud.

Cloud providers are fully aware of these issues and have not stayed idle through the various legal and other problems that have ensued from the lack of regulation of their environment. Academic and professional researchers have developed initiatives to find solutions. And now, the two groups are beginning to get together in earnest in an interdisciplinary effort. At the opening of the International Conference on Cloud Security Management (ICCSM) 2013, Howard A. Schmidt, technological advisor to two past US presidents, stated that "technology is not the answer to everything," and that we "need to be prepared to change course" when thinking of the future.[18] Following his intervention, Jim Reavis, head of the Cloud Security Alliance (CSA), emphasized the fact that at this time, the cloud lacks transparency and visibility, is incompatible with existing legislation, is not regulated by comprehensive standards, and does not use true multitenant technology. There is a risk of concentration without clear separation and the tendency to maintain logical control, but lose physical and conceptual control (Reavis 2013). Thus, the CSA is taking a number of initiatives to address the issues identified by Reavis.

Although the cloud will never be transparent, there is a willingness to substitute transparency with trusted oversight. As a voluntary industry action promoting transparency, then, the CSA has developed the Security, Trust, and Assurance Registry (STAR), which is a public registry of cloud providers evaluations based on a Cloud Control Matrix, a Cloud Control Trust Protocol, and a Cloud Audit on how the cloud provider makes assertions.[19] This registry includes the results of an open certification framework (an approach supported by Internet 2) comprising three steps: self-assessment, third party assessment-based certification and attestation, and continuous monitoring-based certification. However, the CSA recognizes that all of this will not completely protect their users from the nine top threats (Cloud Security Alliance 2013):

- Data breaches
- Data loss
- Account hijacking
- Insecure application programming interfaces (APIs)
- Denial of service
- Malicious insiders
- Abuse of cloud services
- Insufficient due diligence
- Shared technology issues

The CSA is focusing on the following aspects to address all these threats: global legal issues; privacy level agreements; continuous monitoring; harmonization of various requirements, regulations, and standards, especially in relation to smart mobiles and anti-bots; and community policing (the already mentioned trusted oversight). But they cannot do it by themselves. Reavis, in his presentation, made a key understatement: "Metadata are important." Metadata are not just important—they are essential to establish trustworthiness of records. And, what does the CSA mean by "trusted"? Is the CSA framework sufficient for the creation, maintenance, and preservation of trusted records? Not really, especially considering that the threats it seeks to address do not include issues of jurisdiction and loss of contextuality. It would be much more useful to talk about cloud providers' responsibilities toward the materials they store rather about the threats they need to address. This approach is supported by Tim Berners-Lee, the inventor of the World Wide Web, who is calling for a Magna Carta, a bill of rights for its users that would identify the responsibilities of those who provide its services (Kiss 2014).[20] While waiting for an overarching framework regulating jurisdiction and trustworthiness in the commercial cloud, what can be done to protect the records that archival institutions are eager to entrust to it?

One possible solution is to consider a hybrid cloud. Contractual agreements can be developed where a commercial cloud provider offers account administration, installation, server administration, and user technical support while the archival institution provides fee-based server hosting and digital object storage service to a network of archives.[21] This type of solution addresses the most important issues deriving from the use of commercial services and is easier to manage than the more popular multicloud solution, where archives use more than one provider and feature more than one type of cloud platform. The multicloud idea works best in situations where there is one archival institution that is the designated custodian for a number of record creators who use different clouds (e.g., a national archives and the government agencies who have to transfer records to them), but the hybrid cloud works best in cases of archival institutions acquiring public and private, organizational, and personal records from a variety of record creators. Archival institutions with low resources may consider a minimalist approach to the cloud, choosing to adopt only a few simple services, such as storage, computing, or database management. This approach is called "the naked cloud," and in some cases, it can get down to the simple platform, without going through layers of APIs and management tools. The naked cloud may be offered by "hosting providers," who would just keep and service the archival institution servers in their own data center; "managed service providers," who would manage resources on behalf of the archival institution, maintain the platform, offer specific services, and manage security and governance; and "specialized cloud services providers," who offer a dedicated server environment. The naked cloud is useful to archival institutions because they need to use resources that do not autoscale for long periods of time, and it allows them to control the platform and platform services using direct access (Linthicum 2014).

Conclusion

There is no doubt that entrusting records and archives to commercial cloud providers constitutes an enormous and difficult challenge—one that archival institutions must address or else they would fail to fulfill important cultural, educational, scientific, social, governmental, business, and practical needs that depend on trustworthy digital records. As Nathan and Shaffer state, this kind of problem can never be solved forever, and one can always do better. Furthermore, there is no single "solution"; rather, there is a continuous series of ever-evolving processes based on a combination of theory and empirical inquiry that informs the design of systems, policies, practices, procedures, contracts, and possibly laws (Nathan and Shaffer 2013). The Magna Carta advocated by Berners Lee, and the international framework for trustworthiness that the archival research carried out by InterPARES Trust[22] aims to develop will be useful in a variety of endeavors, such as articulating a theory of record keeping and record preservation in the cloud; formulating models for law reform and policy design; developing specialized bodies of knowledge and skills; planning for and managing online repositories; defining the need for better record-keeping technologies and guiding their development; and evaluating the relevance and adequacy of the creation, maintenance, and preservation techniques for specific records. But none of these initiatives can be successful without the willingness of cloud providers to accept procedural and contractual conditions that will support the archival mission, the exercise of archival functions, and the documentation of context, which is vital to understanding and preserving meaning, providing a collective authentication of the materials within each archives, and ensuring controlled and accurate access.

Records are vital instruments of legal, administrative, and historical accountability. Their trustworthiness, as well as the clear identification of the jurisdiction within which they have to be assessed, comprise the foundation of our democratic system. Technological progress has to be embraced, but before doing so, it is necessary to identify the consequences of such action and address relevant issues so that the values of society can be protected and enhanced by the adoption of new ways of fulfilling our responsibilities.

Notes

1. For a full description of what a record is, see Duranti (2009).
2. For further details, see Duranti and Rogers (2012).
3. For example, see DSTRUX (https://dstrux.com), a cloud-based file-sharing product that allows users to set up a self-destruct timer on shared files, so they're automatically destroyed at a certain point in time.

4. A retention and disposition plan or schedule is a document describing the recurring records of an organization or administrative unit, specifying which records are to be kept and for how long, and authorizing, on a continuing basis and after the lapse of specified retention periods and the occurrence of specified actions or events, the destruction of the remaining records or their transfer to their designated custodian for permanent preservation.

5. See Davenport (2013).

6. A "right to be forgotten" has been approved in Europe and is being considered in North America. See European Parliament on Civil Liberties, Justice, and Home Affairs (2013) and Hunton and Williams LLP (2013).

7. Since 2010, US government agencies have moved into Google Apps, Google Mail, and Microsoft Office 365. See, for example, GCN (2012).

8. The term *digital form* is defined as the representation of an object or physical process through discrete, binary values.

9. See Posner (1940); Muller, Feith, and Fruin (1898); Jenkinson (1968); and Cook (1997).

10. For ease of reading, the expression *archival institution,* in a social sense, will be used to encompass archival organizations of all types, public and private, and archival units within organizations.

11. See, for example, Records in the Cloud (http://www.recordsinthecloud.org), the Law of Evidence in the Digital Environment (http://www.lawofevidence.org), and InterPARES Trust (http://www.interparestrust.org).

12. See United Nations (2013) and Anderson (1998).

13. See Council of Europe, Economic Crime Division (2010); Council of Europe, Cybercrime Convention Committee (2012); Seger (2012); and Narayanan (2012).

14. See the Government of India site at https://cloud.gov.in.

15. As an example of the size of the problem, see the BBC report on Edward Snowden's leaks about the hacking of Google and Yahoo! data links by the US government. Available at http://www.bbc.com/news/world-us-canada-24753586.

16. See Moreira (2012) and Mari (2013).

17. For further information about digital records metadata, see Authenticity Task Force (2005), Tennis (2010), and Rogers and Tennis (2012).

18. For the International Cloud Security Management ICCSM 2013 conference website, see http://academic-conferences.org/iccsm/iccsm2013/iccsm13-home.htm.

19. For the CSA Star Registry, see https://cloudsecurityalliance.org/star.

20. This is the projected outcome of the InterPARES Trust project, which will be concluded in 2018 (www.INTERPARESTRUST.OR6). Another key outcome is a Unified Modeling Language (UML) model of preservation in a cloud environment called Preservation As a Service for Trust (PAST), which is being developed in collaboration with the Object Management Group (OMG) and details all the functional requirements that providers must respect for the purpose of issuing an international standard.

21. A real-life example is provided by the collaboration between the Artefactual System, which provides preservation software as a service, and the Council of Prairie

and Pacific University Libraries (COPPUL), in Canada. COPPUL is responsible for promoting the service, signing up new institutions, and seeding the one-time setup costs; Artefactual Systems provides account administration, installation, server administration, and user technical support; and the University of British Columbia Library provides fee-based server hosting and digital object storage service. See http://coppuldpwg.wordpress.com/committees/archivematica.

22. See www.INTERPARESTRUST.OR6.

References

Anderson, D. 1998. The Roles of Flag States, Port States, Coastal States, and International Organizations in the Enforcement of International Rules and Standards Governing the Safety of Navigation and the Prevention of Pollution from Ships under the UN Convention on the Law of the Sea and Other National Agreements. *Singapore Journal of International and Comparative Law* 2:557–578.

Authenticity Task Force. 2005. Appendix 2: Requirements for Assessing and Maintaining the Authenticity of Electronic Records. In *The Long-term Preservation of Authentic Electronic Records: Findings of the InterPARES Project*, ed. Luciana Duranti, 204–219. San Miniato, Italy: Archilab.

Cloud Security Alliance. 2013. "The Notorious Nine: Cloud Computing Top Threats in 2013." Available at https://cloudsecurityalliance.org/download/the-notorious -nine-cloud-computing-top-threats-in-2013.

Council of Europe. 2004. Convention on Cybercrime. CETS No. 185. Budapest, November 23, Available at http://conventions.coe.int/Treaty/en/Treaties/Html/185 .htm.

Council of Europe, Economic Crime Division. (2010). *Cloud Computing and Cybercrime Investigations: Territoriality vs. the Power of Disposal?* (Discussion Paper). Strasbourg. Retrieved August 19, 2014, from http://www.coe.int/t/dghl/cooperation/ economiccrime/cybercrime/documents/internationalcooperation/2079_Cloud _Computing_power_disposal_31Aug10a.pdf.

Council of Europe, Cybercrime Convention Committee. (2012). *Transborder Access and Jurisdiction: What Are the Options?* (Discussion Paper). Strasbourg. Retrieved August 19, 2014, from http://www.coe.int/t/dghl/cooperation/economiccrime/ cybercrime/T-CY/TCY_2012_3_transborder_rep_V30public_7Dec12.pdf.

Cook, T. 1997. What Is Past Is Prologue: A History of Archival Ideas since 1898, and the Future Paradigm Shift. *Archivaria* 43:18–63.

Davenport, C. 2013. "Google and Spain Wrestle over EU Privacy Law," Reuters, February. Available at http://in.reuters.com/article/2013/02/26/eu-google -dataprotection-idINDEE91P07K20130226.

Duranti, L. 1996. Archives as a Place. *Archives & Manuscripts* 24 (2): 242–255.

Duranti, L. 2009. Diplomatics. In *Encyclopedia of Library and Information Science*. 3rd ed., ed. Marcia Bates, Mary Niles Maack, and Miriam Drake, 1593–1601. London: Taylor & Francis.

Duranti, L. and C. Rogers. 2012. Trust in Digital Records: An Increasingly Cloudy Legal Area. *Computer Law & Security Review* 28 (5) (October): 522–531 (quote on 528).

Duranti, L., and A. Jansen. 2013. Records in the Cloud: Authenticity and Jurisdiction," in *Proceedings of the 2013 Digital Heritage International Congress,* Marseille, France, October 28–November 1, 2013. Vol. 2 (Paris: IEEE, 2013): 161–164.

European Parliament Committee on Civil Liberties. Justice and Home Affairs (2013). Draft Report on the Proposal for a Regulation of the European Parliament and of the Council on the Protection of Individual with Regard to the Processing of Personal Data and on the Free Movement of Such Data (General Data Protection Regulation). January 10. Available at http://www.europarl.europa.eu/meetdocs/2009_2014/documents/libe/pr/922/922387/922387en.pdf.

Fritsch, A. 1664. *De iure archivi et cancellariae.* Jenae, Germany.

GCN. 2012. "VA Plugs into the Cloud with Office 365 for 600,000." Available at http://gcn.com/Blogs/Pulse/2012/12/VA-cloud-Office-365-for-600000-users.aspx.

Hunton and Williams LLP. 2013. "Council of the European Union Releases Draft Compromise Text on the Proposed EU Data Protection Regulation." Hunton Privacy Blog. Available at http://www.huntonprivacyblog.com/2013/06/articles/council-of-the-european-union-releases-draft-compromise-text-on-the-proposed-eu-data-protection-regulation.

Jenkinson, H. 1966. *A Manual of Archive Administration*. Revised Edition. London: Percy Lund, Humphries & Co. Ltd.

Justinian (A.D. 529–534). *Corpus Juris Civilis, Novella 15,* "De Defensoribus civitatum," "Et a defensoribus," *Digestum48, no. 19,* "De Poenis," *Codex I, no. 4,* "De episcopali audientia."

Kiss, J. 2014. "An Available Magna Carta: Berners-Lee Calls for Bill of Rights for Web," *The Guardian,* March 12, 2014.

Linthicum, D. S. 2014. "Stripping down Enterprise IT to the Naked Cloud," *TechTarget.* Available at http://searchcloudcomputing.techtarget.com/tip/Stripping-down-enterprise-IT-to-the-naked-cloud.

Lodolini, L. 1991. *Lineamenti di storia dell'archivistica Italiana. Dalle origini alla metà del secolo XX.* Rome: La Nuova Italia Scientifica.

MacNeil, H. 1995. Metadata Strategies and Archival Description: Comparing Apples and Oranges. *Archivaria* 39 (Spring): 22–32.

MacNeil, H. 2000. Providing Grounds for Trust: Developing Conceptual Requirements for the Long-Term Preservation of Authentic Electronic Records. *Archivaria* 50 (Fall): 52–78.

Mari, A. 2013. "Brazilian Government Launches Own Cloud Offering," *Zdnet*. Available at http://www.zdnet.com/brazilian-government-launches-own-cloud-offering -7000020738.

Moreira, Rafael H. R. 2012. "IT and Cloud Computing in Brazil: Public Policies," *CloudConf LATAM 2012*. São Paulo, BR. Available at http://cloudconf.com.br/ arquivos/CloudConf2012_Rafael_Moreira.pdf.

Muller, S., J. A. Feith and R. Fruin. 1898. *Manual for the Arrangement and Description of Archives*, 2nd ed., trans. Arthur H. Leavitt, New York, 1940.

Narayanan, V. 2012. Harnessing the Cloud: International Law Implications of Cloud-Computing. *Chicago Journal of International Law* 12 (2): 783–809.

Nathan, L., and E. Shaffer. 2103. "Preserving Social Media: Opening a Multi-Disciplinary Dialogue," in Luciana Duranti and Elizabeth Shaffer, eds. *The Memory in the World in the Digital Age: Digitization and Preservation*. Vancouver 26–28 September 2013. Conference Proceedings. (Paris: UNESCO, 2013): 410–419.

Posner, E. 1940. Some Aspects of Archival Development since the French Revolution. *American Archivist* 3:159–172.

Reavis, J. 2013. "Keynote Speech," October 18, 2013, ICCSM 2013, Seattle. Available at http://academic-conferences.org/iccsm/iccsm2013/iccsm13-home.htm.

Rogers, C., and J. Tennis. 2012. InterPARES 3 Project. General Study 15. Application Profile for Authenticity Metadata. Available at http://www.interpares.org/ip3/ display_file.cfm?doc=ip3_metadata_application_profiles_final_report.pdf.

Seger, A. 2012. "The Budapest Convention 10 Years On: Lessons Learnt," in "Cyber-criminality: Finding a Balance between Freedom and Security. Selected Papers and Contributions from the International Conference on Cybercrime: Global Phenomenon and Its Challenges," Courmayeur Mont Blanc, Italy, December 2–4, 2011, ed. Stefano Manacorda (Milan, Italy: ISPAC, 2012): 167–177.

Tennis, J. 2010. "Metadata: Interoperability across Systems, Time, and Conceptions," InterPARES 3 Project, Third International Symposium, May 29, 2010. Vancouver, BC, Canada. Available at http://www.interpares.org/display_file.cfm?doc=ip3 _canada_dissemination_cs_tennis_ip3-isym03_2010.pdf.

United Nations. 2013. United Nations Conventions on the Law of the Sea Agreement Relating to the Implementation of Part XI of the Convention. Available at http://www.un.org/Depts/los/convention_agreements/convention_overview _convention.htm.

8 Software Copyright in the Cloud[1]

Lothar Determann and David Nimmer

It was never a happy marriage. Computer software and copyright law came from different families, embodied disparate values, and pursued separate interests. So, even though the latter became the vehicle to secure legal protection for the former, the union was never smooth—even on the wedding day. At present, the plates are flying with ever more reckless abandon, as the open-source movement has been active to turn copyright into so-called copyleft, courts around the world are reshaping the first sale doctrine, and software manufacturers flee from distribution to service models into using the cloud. With a perfect storm brewing, this chapter steps in to offer some gentle marital counseling.

Part of the initial bargain that brought software into the copyright fold was that users would obtain privileges in software via two legal devices—the first sale defense and the essential step doctrine. Yet, in recent years, software developers have sought to maximize their rights by enclosing their physical products with shrink wrap or other purported contractual terms. Through that stratagem, they have sought to avoid the privileges that would otherwise be available to software users via the first sale doctrine. In that endeavor, they have largely achieved success within the United States, albeit not without some backlash. Yet the European Court of Justice dealt software makers a blow in July 2012 by dramatically expanding the scope of "exhaustion," the European analog to the US first sale doctrine (Judgment of the European Court of Justice, *UsedSoft GmbH v. Oracle Int'l Corp.* 2012). Thus, the international status of these efforts is currently in flux. Moreover, even within those two jurisdictions, the results have been less than categorical—for instance, in March 2013, the US Supreme Court held that copies made and first sold abroad can be imported into the United States against the US copyright owner's will, potentially presaging a retreat from the expansive interpretation of license terms evident in prior opinions (*Kirtsaeng v. John Wiley &*

Sons, Inc., 2013). Correlatively, more recent developments within Europe call into question the European Court of Justice ruling of 2012—some portending its limitation, others its radical expansion.

As if those developments were not dizzying enough in their own right, the cloud injects even more volatility into the mix and may turn things upside down. By keeping software copies on their own servers and making software functionality available remotely as part of cloud offerings on a subscription basis, the cloud promised to enable software publishers to place their code outside the framework of copyright exhaustion under the first sale doctrine and the "distribution trigger" in open-source code license terms. Users' inability, in the cloud context, to directly access the underlying software threatens to exert various side effects, notably those affecting software interoperability. New kids on the block lose the ability to reverse-engineer hosted software. Established platform providers gain the ability to prevent interoperability based on laws prohibiting interference with computers and technical protection measures.

These developments risk upsetting the delicate balance between exclusive rights for copyright owners and access rights for the public—a balance that courts and legislatures have carefully established over the years—to foster creativity and innovation. With unprecedented pressure on traditional distribution models, how will copyright law cope? Having no idea of the ultimate goal toward which the law is heading, we attempt to illuminate the immediate path ahead in the light of past events that have brought matters to their current location. The first section, "History and Application of Copyright Protection for Software," starts with a brief overview regarding the history and current state of software copyright law to set the stage for our assessment. The second section, "Economics and Technology of the Cloud," brings the cloud into the picture: we describe the nature of the cloud, as well as its technological and economical disruptive force potential. The effects of the cloud on software copyright law is then examined in the third section, "The Cloud's Impact on Software Copyrights," followed by a look at possible developments ahead in the fourth and final section, "Some Weather Forecasts."

History and Application of Copyright Protection for Software

From the beginnings of computer technology, copyright law was an unlikely candidate to protect intellectual property when it came to software. After all, copyright is intended, at its roots, to protect creative expression, such as paintings, music, novels, and sculptures. Yet the value in most software inheres not in its creative expression, but instead in its technical functionality—a matter that copyright law was never intended to protect. In fact, the Copyright Act expressly carves out ideas, procedures, processes, systems, and methods of operation from its scope of protection.

Nevertheless, copyright law ended up as the legal vehicle providing the primary source of intellectual property law protection for software (Menell 1987). It took considerable bending and tweaking to make it work (see Lemley 1995a, 3–6; Samuelson et al. 1994; Menell 1987, 1329). Even the rise of open-source licensing and "copyleft" (Determann 2006) can be viewed as an affirmation of software copyright law, insofar as copyleft and the broader trend of "sharing nicely" (Benkler 2004, 334–336) were enabled precisely through leveraging the adaptation right afforded to copyright owners—a feature that patent and trade secret laws pointedly do not offer (Determann 2006, 1442).

Conferral of Rights on Copyright Proprietors
Computer Software Amendment of 1980 By adopting the Computer Software Copyright Act of 1980 (Pub. L. 96–517, § 10, 94 Stat. 3028), the US Congress made the decision that copyright law serves as the appropriate vehicle for courts to afford protection to computer programming.[2] Computer programs (both object and source code versions) therefore now generally find protection under the Copyright Act (see, e.g., *Harcourt, Brace, & World, Inc. v. Graphics Controls Corp.* 1971; *Williams Electronics, Inc. v. Artic Int'l, Inc.* 1982); for an overview, see Lemley et al. (2000, 1–45, 97–98; 2003, 33–35). The underlying code constitutes a literary work (*Apple Computer, Inc. v. Franklin Computer, Inc,* 1983, 1246–1249). The output of software, such as screen displays and graphical user interfaces (GUIs), does not constitute software in and of itself, but it can be protected separately from the computer program that creates it in the form of literary, pictorial, or graphic works (*Stern Electronics, Inc. v. Kaufman* 1982; *Data East USA, Inc. v. Epyx, Inc.* 1988; *Apple Computer, Inc. v. Microsoft Corp.* 1994).

In 1991, a unanimous US Supreme Court rejected the "sweat of the brow" doctrine, which stood for the proposition that authors could achieve copyright protection for works that showed little originality but took a lot of work to create, such as a phone directory in the case decided by the US Supreme Court. Copyright law is designed to protect creative expression as an incentive for further creative activity (*Feist Publications, Inc., v. Rural Telephone Service Co.* 1991). Given that the value in software is usually measured by its functionality and efficiency (*Bucklew v. Hawkins, Ash, Baptie & Co.* 2003, p. 928), aspects that are expressly excluded from copyright protection,[3] courts must face the prospect of having to fit a square peg into a round hole (*Computer Associates. Int'l, Inc. v. Altai, Inc.* 1992, p. 712). Courts have developed a number of tests and approaches to separate software's protectable creative elements from its nonprotectable functional elements (*Computer Associates Int. Inc. v. Altai Inc.* 1992, p. 714; *Gates Rubber Co. v. Bando Chemical Industries, Ltd.* 1993, 836–838; *Lotus Development Corp. v. Borland Int'l* 1995, p. 815–817; *Lexmark International, Inc. v. Static Control Components, Inc.* 2004, p. 534–536; *Chamberlain Group v. Skylink Technologies, Inc.* 2004; EU Court of Justice, Case C-406/10, *SAS Institute Inc. v. World Programming Ltd.* 2012, para. 46). Creative elements are protected against literal and nonliteral copying; by contrast, functional ingredients can be freely duplicated, even in the limited case when idea and expression (or functionality and creativity) merge—for example, because a particular technical solution can be programmed efficiently only in one particular manner (*Google v. Oracle* 2012); *Computer Associates Int'l, Inc. v. Altai, Inc.* 1992, 707–708; Case C-406/10, *SAS Institute Inc. v. World Programming Ltd.* 2012, para. 46). Thus, software copyright analysis must begin with a thorough examination of the dichotomy between creativity and functionality (*Feist Publications, Inc., v. Rural Telephone Service Co.* 1991, p. 362).[4] This analysis involves filtering out ideas, processes, methods, facts, and elements dictated by external factors or efficiency, material in the public domain, expression that has merged with any of the foregoing, and expression that is so standard or common as to be a "necessary incident" to any of the foregoing (*Gates Rubber Co. v. Bando Chem. Industries, Ltd.* 1993, 837–838).

International Dimensions

Copyright law has established itself globally as the primary intellectual property regime for software. Jurisdictions that initially rejected this approach have since adopted it.[5] In the thirty member states of the European Economic Area (EEA),[6] for example, national copyright law is partially harmonized by directives of the European Union (EU), in particular the EU Software Directive (Directive 2009/24/EC of April 23, 2009 on the legal protection of computer programs) and the EU Copyright Directive (Directive 2001/29, 2001 O.J. (L 167) 10). The EU Software Directive grants copyright protection to computer programs as literary works (Directive 2009/24, 2009 O.J. (L 111) 16). As US copyright law (17 U.S.C. § 102(a)-(b)), the EU Software Directive protects only creative elements of computer programs and not functionality, technical interfaces, programming language, or data file formats (Directive 2009/24, 2009 O.J. (L 111) 16; EU

Court of Justice, Case C-406/10, *SAS Institute Inc. v. World Programming Ltd.* 2012), at para. 46). GUIs as such are not covered by the EU Software Directive. Unlike the code that creates the GUI, the GUI itself does not constitute a computer program. A GUI can be covered by "ordinary" copyright law, but only if and to the extent that it is sufficiently original and not merely dictated by functional requirements (EU Court of Justice, Case C-393/09 *Bezpečnostní softwarová asociace—Svaz softwarové ochrany v Ministerstvo kultury* 2010, at paras. 42, 49, 51).

Reservation of User Privileges

First Sale Doctrine   Enactment of the Computer Software Copyright Act of 1980 inevitably brought numerous established features in its wake. Had Congress chosen a different vehicle, there would have been no importation into the software domain of such incidents of Title 17 as the necessity to place a copyright symbol on computer code;[7] it would have been unnecessary to register the code for protection with the US Copyright Office; and its infringement need not have been gauged through a standard called "substantial similarity" (*Computer Associates Int'l, Inc. v. Altai, Inc.* 1992, p. 715; Nimmer, Bernacchi, and Frischling 1988), in turn calibrated by another doctrine called "fair use" (Nimmer 2015, § 13.03[F][5]; Nimmer, Bernacchi, and Frischling 1988, 651–656).

Among the many other antecedent doctrines of copyright law imported into the software context by virtue of the 1980 amendment is the first sale doctrine. More than a century ago, in *Bobbs-Merrill Co. v. Straus*, the US Supreme Court ruled that a book publisher could not use copyright law to enforce minimum resale price covenants against secondary book purchasers, inasmuch as the copyright owner's right to control distribution was exhausted after the first sale of each book (*Bobbs-Merrill Co. v. Straus* 1908). That ruling, about an otherwise very forgettable novel called *The Castaway,* birthed a vital feature of copyright law, the first sale doctrine, which subsequently was adopted into legislation and treaties around the world as part of the overall effort to balance exclusion and access rights. Many aspects of the first sale doctrine appear relatively uncontroversial today. For books and many other products, the copyright owner exhausts exclusive distribution rights regarding a particular copy with the first sale. After selling a copy or consenting to a sale, the copyright owner is compensated and cannot use copyright to control further distribution.

Copying as an Essential Step in Using a Program   With respect to software, however, the first sale doctrine alone cannot protect consumers to the

same extent that it does with respect to books, paintings, musical composi-
tions, or other works. With respect to novels and cookbooks, for example,
the first sale doctrine allows their readers, once they have finished, to resell
the products through secondhand bookstores, and likewise allows libraries
to obtain a copy and lend it to patrons. But that doctrine attaches solely
to copyright law's *distribution* right; it has no purchase on the coordinate
reproduction right. In other words, the first sale doctrine affords users no
ability under law to *copy* the subject work. Yet, given that readers have no
need to photocopy novels or rewrite recipes, the first sale doctrine affords
them all the latitude they need.

But things are very different in the software world. Just to enjoy the
software copy that they have acquired,[8] users need to reproduce it. Consider the difference—for instance, after John buys a novel in the form of
a published book, he can read and reread it a thousand times, no copying
necessary; after Jane buys a DVD containing software, by contrast, she
cannot use it even once on her computer without copying its contents.
Software users typically need to make one permanent copy in the process
of installing the software on the computer's hard disk or other persistent
storage memory. The first sale doctrine, being limited to the distribution
right, confers no such reproduction right. The upshot, as we have just seen,
is that users risk infringement liability simply by running the very software
copy they have acquired so they can use it. Congress redressed this situation by targeted legislation—the same 1980 amendment that conferred
protection on software simultaneously added a provision allowing any
lawful owner[9] of a software copy to make such additional copies as are
necessary to use the acquired software.[10] The provision in question is codified as section 117 of the Copyright Act. Like section 109 (the statutory
codification of the first sale doctrine), this provision applies to "the owner
of a copy of a computer program" (17 U.S.C. § 117(a)).[11]

Reverse Engineering   From a technical perspective, in order to function
in combination, programs have to be interoperable; that is, capable of
exchanging and mutually using information (Wikipedia n.d.). Software
manufacturers typically try to ensure that their own programs are interoperable with each other (in order to market seamlessly integrated software
suites). With respect to programs made by other companies, however,
software manufacturers have different agendas, depending on the market
situation. For example, companies with an established platform may wish,
at times, to prevent interoperability with third-party software, in order to
protect their market share for add-on programs[12] or to foster hardware sales

(*Sony Computer Entertainment, Inc. v. Connectix Co.* 2000; *Lexmark Int'l, Inc. v. Static Control Components, Inc.* 2004; *Chamberlain Group v. Skylink Technologies, Inc.* 2004). New market entrants may sometimes try to achieve or promote interoperability with third-party software in order to establish their platforms or to be able to offer add-ons or substitute programs for already established platforms.[13]

In the interest of optimizing the balance between protecting exclusion and access rights and encouraging innovation, courts have invoked the fair use doctrine of copyright law to allow intermediate copying of software code for purposes of reverse engineering and creating interoperable (*Sega Enterprises, Ltd. v. Accolade, Inc.* 1992) and even substitute (*Sony Computer Entertainment v. Connectix Corporation* 2000) software products. Courts have also allowed the circumvention of technological protection measures to achieve interoperability of software-hardware combinations (*Chamberlain Group v. Skylink Technologies, Inc.* 2004; *Lexmark International, Inc. v. Static Control Components, Inc.* 2004). Those constructions underwrite copyright law's purpose of promoting creativity and innovation in the software field.

Divergent Interpretations

Starting in the United States   Given that software constitutes a form of "literary work" in the eyes of the Copyright Act (17 U.S.C. § 101), and that traditional exemplars of that genre—such as paperback novels, cookbooks, and multivolume textbooks—can be freely vended by secondhand bookstores and lent to library patrons, it follows that software is subject to the same exploitation potential. The danger thereby arises that one customer could buy an expensive software suite and rent it to successive "library customers" for them to make their own copies. Congress took explicit note of that danger. In 1990, it amended the first sale doctrine to forbid rental of software.[14] At present, therefore, libraries are forbidden from lending software except under specified circumstances (such as university libraries) (17 U.S.C. § 109(b)(1)(A); Nimmer 2015 § 8.12[B][8]).

Of course, that amendment leaves software users perfectly free to sell the copies of software in their possession,[15] even if they cannot rent the software itself. Software companies have tried to avoid the implications of that state of affairs by labeling commercialization transactions whereby users acquire copies of software as a license rather than a sale of the physical medium.[16] They have drafted shrink-wrap agreements to the effect that software copies are only licensed, never sold, and that they never transfer ownership to those physical products embodying their software. Without an authorized first sale, software copies cannot even be used on a computer without additional permission from the copyright owner. Thus, someone in possession of a copy of software cannot use it for its intended purpose except insofar as those rights are explicitly granted in the subject license.

At this point, we enter highly contested terrain. Dissension extends to courts, scholars, and even entire countries. Without purporting to cover the field, some highlights deserve brief mention (Carver 2010; Kim 2008; Chin 2004; Braucher 2006; Madison 2003; Maggs 2003; Rice, 2004; Rothchild 2004; Fisher 2007). One point of view, adopted by some courts and scholars (including one of the current coauthors of this chapter), focuses on the particular medium embodying the software (Nimmer 2015, § 8.12[B][d][i][III]). If that medium falls within the dominion of the user, then it is a sale.[17] Thus, just as someone who has paid $15 for the hardcover or paperback version of *The Castaway* can freely write in its margins, tear out chapter 3, burn the whole, repurpose it as a paperweight, or shellac it to use as a doorstop, the same considerations apply to someone who has paid $495 for a set of CD-ROMs that embody AutoCAD software—that individual is likewise free to punch a hole in disc 2, repurpose disc 1 as a Frisbee, burn all three discs, or shellac the set to use as a doorstop. In *Vernor v. Autodesk, Inc.* (2008), at the trial court level, Judge Richard Jones adopted this viewpoint concerning AutoCAD software.

The contrary point of view, adopted by some courts and scholars (including the other coauthor of this chapter), defers more or less to the characterization of the transaction concerning a software copy in the first agreement with the copyright owner. If the copyright owner does not agree to a sale of a software copy, then neither the first acquirer nor any downstream buyers can become an "owner," who thereby acquires rights under section 109 or 117 of the Copyright Act. Among the subscribers to this viewpoint, opinions vary as to just how much deference is due the wishes of the copyright owner. Some maintain that the copyright owner should be able to preclude a sale simply by stating in a formal agreement that a license is intended (*MAI Systems Corp. v. Peak Computer, Inc.* 1993, p. 518). Others believe that a more substantive analysis is warranted to determine how "sales-like" the commercial terms of the transaction really are, regardless of what the agreement is called (*DSC Communications Corp. v. Pulse Communications Inc.* 1999, p. 1360; Determann and Fellmeth 2001). However, despite such distinctions, all varieties of this viewpoint allow the software industry to opt out of the first sale doctrine.

Defenders of this latter position focus on the economics and value-propositions of the software industry (Nadan 2004). A computer program can be of immense value to a large enterprise, which is consequently willing to pay hundreds of thousands of dollars for a license; by contrast, a student, an educational institution, or a small business derives a much smaller economic benefit, and, concomitantly, can afford to pay much less. If the software copyright owner had to charge each user the same price to recoup development costs, it would have to pick a price somewhere in the middle and miss out on prices that large enterprises would be willing to pay, at the same time rendering the programs unaffordable for students. If copyright owners charge different prices and do not control distribution, however, they create a potential for arbitrage. For example, a student or educational institution could buy a software copy at a low price, resell at a higher price to a large enterprise, and pocket the arbitrage margin; the copyright owner hence misses out on an opportunity to sell at a higher price to the large enterprise. Alternatively, a large enterprise could purchase multiple licenses at favorable volume prices and sell some copies to other businesses; the copyright owner misses out on an opportunity to sell single copies with no discount. Given the relatively high potential for value differential with respect to computer programs and user bases, software companies have been particularly keen on controlling distribution and avoiding arbitrage.

Reverting to *Vernor v. Autodesk* (2010), Judge Callahan on appeal vacated the judgment.[18] The Court of Appeals for the Ninth Circuit decided to defer to the copyright owner and its "license terms," ruling, "Generally, if the copyright owner makes it clear that she or he is granting only a license to the copy of software and imposes significant restrictions on the purchaser's ability to redistribute or transfer that copy, the purchaser is considered a licensee, not an owner, of the software." The effect, as the same appellate court expressly conceded four years earlier, is that "the first sale doctrine rarely applies in the software world because software is rarely 'sold'" (*Wall Data Inc. v. L.A. County Sheriff's Department* 2006, p. 785 & n.9). At this point, the prevailing view in the United States inclines toward this latter viewpoint (*SoftMan Products Co. v. Adobe Systems Inc.* 2001, p. 1084; *DSC Communications Corp. v. Pulse Communications Inc.* 1999, p. 1360; *Novell v. Network Trade Center* 1997, p. 1230; *Davidson v. Internet Gateway* 2004, p. 1177; *ISC-Bunker Ramo v. Altech, Inc.* 1990, p. 1314; *Data Products v. Reppart* 1990, p. 1601; *Microsoft Corp. v. Harmony Computers & Electronics* 1994, 212–213).

Moving to Europe   As we shift focus eastward, it is necessary to note at the outset that the European legislative framework provides for more rigid versions of fair use and essential step doctrines relating to software. Under the EU Software Directive, a software user needs authorization from the copyright owner with respect to "the permanent or temporary reproduction of a computer program by any means and in any form, in part or in whole," including by way of "loading, displaying, running, transmission, or storage of the computer program" (Directive 2009/24/EC, 2009 O.J. (L 111) 16, Article 4(1)(a)). But any "person having a right to use a copy of a computer program shall be entitled, without the authorisation of the rightholder, to observe, study, or test the functioning of the program in order to determine the ideas and principles which underlie any element of the program if he does so while performing any of the acts of loading, displaying, running, transmitting, or storing the program which he is entitled to do." This statutory right cannot be restricted by contract. In addition to this statutory right to copy for purposes of reverse engineering, Article 5(1) of the EU Software Directive provides a defense similar to section 117(a) of the Copyright Act. If and to the extent that reproduction is "necessary for the use of the computer program by the lawful acquirer in accordance with its intended purpose, including for error correction," the software user does not need authorization from the copyright owner except as otherwise agreed in a contract (Directive 2009/24/EC, 2009 O.J. (L 111) 16, Articles 5(1) and (3), 8).[19] Thus, if the copyright owner does not address the topic in a software license agreement, or if a secondary user does not accept or assume the copyright owner's software license agreement , the lawful user is free to reproduce the software copy as necessary to use the program in accordance with its intended purpose. These statutory rights extend to lawful users and acquirers, respectively, not only to owners of a copy as under the comparable feature of the Copyright Act.

The right to "communicate to the public" copyrighted works under the EU Copyright Directive (for example, by streaming or arranging for the download of music files over the Internet) is not exhausted by a first communication (Directive 2001/29/EC, 2001 O.J. (L 167) 10, Article 3(3)). But a first sale of a software or music file exhausts distribution rights under the EU Software Directive and EU Copyright Directive, respectively. The first sale doctrine, as applied to software copyrights, is framed in the same way as its counterpart in the Copyright Act: "The first sale in the Community of a copy of a program by the rightholder or with his consent shall exhaust the distribution right within the Community of that copy, with the exception of the right to control further rental of the program or a copy thereof." Notably, a sale is required, and mere acquirers or lawful users of software copies are not expressly protected (unlike the case with respect to reverse engineering and reproduction as an essential step of using software).

Yet, in Europe, courts have taken a different viewpoint on what kinds of transactions qualify as sales (Determann and Fellmeth 2001). In general, European courts tend to give much less weight to contract terms, particularly in standard contracts imposed by software companies in the form of shrink-wrap or click-through license agreements (Maxeiner 2003; Determann 2007; see also Lemley 1995b, 1246, 1261, 1267–84; Radin 2012; Gallegos 2011). Moreover, EU law is decidedly opposed to allowing companies to segment the "Common Market" in the European Economic Area (EEA). The European Court of Justice, as the European Union's "engine of integration," strives to strengthen European economic unification (Gabel and Carrubba 2009). Given that copyrights are territorial and convey national rights in each of the 30 EEA states, copyright laws have a tendency to obstruct (or allow companies to obstruct), rather than support borderless trade in Europe. Consequently, the EU Court of Justice has traditionally leaned toward standing up for defenses and exceptions under copyright law, rather than protecting intellectual property.

Based on this foundation in policy principles, on July 3, 2012, the EU Court of Justice held in *Oracle v. Usedsoft* that a software copyright owner cannot prevent the resale of software copies that are downloaded with the copyright owner's consent over the Internet, even if the initial acquirer agrees with the software copyright owner that the software copies are licensed only to the initial acquirer and shall not be resold (Determann and Batchelor 2012). The EU Court adopts the view—previously taken by German courts—that any transfer of possession without a time limit for a lump-sum fee constitutes a sale and triggers the first sale doctrine.

The EU Court also expands this view to apply to software downloads and indicates that someone who acquires a software copy lawfully (from the copyright owner, with the copyright owner's consent, or from a secondary distributor after exhaustion kicks in) may make and sell an additional copy so long as the original software copy is made "unusable" (*UsedSoft GmbH v Oracle International Corp.* 2012). This argument was recently expressly rejected in the United States with respect to digital music files (*Capitol Records, LLC v. ReDigi Inc.* 2013). Consequently, downloaded software copies can be resold much more easily in Europe because they can be freely separated from media or devices where they are originally installed.

Going even further, the EU Court indicates that, after copyright exhaustion kicks in, secondary purchasers may also transfer licenses relating to software copies that are transferred in saleslike transactions. The legal basis for this assertion remains unclear, given that the first sale doctrine does not itself address the transfer of license agreements. Nevertheless, the EU Court of Justice seems to view such an expansion of the first sale doctrine as beneficial from a policy perspective, to ensure that the doctrine has more force. Finally, the EU Court of Justice ruled that any contractual agreements to the contrary would not be enforceable, regardless whether they are negotiated and concluded between two sophisticated companies with similar bargaining strength.

Following the EU Court of Justice's decision, German courts have already blessed the resale of software copies that were licensed by educational institutions subject to heavy discounts and restrictive licenses and subsequently sold to UsedSoft for the purpose of further resale and margin arbitrage (*Adobe v. UsedSoft* 2012).

Emblematic of the turmoil in this field is that US courts have moved in one direction, European courts in the other. Scholars remain divided; one need only add that (perhaps ironically) the American coauthor of this chapter sides with the governing view in Europe, whereas the European sides with the precedential view articulated in the United States.

Departure from Statute Goals? This rundown reveals severe climatic changes in recent decades. When adopted, software was slotted into the realm of "literary works" protected by copyright, so as to afford rights to proprietors while simultaneously reserving salient privileges to users. The safeguards of preexisting copyright law—free alienability of tangible manifestations via the first sale doctrine and application of copyright's all-purpose defense, the fair use doctrine—applied automatically. In addition, the 1980 law that recognized software protection concomitantly relaxed the reproduction strictures applicable to this new domain by virtue of the tailored addition of section 117 to the statute.

Yet, as we have seen, *Vernor* and similar cases recognize plenary protection for software copyrights on the proprietors' side of the ledger, without any of the corresponding safeguards on the users' side. In particular, that case overtly denies application of the first sale doctrine through the simple expedient of replacing "for sale" with "for license" in a single-pay transaction by which possession of tangible media changes hands forever. It also explicitly rejects application of the essential step defense, which is likewise a privilege belonging only to the "owner of a copy" of the software in question. And it even approves, in that context, the elimination through that "license" of the user's ability to reverse-engineer the software in question[20]—a privilege that the fair use doctrine itself grants, according to antecedent Ninth Circuit authority. In short, *Vernor's* tally is: Copyright Owners 4, Users 0.[21]

The law is in flux. The marriage of copyright law to software protection has reached a state in which unforeseen developments have rendered the nuptial conditions suspect. Had Congress known in 1980 that software publishers would be able to unilaterally ratchet up their rights—such that they would continue to enjoy complete copyright protection over their handiwork, untrammeled by the expected limitations of the first sale doctrine, essential step defense, and the quintessential matter of fair use[22]—it is unclear whether Congress would have even enacted the amendment. These considerations warrant another look at the legal landscape. But the situation is actually even more stark. To appreciate why, we must focus our attention on the cloud, which we will do next.

Economics and Technology of the Cloud

Software Commercialization Models

Software developers have always had numerous vehicles to exploit their innovations, including the following:

- *Internal use*: Keep the software secret and use it internally as a competitive advantage for other business activities (e.g., manufacturing, financial services, administration, business planning, marketing, and product development).
- *Contract development*: Sell development services and work product, including title to the intellectual property rights to the software.
- *Distribution of copies*: Sell, lease, or give away copies of software (possibly subject to license agreement) to enterprises or consumers for a fee, with the purpose of collecting personal data; establishing a platform; or generating goodwill in the open-source community.
- *Distribution of hardware-software combinations*: Sell or lease products with preinstalled software (e.g., personal computers, enterprise servers, laptops, and smartphones).

In the first business model (internal use), the software developer does not make the software available at all. In the other three models, the developer transfers possession of software copies to users. Between these all-or-nothing cases regarding transfer of possession lies another group of business models, through which a software company retains physical possession of the software copies (and the hardware on which the software runs) and enables users to remotely access and use the software functionality. Such business models have been on the rise over the last fifteen years under such names as application service provider (ASP), infrastructure as a service (IaaS), platform as a service (PaaS), and software as a service (SaaS). More generally, they go under the name "cloud models" (Determann 2013a), and this term is used throughout the remainder of this chapter to refer collectively to service-based software exploitation models.

Economically, cloud models feature a number of aspects traditionally associated with services and leases, but without meeting all legal elements of these models.

As in a lease-and-services context, the software user pays recurring fees and receives benefits during an agreed-upon, limited term. Unlike in traditional lease arrangements, however, the user in the cloud context does not have physical possession of software copies. The user is not responsible for maintaining the cloud offering (as a lessee typically would in the context of a lease). The cloud user relies on the cloud provider with respect to software availability, operability, and data security. Unlike in the lease context, the cloud user does not return anything to the cloud provider at the end of the agreed term. Instead, the cloud provider returns the user's data.

As in the services context, the user does not have to take care of hardware or software installation, maintenance, repair, updates, interoperability, or other functions. However, unlike in traditional service arrangements (e.g., word processing or outsourced accounting services), it is the cloud user who operates the software and creates (and owns *ab initio*) the work product generated with the cloud offering (e.g., Microsoft Word documents, Microsoft PowerPoint slides, and Microsoft Excel spreadsheets).

Cloud models do not resemble sales from an economic perspective. The cloud provider does not transfer possession to anything, the arrangement is not perpetual, and the user pays a recurring fee rather than a one-time purchase price. Cloud models are as unlike sales as the internal use model. But cloud models do not resemble the internal use model, either: The cloud provider does not use the software to support other business activities (such as manufacturing or other services). The software functionality *is* the service.

What advantages do cloud models have over the more traditional models summarized thus far? Software users appreciate access to state-of-the-art software functionality without the burden of having to deal with infrastructure, hardware, updates, maintenance, and other aspects of business, which is not a core competency for many organizations.

Also, change management (e.g., updates, upgrades, and bug fixes) can be less burdensome. Users typically do not have to pay a large upfront sum with subscription models. In addition, the overall costs of software and computing resources over time can be reduced because cloud providers bundle purchasing power and reduce redundancies by deploying computing capacity dynamically; that is, only when it is needed by a particular user. To enjoy these benefits, more and more software users are willing to hand over their data to cloud providers, even though data security and third-party access to data are a concern for some organizations—more so, in fact, than in the context of any of the more traditional business models (Determann 2011, p. 1).

Examples of Cloud Offerings

Cloud providers offer different commercial terms and technological deployments. Their offerings depend on the provider's business model, whether the provider develops its own software or largely uses programs made by other companies, and other factors, such as software functionality, industries, and targeted user groups (i.e., enterprise, consumers, and prosumers). A given cloud provider may offer third-party software application products (such as Word, PowerPoint, or Adobe Acrobat) to enterprise and consumer customers (see, e.g., OnLive n.d.). Another may host computer games or components thereof, made by third parties (see, e.g., *MDY Industries, LLC v. Blizzard Entertainment, Inc.* 2010, p. 945). Still other providers may develop and host their own enterprise applications for customer relationship management, human resources systems, or enterprise resource planning (see, e.g., Salesforce n.d.; SugarCRM n.d.; NetSuite n.d.; Workday n.d.).

Our analysis herein refers to a simplified, typical technical scenario. The cloud provider acquires software copies by developing them internally or procuring them from outside sources. Then it creates the cloud offering by combining application programs with operating system software, drivers, and programs that facilitate remote access, and installing the software combination on the hard disks of servers in secure locations with connections to the Internet. When the cloud provider turns the cloud service on, it uploads a software copy into the random access memory (RAM) of one or more servers for its customers to use.

Customers enter into an agreement with the cloud provider, pay a recurring fee, and receive access credentials (i.e., user IDs and passwords). Customers can then access the cloud offering with general-purpose web browsers (e.g., Firefox, Chrome, Safari, or Microsoft Internet Explorer). The work product that the customer creates with the cloud offering consists of data (e.g., in the form of a PowerPoint slide deck or Word document) stored on the cloud provider's server. The customer can view the work product via the GUI that is reproduced via the web browser on the remote computer. If the customer downloads (i.e., copies) the work product to its remote computer, the cloud provider's server may deliver the work product in files that contain standard file format specifications so that the user can process the files on remote computers. If the cloud provider's offering includes objects for inclusion into work product (e.g., clip art for Power-Point slides), customers can view or download copies of such objects, too.

Multiple Cloud Users

Cloud service providers can configure their software such that one RAM copy can simultaneously serve multiple users. In a multitenant, multi-threaded setup, dozens (or even many thousands) of users could use the same RAM copy without the need to create additional copies of the application software that provides the program functionality to the remote users' computers. Does that activity implicate the copyright owner's rights? We begin with the core reproduction right (17 U.S.C. § 106(1), and then radiate outward to consider the other rights belonging to the proprietor (17 U.S.C. § 106(2)-(6)).

Counting copies for purposes of copyright law analysis produces the following results: A company that wants to offer software as a service via the cloud typically has to create two copies: namely, one permanent copy of the underlying code on its server and one RAM copy in working memory. In that regard, the cloud scenario does not involve more copies than a traditional desktop scenario. However, in the cloud context, the one RAM copy can be accessed by multiple users—very much unlike the desktop scenario.

Let us turn from setup to usage. Once the cloud solution is up and running, users make access requests from remote computers. Each time the software is executed, numerous fractional excerpts of the RAM copy are reproduced in cache memory spaces and the CPU of the cloud provider's server. But, as in the desktop scenario, such fractional excerpts of the RAM copy do not implicate the software owner's reproduction right. Instead, the individual command lines reproduced in the CPU or cache registers close to the CPU tend to be too fleeting to count as copies, too small to show originality, and too functional to constitute protectable expression. Thus, two copies can serve far more users in the context of cloud offerings than in the desktop context.

We must further consider whether users' viewing of GUIs on remote computers increases the copy count. In the cloud context, users can never see the software itself, which stays hidden on the cloud provider's server (on hard disk, in RAM, cache, and CPU). Many computer programs do not embody any meaningful GUI; therefore, with them, the analysis ends without any more copies added to the count. But some programs do, and in the cloud context, multiple remote users can see the GUI of the software. In response to access requests, the cloud provider sends copies of Hypertext Markup Language (HTML) commands for the purpose of displaying an image of the GUI on each remote computer. Thus, there could be one GUI copy per remote user. Are more actionable reproductions thereby implicated? The answer is often "No," as such GUI copies may not count for the purposes of copyright infringement. The first reason for this conclusion is that many GUIs are bare of copyrightable material; after all, GUIs tend to be highly functional and uniformly aligned with formats in the public domain to accommodate user expectations. But even when dealing with the exceptional GUI that reflects a creative contribution of expression, a cloud provider could avoid displaying it remotely by suppressing it. Specifically, the cloud provider need only prepare its own add-on GUI to mask the original GUI. This superimposition need not impair the software's functionality, as the GUI is not software per se, but rather the output of software.

Thus, in cloud scenarios, one software copy can be utilized by far greater numbers of users without needing more copying than in the more traditional desktop scenario. The result is that the copyright owner's reproduction right is not implicated any more than in the desktop scenario, even when the user of a single software copy installs it on a cloud server for use by thousands of other users.

Turning from the reproduction right to the other rights belonging to the copyright owner, the software proprietor's rights under copyright likewise will often not be implicated (Determann 2014). In terms of the adaptation right (17 U.S.C. § 106(2)), cloud providers at times may have to modify code that was not originally written for cloud deployment. If the provider can deploy remote access functionality with independently created programs, however, then neither the cloud provider nor the users would seem to implicate the adaptation right belonging to the owner of the underlying software.[23] Moreover, it would seem that whatever combinations or modifications may occur in RAM or the CPU cache do not reach sufficient levels of creativity or fixation to amount to adaptation.[24] Thus, if the software supplier delivers software in "cloud-ready" form, or the cloud provider can achieve cloud-readiness with independently created or licensed programs, then the adaption right of the underlying programs should not be implicated.

Turning to the distribution right (17 U.S.C. § 106(3)), the cloud provider does not transfer copies of the implicated software to the customer's computer—neither complete copies stored on read-only memory (ROM) nor partial copies stored in RAM or in cache. Instead, all copies remain on the cloud provider's server.[25] Accordingly, the distribution right of the underlying programs should not be implicated by the cloud model, either.

Confronting next the public performance right (17 U.S.C. § 106(4)),[26] the act teaches that "[t]o 'perform' a work means to recite, render, play, dance, or act it, either directly or by means of any device or process or, in the case of a motion picture or other audiovisual work, to show its images in any sequence or to make the sounds accompanying it audible" (17 U.S.C. § 101). The enumerated activities (i.e., recite, render, play, dance, and act) all require that the work in question be presented to a human audience in a manner such that it can be perceived visually or audibly. By contrast, the internal execution of code within a computer's bowels does not cause or allow perception by a human audience.[27] A quick answer[28], therefore, is that the performance right of the underlying programs likewise should not be implicated by the cloud model.

Wrapping up with the public display right (17 U.S.C. § 106(5), it is doubtful that any material displayed remotely[29] on users' screens (outside the GUI, which can simply be replaced as discussed previously) itself amounts to copyrightable expression sufficient to warrant an infringement cause of action.[30] It therefore seems overwhelmingly likely that the public display right in the underlying programs will not be implicated by the cloud model, either.

The foregoing considerations introduce new dynamics. In theory, they create a tremendous risk to software copyright owners—no longer will each user need to acquire his or her own copy, but one cloud provider may be able to simultaneously service myriad such users, to the owner's detriment. Yet, in the United States at least, that risk might be mitigated by the same ruling confronted previously, which magnifies the rights of such owners—namely, *Vernor*. To the extent that software purveyors continue to succeed in establishing that they never part with ownership of copies but only "license" those copies, then they can simply insert into the "license" terms a clause prohibiting cloud exploitation. In that manner, their loss of rights under copyright law will prove to be of no moment, as contract law will step into the breach.[31]

Nonetheless, the implications of software provision through the cloud do not thereby shrink into insignificance. First, as we have seen, European law views software copies as regularly being "sold" rather than "licensed," so that same lenity cannot apply there. Second, that freedom is magnified under United Kingdom law, under which reproducing even highly creative websites or GUIs does not require consent from copyright owners. Third, danger to copyright owners is not altogether absent in the United States either, given that not all courts follow *Vernor*'s rule, and the Supreme Court may reconsider it if and when the occasion arises. Fourth, even if no chinks ever develop in *Vernor*'s armor, a proprietor may surrender possession of a given copy, for whatever reason, outside of license terms.[32] It only takes one such copy—if a cloud purveyor could get its hands on that single exemplar, it would then place itself in a position to take advantage of the various features cataloged, as already described, such that it would escape liability for copyright infringement, notwithstanding making the third party's software accessible to thousands of third parties.[33]

The Cloud's Impact on Software Copyrights

Based on this review of past challenges relating to software and copyrights, along with the development of cloud exploitation models, the stage is set to assess the cloud's impact.

Challenges to Copyright Law's Goals

We have already seen how an aggressive implementation of *Vernor* could set at naught the delicate balance underlying software protection. In particular, it could undermine the first sale doctrine, the essential step defense, and the application of fair use to software. Still, the discussion has also noted that aggressive implementation might not pass legal muster—in other words, the Supreme Court might halt *Vernor*'s advance before matters reached such a state, at least in the context of traditional book publishing.

Nonetheless, one must frankly concede that no such ameliorative construction seems likely in the cloud context. The three specifics are each examined in turn next.

First Sale Doctrine A software copyright owner can avoid the first sale doctrine by commercializing its software as a service rather than by way of sale. Cloud service transactions involve recurring payments, temporal use limitations, and no transfer of possession. Such transactions do not resemble sales by any standards. Besides moving to services models, software copyright owners have a few other options to reduce the risk that the first sale doctrine applies, even under EU laws. Software companies can include "sales-unlike" clauses in contracts,[34] apply technological restrictions,[35] charge extra for resales or transferable licenses, or charge more for support on transferred licenses, grant "real" reproduction licenses that cannot be transferred based on exhaustion principle (e.g., enterprise licensing), etc. But with a shift to cloud models, copyright owners would be able to preclude secondary markets more clearly and effectively.

This state of affairs corresponds to *Vernor*'s ruling. Nonetheless, the differences are as important as the points of commonality. First, and most important, we have already seen that Europe applies the opposite construction. Nonetheless, the impact of the cloud would be to Americanize the content of European law in this regard. By moving to cloud business models, a software copyright owner would be able to continue to control distribution of its software, thereby sidestepping any first sale under EU law.

Second, internal to US law, the cloud eliminates any conceptual fog hanging over *Vernor*'s construction. As previously explicated, the problem with the Ninth Circuit's logic inheres in the court's construction that a proprietor's permanent parting with physical ownership for a one-time fee constitutes anything other than a sale. Nonetheless, even the case's harshest critics concede that the cloud does not result in a sale of physical products (Nimmer 2015, § 8.12[B][1][d][iii]). In other words, when a user does not obtain permanent dominion over CD-ROMs containing AutoCAD but simply rents access to that software product by the hour, then all parties agree that no "sale" has taken place. Accordingly, the cloud itself affords no room to vindicate the ruling of earlier cases contrary to that Ninth Circuit ruling.

Third, the aggressive extension of *Vernor* under current copyright law to books, as postulated previously, seemed dicey at best. By contrast, purveying eBooks over the cloud is straightforward and beyond challenge. By no means do users thereby gain dominion over physical products that the first sale doctrine would thereby allow them to resell (Nimmer (2015, § 8.12[E])). Accordingly, a user privilege whose pedigree traces back to 1908, which is codified in section 109 of the act, could effectively be set at naught. The upheaval to traditional notions of copyright law could not be more pronounced.

On the other hand, a move toward embracing the first sale doctrine as radically as under *UsedSoft* could cause the cloud to extremely marginalize the software copyright owner's rights and economic opportunities. Once a software developer parts with one software copy under an agreement meant to characterize the transaction as a nonexclusive, limited license, a licensee-turned-owner under *UsedSoft* could deploy such a copy in a cloud context and offer it to thousands of other users in competition with the software developer. If US courts do not follow *UsedSoft* or import European views on copy ownership in cross-border cases (Determann 2013b), cloud providers might find a home in Europe for cloud offerings and provide them remotely to users in the United States, hence disrupting US copyright exploitation without actually causing copies to be made in the United States.

Essential Step Defense   The previous subsection illustrated how copyright owners can unilaterally eliminate users' distribution privileges through purveying their wares on the cloud. Different considerations apply to extending that state of affairs to users' reproduction privileges in software. To recall, part of the aggressive application of *Vernor* imagined that copyright owners of software would charge $490 to "license" a physical copy of software, and then would proceed to charge more for using it (e.g., by loading it into RAM). How do those aspects translate to the cloud?

As a theoretical matter, the danger is every bit as great that this aspect of users' privileges will be equally forfeited. As a practical matter, however, there is reason to be more sanguine. Granted, cloud purveyors can impose any charges that the market will bear—for instance, $2 for the first four hours of using Program X, and then $1,000 for every minute thereafter. Nonetheless, it is doubtful that those purveyors will be able to have an additional charge for "licensing" a physical copy of the software, only to impose a hidden "use" charge later. The reason is that there is no physical copy at the outset for which the cloud purveyor could colorably entice users to pay. In other words, it seems most likely that the charge will be for use. Either the market will bear that charge or not. The same potential for abuse ventilated thus far, therefore, seems to be absent with regard to the essential step defense.

Fair Use   Differences are equally at play when we transfer our attention to the next aspect at risk from an aggressive application of *Vernor*— namely, the fair use defense. The reason is that traditional forms of reverse engineering seem to be impractical in the context of cloud offerings (Zieminski 2008). Included here is the process of copying, analyzing, and disassembling object code for the purpose of separating unprotectable functional elements from copyrightable expression. This state of affairs results not so much from limitations established by copyright law, but rather from the cloud provider's technological ability to control and restrict access to the underlying code residing on the cloud provider's server.[36] In other words, in the cat-and-mouse competition between software publishers and competitors, the latter have been able to reverse-engineer in the past, given the business models and technical controls then extent. The advent of the cloud promises to overturn that state of affairs.

Of course, future competitors could attempt self-help by removing the software publishers' technical measures and attempting to reverse-engineer the product anyway. Unfortunately for them, however, those who attempt to access the software underlying cloud offerings for the purpose of reverse engineering face civil and criminal penalties under laws prohibiting unauthorized access to computers and circumvention of technical protection measures. Included in that scope are aspects of the Digital Millennium Copyright Act (17 U.S.C. § 1201), the Computer Fraud and Abuse Act (18 U.S.C. § 1030), and equivalent laws in the European Union (Determann 2013c).

These same kinds of laws—protecting computers against interference—can be used not only to prevent the creation of interoperable software products through reverse engineering, but also to establish hurdles against interoperability of independently created software programs more absolutely. In the age of the cloud, software offered as a service on one computer has to access software offered as a service on another computer in order to communicate data. Such access can also be hindered based on laws restricting computer interference and circumvention of technical protection measures (*MDY Industries, LLC v. Blizzard Entertainment, Inc.* 2010, p. 945; *Craigslist, Inc. v. 3taps, Inc.* 2013). Courts have rejected arguments by defendants that the fair use doctrine under copyright law must allow them access to hosted software copies, in derogation of the website operator's terms of use or in violation of technical protection measures, even if the online access was for the purpose of developing or deploying interoperable applications (*Ticketmaster LLC v. RMG Techs., Inc.* 2007; Determann and Gutierrez 2008; *MDY Industries, LLC v. Blizzard Entertainment, Inc.* 2010, p. 945; Zieminski 2008; *Facebook, Inc. v. Power Ventures, Inc.* 2012, p. 1028; *Craigslist, Inc. v. 3taps, Inc.* 2013). Therefore, cloud providers can largely rely on technical protection measures and contractual website access restrictions to protect the underlying code. Once such measures and access restrictions are in place, others cannot access the software underlying the cloud offering except in compliance with the authorizations contained in the applicable contracts.

Therefore, the move to cloud models has the potential for less interoperability and adverse effects on innovation. Whether this potential will materialize remains to be seen. Currently, many cloud platforms encourage the development of compatible applications and have spurred a flurry of development (*Vault Corp. v. Quaid Software Ltd.* 1988, p. 270; App Store n.d.). On the other hand, frictions have developed, and software copyright owners with established platforms have been able to prevent the development of add-on offerings that they probably could not have achieved in the context of more traditional distribution models (*Ticketmaster LLC v RMG Technologies, Inc.* 2007; Determann and Gutierrez 2008; *MDY Industries, LLC v. Blizzard Entertainment, Inc.* 2010, p. 945). If this situation becomes a problem and stifles innovation significantly, changes to the legislative framework may have to be considered, including similar defenses for access and reverse engineering of software for interoperability purposes in the cloud as in more traditional distribution models.

Other Impacts

Of course, the cloud also poses challenges to other aspects of copyright law, which we will explore next.

Open-Source License Terms Today, most commonly used open-source license terms permit reproduction and adaptation freely and unconditionally (OSI n.d.). In order to preserve developers' freedom to tinker with code, the license terms typically refrain from applying any restrictions until the developer distributes a copy to third parties (see, e.g., GPL Sections 0 and 2). Consequently, companies that operate service businesses have been able to use most open-source code without being legally obligated under the applicable license terms to give back to the community (Gue 2012). Cloud models sidestep some of the attempts by the open-source movement to keep software free and available—in cloud models, the code is locked up in servers and not available for further improvement and development.

This matter presents a choice to the drafters of open-source license terms. Licensors can tie release obligations or other restrictions not only to distribution, but also to offering modified or unmodified software on a services basis, given that cloud offerings always implicate reproduction rights. The GNU GPL v. 3 (Affero version) already embodies such a provision (GNU Operating System n.d.), and other licenses may follow suit (Gue 2012). Thus, the move to service models may prompt some open-source code licensors to consider updating their license terms. In the meantime, companies can sidestep most commercial concerns relating to open-source or free software code by switching from traditional forms of software distribution to cloud models.

Unauthorized Access to Copyrighted Material

Piracy   Software pirates around the world engage in blatant, literal copying of code without the copyright owner's authorization (BSA 2012). This problem primarily afflicts software commercialization models that are based on the delivery of software copies on physical media or by way of download (see, e.g., Piracy n.d.). In the cloud context, pirates find it much more difficult to get ahold of software copies, given that the code remains on heavily secured servers and is not widely disseminated (Asay 2010). In the best-case scenario, cloud offerings will undermine much of the very incentive underlying piracy, as users are afforded the ability to obtain the works they want when they want them from wherever they happen to be located—all for (hopefully) a reasonable price.[37]

Nonetheless, the software copyright owners' economic interests can be adversely affected by cloud customers' sharing of access credentials in violation of cloud agreements or by criminals hacking into cloud systems (De Borja 2012). At present, those activities seem easier to prevent and prosecute than literal reproduction of physical software copies. Therefore, hosted software in cloud models tends to far be less vulnerable to software piracy than in more traditional distribution models (Asay 2010).

Facilitation of Multiple Cloud Users   Wholly separate from the prospect of copyright owners' commercializing their own software via the cloud is the concept of third parties beginning to compete with those copyright owners in the exploitation of their own products. A user who obtains one physical copy of that software can offer access to it, via the cloud, to tens of thousands of third parties, thus obviating the need for any of those myriad users either to obtain their own copy or to access the proprietor's own cloud offering. Viewed through that prism, the cloud portends disaster to those copyright owners—any positive effect that it exerts on their bottom line through universalizing the effects of *Vernor* are more than counterbalanced by the dangers of cloud exploitation being used to escape copyright liability.

As noted previously, the legal underpinnings of that model have yet to be fully clarified. Much may depend on the precise technical specifications employed by various cloud purveyors and how many distinct copies they need to generate to service their customers. At present, all that can be stated is that dangers and opportunities abound for all interested parties.

Some Weather Forecasts

With the benefit of the foregoing exposition, it is time to evaluate the cloud and its implications for copyright, affecting software and beyond. Given that the phenomenon is still at its outset, the time is premature for a marriage counselor to conclude either that there are irreconcilable differences or that a bit of effort from both parties will ensure another three decades of pragmatic cohabitation. Instead, the savvy observer must simply observe current tensions in light of past history, extending strictly tentative diagnoses regarding the balms needed for future harmonious relations.

Gloomy Prospects: Dark Clouds Undermine the Goals of 1980

Resolved, the cloud is unprecedented, both in its technology and the stress that it places on traditional copyright categories.

Congress embraced software within the copyright domain, *faute de mieux*, and subject only to a carefully developed balance: At the same time that it conferred rights on that subject matter under section 102 of the Copyright Act, it did three things. It adopted the limitations on the distribution right incorporated into section 109; it explicitly added new limitations on the reproduction right under section 107; and it acted against the backdrop of copyright law's ubiquitous defense, the infinitely malleable fair use doctrine.

As set forth in the previous sections of this chapter, certain interpretations of existing law (celebrated by some, bemoaned by others) yield a tally of Copyright Owners 4, Users 0. For those who bemoan those results, current law contains at least some prospect for amelioration. Given that they decry *Vernor*'s construction of the statute as faulty, they hold onto the hope that other circuits, eventually joined by the Supreme Court, will ultimately jettison that ruling and set the law back on its proper course.

No such hope arises with the cloud, however. Even *Vernor*'s critics concede that those who purvey software via the cloud may invoke existing law to eliminate any user privileges of further distribution. Moreover, they may equally deny any user privileges of further reproduction, even if that particular danger is noticeably muted in the cloud context. Finally, cloud offerings effectively lie beyond the realm of fair use exploitation. As such, all use becomes fared (Bell 1998), with no latitude remaining for one of the fundamental protections encapsulated in the text of the 1976 law itself.

These deformations push the law so far out of its intended path that reformation becomes essential. As Melville Nimmer, the vice-chair of the Commission on New Technological Uses of Copyrighted Works (CONTU) commented, in the report on which Congress relied when extending copyright protection to software in 1980, certain "line[s]of demarcation" must be borne in mind, not because they were needed as of 1978 when the CONTU report was issued, but rather because they "may prove useful in the years to come if the current recommendation for protection of all software should prove unduly restrictive."

That time has now dawned. The cloud is its midwife.

In fact, the cloud's deformation is much worse than even the vice-chair imagined three and half decades ago. Not only does the cloud eliminate the first sale doctrine as to software, but it exerts the same effect on all literary works. Since 1908, *Bobbs-Merrill Co. v. Straus* and its statutory codification have safeguarded the privilege for readers of novels to resell them at secondhand bookstores. In a world of eBooks, that privilege is no more.

The same deprivation applies across the board, moreover—far beyond the sphere of literary works. Video rental stores traditionally offered movies to their customers. That instantiation serves for audiovisual works the role that libraries have traditionally served for literary works. Those outlets are in the cloud's universe. And the same applies to music and other works subject to copyright protection as well. In fact, the only secondary market for works of authorship, in a future dominated by the cloud, promises to be in the realm of fine art. Thus, purchasers of a painting to hang on their living room wall will be able to resell the work, as will the sculpture garden that wishes to cycle out an old maquette for a new bronzework.[38] Outside those peripheral applications, however, the first sale doctrine will be rendered everywhere obsolete.

Thus will the dream be universalized of those "license" advocates who, long ago, rendered the first sale doctrine a dead letter. In their wake, Fred Hoyle's dystopic vision of *The Black Cloud* (1957) becomes our reality. To save us from that darkness, legislative redress is needed.

A Cheery Rebuttal: Return to an Earlier Sensibility

Resolved, the cloud is not unprecedented, and simply returns many traditional copyright categories to their historic role.

On the other hand, a broader view of history yields different insights. We change our field of vision here from the literary works that have occupied this chapter thus far—whether those denominated *software* or more traditional forms, such as *novels*—in order to scrutinize the realm of music. Here, we enter very different territory.

Whereas *Bobbs-Merrill Co. v. Straus* litigated the status of *The Castaway* over a century ago, at a time that any interested reader could obtain her own personal copy of the work in question, matters were very different at the time for music lovers. Throughout much of history, music has been experienced exclusively as a service, or something that one needs to receive from a service provider in order to enjoy. The advent of sound recordings—especially digital sound recordings—"product-ized" the medium, allowing consumers to take music with them wherever they go, manipulate it, and engage with it at will. Internet music streams, however, remove consumers' control over the access and playback of music, transforming digital music once again into a service (Anderson 2011, p. 162).

The same considerations apply to movies. The motion picture industry was in its infancy when *The Castaway* hit bookstores. For many decades thereafter, the only way to experience a movie was to wait until it came to one's local cinema, or, if you did not want to go out, when a local television station broadcast it later (Nimmer 1996, 14–16). The situation changed only with the advent of the Betamax video recording format in the 1970s.

Therefore, we can appreciate that, before high-fidelity recording and before videotape recording capabilities, users had none of the privileges canonized in these pages. During those intervals, they had no ability to obtain ownership of songs or movies; instead, they had to wait for others to perform them. (In addition, they certainly enjoyed no "essential step" defense in that context.) And their rights of fair use were also extremely circumscribed, given that there was no practical way of quoting at length from the music and movies that had been evanescently performed and then passed into the ether.[39]

Viewed from this perspective, the cloud simply returns music to its origins,[40] and the same applies to film. By replacing products with streams, the cloud brings back to the fore the effective copyright status of large swaths of works that existed for many decades in the past.

If the enjoyment of movies in the 2030s matches that of the 1930s—in which the proprietor could charge for each and every viewing[41]—no cosmic injustice requires redress. Instead, the long eye of history can find bemusement in the swirls and eddies of time, in which nothing is really new under the sun.

Highs and Lows in Turbulent Transitions

Whatever the long-term weather forecast may hold for clouds, there is one prediction that we do not hesitate to make at this juncture: there will be turbulent transitions.[42] Software in the cloud places entirely different pressure points on copyrights than software on desktops. Phases of high pressure will alternate with low pressure systems that will move in as the marketplace, technological measures, courts, and perhaps even legislatures adjust. Nevertheless, whatever future you envision today inevitably will be upset by tomorrow's reality. We have no choice but to live and learn.

Notes

1. © 2015 by Lothar Determann and David Nimmer. Opinions expressed herein reflect only the authors' views; they should not be imputed to their universities, firms, clients, or others. The substance of this chapter will be published first in the 30th volume of the *Berkeley Technology Law Journal;* see Lothar Determann & David Nimmer, "Software Copyright's Oracle from the Cloud," *Berkeley Technology Law Journal 30.*

2. Congress acted against the backdrop of a special commission that it had charged with investigating this arena. In his Commission on New Technological Uses of Copyrighted Works (CONTU) concurrence, Vice-Chair Melville Nimmer issued a warning that will be reprised later in this chapter:

We may need a line of demarcation to distinguish between programs which control the air-conditioning in a building and those which produce works which themselves qualify for copyright protection (e.g., program designed for a computer game). This suggestion is made not because I recommend its immediate implementation, but rather because it may prove useful in the years to come if the current recommendation for protection of all software should prove unduly restrictive. (National Commission on New Technological Uses of Copyrighted Works [1979, p. 207]. See Nimmer [2004, 1263–1265].)

3. See also Lemley and O'Brien (1997) (arguing that copyright protection for software inhibits efficiency); Menell (1989); Samuelson et al. (1994). Cf. Ginsburg (1994); Miller (1993); Dogan and Liu (2005, p. 204) (discussing judicial treatment of computer software copyright protection in light of its dual nature).

4. See *Bateman v. Mnemonics, Inc.* (1996, 1543–1545); *Apple Computer, Inc. v. Franklin Computer Corp.* (1983, p. 1443); *Engineering Dynamics, Inc. v. Structural Software, Inc.* (1994, p. 1342); *Kepner-Tregoe, Inc. v. Leadership Software* (1994, p. 534); *Gates Rubber Co. v. Bando Chemical Industries, Ltd.* (1993, p. 836); *Atari Games Corp. v. Nintendo*

(1992, p. 839); *Control Data Systems, Inc. v. Infoware, Inc.* (1995, p. 1322); *CMAX/Cleveland, Inc. v. UCR, Inc.* (1992, 352–353); *Brown Bag Software v. Symantec Corp.* (1992, 1475–1476); *MiTek Holdings Inc. v. Arce Engineering Co.* (1996, 1554–1556).

5. An example is Germany: Software had been expressly recognized in Section 2 of the German Copyright Act as a category of copyrightable works since 1985. Urheberrechtsgesetz, UrhG [Copyright Law], September 9, 1965, as amended May 8, 1998 § 2 no. 2 (F.R.G.). However, prior to the implementation of the EC Software Directive into German law in 1993, German courts had required a very high level of originality before they would afford copyright protection for software. The leading cases are from 1985 and 1991: Bundesgerichtshof (BGH) [Federal Court of Justice] 1985, 12 Gewerblicher Rechtsschutz und Urheberrecht (GRUR) 1041 (F.R.G.) (known as the collection program case—Inkasso-Programm) and Bundesgerichtshof (BGH) [Federal Court of Justice] 1991, 19 Neue Juristische Wochenschrift (NJW) 1231 (F.R.G.) (known as the operating system case—Betriebssystem). Many programs that would have easily qualified as copyrightable in the United States were not found to be so in Germany. For an overview of software copyright protection in the European Union; see Samuelson (1994).

6. The EEA consists of 28 EU member states, plus Norway, Iceland, and Liechtenstein.

7. Of course, in 1989, incident to joining the Berne Convention, the severity of that requirement was greatly alleviated. See Nimmer 2015, § 7.02.

8. We use the word *acquired* here in a general sense, in order to avoid prejudicing the inquiry to come: Does a user who *acquires* diskettes containing computer software by paying $500 on a one-time basis to the manufacturer thereby "purchase" the physical good in question, or succeed to a different legal relationship with respect to that physical good? (Note that the question is *not* that user's relationship to the copyright in question, which is an intangible. See fn. 16 *infra*. Instead, the first sale question arises based on the user's relationship to a physical product.) Items in point could include diskettes, thumb drives, hard drives, or CD-ROMs. Properly construed, those items would even include a digital download of bits. See Nimmer, 2015, § 8.12[E].

9. As will be seen by the wording of the statute quoted in the next footnote, the copy that has been acquired, in order to fall under the first sale doctrine, must be *owned* by the user. Thus arises the *Vernor v. Autodesk, Inc.* (2010) construction to be explicated at length later.

10. "[I]t is not an infringement for the owner of a copy of a computer program to make or authorize the making of another copy or adaptation of that computer program provided: (1) that such a new copy or adaptation is created as an essential step in the utilization of the computer program in conjunction with a machine and that it is used in no other manner" (17 U.S.C. § 117(a)(1)).

11. The language of the other provision actually refers more generally to "the owner of a particular copy" of a program. 17 U.S.C. § 109(a).

12. See *Sega Enterprises Ltd. v. Accolade, Inc.* (1992).

13. Cerulean Studios, for instance, offers a software program entitled "Trillian." Trillian is essentially a third-party user interface for various instant-messaging programs. It claims to support AOL Instant Messenger (AIM), ICQ, Microsoft's MSN Messenger, Yahoo! Messenger, and traditional Internet Relay Chat (IRC). It acts as both an add-on and a full substitute for all the major instant-messaging programs. It does so without requiring the user to install the various instant-messaging software programs that it interfaces with (Cerulean Studios n.d.)

14. The amendment in question is the Computer Software Rental Amendments Act of 1990. It is codified as a part of the first sale doctrine, as it limits the user privileges that would otherwise be as available to owners of copies of software as is available to owners of copies of novels and cookbooks, namely to rent them out.

15. Later, this chapter will draw further distinctions between possession and ownership.

16. The question pointedly is *not* whether a license or sale of the intangible copyright has been acquired. Plainly, someone who pays $25 for the paper and cardboard comprising a novel is only a licensee to the copyright, the same as someone who pays $500 for set of CD-ROMs comprising a software suite is similarly only a licensee to the copyright.

17. Emblematic here is the following:

The Court finds that the circumstances surrounding the transaction strongly suggests that the transaction is in fact a sale rather than a license. For example, the purchaser commonly obtains a single copy of the software, with documentation, for a single price, which the purchaser pays at the time of the transaction, and which constitutes the entire payment for the "license." The license runs for an indefinite term without provisions for renewal. In light of these indicia, many courts and commentators conclude that a "shrinkwrap license" transaction is a sale of goods rather than a license. (*Softman Products Co., LLC v. Adobe Systems, Inc.* [2001]).

18. Technically, this appeal relates to Judge Jones's later opinion in this case, rather than the published opinion cited previously.

19. Contractual clauses that seek to restrict use of the software program for purposes of decompilation are invalid (*SAS Insttiute Inc. v. World Programming Ltd.* 2012, para. 57 and 58).

20. As recited in the Ninth Circuit opinion, one provision in Autodesk's license stated, "YOU MAY NOT: (1) modify, translate, reverse-engineer, decompile, or disassemble the Software." The Ninth Circuit expressly cited that limitation among the "use restrictions" that caused it to "conclude that [Autodesk's] customers are licensees of their copies of [the software in question] rather than owners" (*Vernor v. Autodesk* 2010, 1104, 1111–1112).

21. As set forth previously, the metrics in place are (1) copyright protection, (2) the user's ability to resell, (3) the user's ability to invoke section 117, and (4) the user's ability to invoke fair use.

22. "Although the traditional approach is to view 'fair use' as an affirmative defense, this writer, speaking only for himself, is of the opinion that it is better viewed as a right granted by the Copyright Act of 1976" (*Bateman v. Mnemonics, Inc.* 1996, 1542 n.22).

23. Specific cases might hinge on how much the underlying program had to be modified, as opposed to how much new expression the cloud provider had to have in order to achieve remote access functionality.

24. Arguably to the contrary of that perspective is *Dun & Bradstreet Software Services, Inc. v. Grace Consulting, Inc.* (2002, p. 204). But that case does not seem to reflect a widely shared perspective. Moreover, if it does state good law, then its holding would equally affect desktop-type deployments, so that aspect is not peculiar to the cloud (Determann 2006).

25. In the cloud context, customers do not even possession of new copies of the code. Instead, those customers can only download the output that they create with the software (e.g., Word documents, PowerPoint slides, Excel spreadsheets) to their own computers, not copies of the software that runs on the cloud provider's servers to create the output (e.g., Word, PowerPoint, or Excel application software). See Widmer (2007, p. 95).

26. Note that this right is inapplicable to certain types of copyrightable works. But it does apply to literary works, and therefore encompasses software. The Copyright Act also embodies another right of public performance, applicable only to sound recordings. See 17 U.S.C. § 106(6). As that subject matter is distinct from the instant subject, this chapter confronts that matter no further. See Nimmer (2015, § 8.22).

27. Of course, software designed to run a video game could be performed. Likewise, software that embodies video or audio tutorials could see those aspects streamed, which in turn would create a public performance. The discussion in the text is extremely cursory. Consider the following counterpoint:

At best, defendant Yeo's alleged publication of the ChainRxn video game for play by Facebook users constituted a public performance of plaintiff's copyrighted work under 17 U.S.C. 106(4). Just as Congress considered the "reading a literary work aloud" as a performance rather than display of a literary work, the reading of Boomshine's copyrighted source or machine code by a computer (resulting in the presentation of the video game to the user) could be seen as an analogous performance of the underlying work. *See* Committee on the Judiciary (1976, p. 63). Admittedly, this area of the law is still developing." (*Miller v. Facebook, Inc.* [2010]).

28. Bearing in mind the caveats of the previous footnote, the Ninth Circuit has held that public performance rights could not be implicated by the mere playing of interactive video games in public, given that the concept of playing as performance had been narrowly interpreted to apply only to films and music. Allowing copyright owners of games to control if and where games are played would unreasonably strengthen the owners' interests at the expense of the public interest in access to games (*Allen v. Academic Games League of America* 1996).

29. As to public display that takes place "at the place where the copy is located," it is immune from liability under an extension of the first sale doctrine (17 U.S.C. § 109(c)).

30. US courts have denied copyright protection for command-line arrangements in office software products on the basis that these constitute methods of operation, excluded from copyright protection (*Lotus v. Borland* 1995). Similarly, commonly used icons and symbols lack sufficient originality or are dictated by extrinsic factors (user expectations and familiarity) (*Apple Computer, Inc. v. Microsoft Corp.* 1994).

31. Of course, to be efficacious, the subject terms must constitute a *condition* to the license, rather than a *covenant*. That distinction proved fatal to the copyright claim in the companion case to *Vernor*. Specifically, copyright owner Blizzard in that case sought to impose liability on counterdefendant MDY. It failed in that endeavor, when the Ninth Circuit interpreted the provision under investigation to be a mere covenant, whose violation accordingly did not give rise to an infringement claim (*MDY Industries, LLC v. Blizzard Entertainment, Inc.* 2010, 939–942).

32. One could imagine a beta copy that was not shrink-wrapped; settlement of litigation that leaves a copy in a remote party's hands; a mistake at the factory such that the product was shipped with its shrink-wrap terms absent or printed defectively; or a variety of other factors.

33. Other pitfalls also loom, such as the distinction between covenant and condition if the operative cause of action is for copyright infringement, and lack of privity if it is breach of contract. See fn. 31 supra.

34. See Determann and Batchelor (2012): Software companies can consistently use terminology to clarify that they are selling licenses, services, or access to software, not software copies, and include "unlike-sales" commercial terms, for example, "field of use" restrictions, a contractual obligation to return old software copies at the time of upgrades, access limitations (authorized or concurrent users), etc.

35. Software that is frequently updated, upgraded, and changed, without reverse version interoperability, is more difficult to resell—but it may also be less attractive to users. Dongles and expiring activation codes can also be used to control changes on the user side, regarding hosting equipment, authorized users, and other details—but such restrictions are not favored by users or data privacy laws.

36. In addition, the pertinent contracts promulgated by the cloud provider can be to the same effect.

37. "Combining cloud computing and content streaming technologies could thus reduce online piracy of entertainment content by providing the consumer with value—the ability to access content from almost anywhere— while providing content owners, creators, and providers with an unprecedented means to control their digital works" (Winegust 2012, p. 10).

38. But even those resales will become more complicated, to the extent that the Copyright Act is amended to adopt the *droit de suite* (a resale royalty right),

a prospect currently under consideration (US Copyright Office 2013; Nimmer 8C.04[A][1]).

39. As to movies, there was no practical way to "perform" them at home. With music, by contrast, anyone with the requisite skill was welcome to play the tune on the living-room piano. Presumably, even a neighborhood gathering to sing familiar tunes would enjoy a robust fair use defense.

40. "Music began as a service and has remained exclusively so for most of its existence. Until very recently in human history, a person wishing to hear music required the performance of a musician" (Anderson 2011, p. 162).

41. In the twentieth century, the charge from the studios was either to theaters or to broadcast networks. In this century, the charge will be directly to consumers—to whom the charge was previously passed on by those intermediaries.

42. High honors go here to the prospects of cloud purveyors offering proprietary software without authorization to thousands of remote users, as discussed previously.

References

Allen v. Academic Games League of America, 89 F.3d 614 (9th Cir. Cal. 1996).

Anderson, J. 2011. Stream Capture: Returning Control of Digital Music to the Users. *Harvard Journal of Law & Technology* 25 (1): 159–178.

App Store. (n.d.). Apple. Retrieved August 26, 2013, from http://www.apple.com/iphone/from-the-app-store.

Apple Computer, Inc. v. Franklin Computer Corp., 714 F.2d 1240 (3d Cir. 1983), cert. denied, 464 U.S. 1033 (1984).

Apple Computer, Inc. v. Microsoft Corp., 35 F.3d 1435 (9th Cir. 1994).

Asay M. (2010). The BSA's Fading Twentieth-Century Piracy Fight: Misreading the Data. *The Register*, September 24. Retrieved on August 28, 2013, from http://www.theregister.co.uk/2010/09/24/piracy_open_source_bsa/.

Atari Games Corp. v. Nintendo, 975 F.2d 832, 839 (Fed. Cir. 1992).

Baker v. Selden, 101 U.S. 99 (1879).

Bateman v. Mnemonics, Inc., 79 F.3d 1532 (11th Cir. 1996).

Bell, T. W. 1998. Fair Use vs. Fared Use: The Impact of Automated Rights Management on Copyright's Fair Use Doctrine. *North Carolina Law Review* 76 (2): 557–620.

Benkler, Y. 2004. Sharing Nicely: On Shareable Goods and the Emergence of Sharing as a Modality of Economic Production. *Yale Law Journal* 114 (2): 273–358.

Bobbs-Merrill Co. v. Straus, 210 U. S. 339 (1908).

Börsenverein des Deutschen Buchhandels. (2013). www.boersenverein.de/sixcms/ media.php/976/LG_Bielefeld_vom_05.03.13_Klage_Verbraucherzentralen.pdf.

Braucher, J. 2006. Contracting Out of Article 2 Using a "License" Label: A Strategy that Should Not Work for Software Products. *Loyola of Los Angeles Law Review* 40 (1): 261–280.

Brown Bag Software v. Symantec Corp., 960 F.2d 1465 (9th Cir. 1992).

BSA. (2012). Shadow Market: 2011 BSA Global Software Piracy Study. Retrieved August 28, 2013, from http://portal.bsa.org/globalpiracy2011.

Bucklew v. Hawkins, Ash, Baptie & Co., 329 F.3d 923 (7th Cir. 2003).

Bundesgerichtshof [BGH] [Federal Court of Justice] 1985, 12 Gewerblicher Rechtsschutz und Urheberrecht [GRUR] 1041 (F.R.G.) (known as the collection program case—"Inkasso-Programm") and Bundesgerichtshof [BGH] [Federal Court of Justice] 1991, 19 Neue Juristische Wochenschrift [NJW] 1231 (F.R.G.) (known as the operating system case—"Betriebssystem"). C-479/04 Laserdisken APS v Kulturministeriet [2007] All ER (EC) 549, [2006] ECDR 30, para. 24.

Capitol Records, LLC v. ReDigi Inc., Case No. 12 Civ. 95 RJS (S.D.N.Y. Mar. 30, 2013).

Cartoon Network LP, LLLP v. CSC Holdings, Inc., 536 F.3d 121 (2nd Cir. 2008).

Carver, B. W. 2010. Why License Agreements Do Not Control Copy Ownership: First Sales and Essential Copies. *Berkeley Technology Law Journal* 25 (4): 1887–1954.

Cerulean Studios. http://www.ceruleanstudios.com (last visited May 31, 2013).

Chamberlain Group, Inc. v. Skylink Technologies, Inc., 381 F.3d 1178 (Fed. Cir. 2004), cert. denied, 125 S. Ct. 1669 (2005).

Chin, A. 2004. Antitrust Analysis in Software Product Markets: A first Principles Approach. *Harvard Journal of Law & Technology* 18 (1): 1–83.

CJEU Case C-355/96, Silhouette International Schmied GmbH & Co. KG v Hartlauer Handelsgesellschaft mbH (1998).

CMAX/Cleveland, Inc. v. UCR, Inc., 804 F. Supp. 337 (M.D. Ga. 1992).

Columbia Broadcasting System, Inc. v. Scorpio Music Distributors, 569 F. Supp. 47 (E.D. Pa. 1983), aff'd mem., 738 F.2d 424 (3d Cir. 1984).

Committee on the Judiciary. (1976). Copyright Law Revision. House of Representatives, Report No. 94–1476, 94th Congress. Washington DC: Government Printing Office.

Computer Associates Int'l, Inc. v. Altai, Inc., 982 F.2d 693 (2d Cir. 1992).

Computer Software Copyright Act of 1980. (1980). Pub. L. 96–517, Sec. 10, 94 Stat. 3028.

Computer Software Rental Amendments Act of 1990, Pub. L. No. 101–650, Sec. 801, 104 Stat. 5089.

Control Data Systems, Inc. v. Infoware, Inc., 903 F. Supp. 1316 (D. Minn. 1995).

CPU cache. (n.d.). Wikipedia. Retrieved August 26, 2013, from http://en.wikipedia .org/wiki/CPU_cache.

CPU register. (n.d.). Wikipedia. Retrieved August 26, 2013, from http://en.wikipedia .org/wiki/CPU_register.

Craigslist, Inc. v. 3taps, Inc., Case No. CV 12–03816 CRB (N.D. Cal. 2013).

Data East USA, Inc. v. Epyx, Inc., 862 F.2d 204 (9th Cir. 1988).

Data Products v. Reppart, 18 U.S.P.Q.2d 1058 (D. Kan. 1990).

Davidson v. Internet Gateway, 334 F. Supp. 2d 1164 (E.D. Miss. 2004).

De Borja, F. (2012). Can Cloud Computing Stop Software Piracy? *Cloud Times*, September 7. Retrieved on August 28, 2013, from http://Cloudtimes.org/2012/09/07/ can-Cloud-stop-software-piracy/.

Determann, L. 2006. Dangerous Liaisons—Software Combinations As Derivative Works? Distribution, Installation and Execution of Linked Programs under Copyright Law, Commercial Licenses and the GPL. *Berkeley Technology Law Journal* 21 (4): 1421–1498.

Determann, L. (2007). Notice, Assent Rules for Contract Changes after *Douglas v. US District Court*. BNA *Electronic Commerce and Law Report* 12 (32).

Determann, Lothar. (2011). Data Privacy in the Cloud: A Dozen Myths and Facts. *Computer and Internet Law* 28:11, 1–8.

Determann, L. (2013a). Data Privacy in the Cloud—Myths and Facts. *Privacy Laws and Business* (121, February 2013): 17–22.

Determann, L. (2013b). Importing software and copyright law. *The Computer and Internet Lawyer* 30: 1–10.

Determann, L. 2013c. Internet freedom and computer abuse. *Hastings Communications and Entertainment Law Journal* 35 (3): 429–454.

Determann, L. (2014). What Happens in the Cloud—Software-as-a-Service and Copyrights, *Berkeley Technology Law Journal* 29: 1095–1130; on SSRN: http://ssrn .com/abstract=2374136.

Determann, L, and W. Batchelor (2012).Used Software Sales and Copyright Exhaustion. *BNA Electronic Commerce and Law Reporter* 17 (December 12, 2012), 2149.

Determann, L., and A. X. Fellmeth. 2001. Don't Judge a Sale by Its License: Software Transfers under the First Sale Doctrine in the United States and the European Community. *University of San Francisco Law Review. University of San Francisco. School of Law* 36 (1): 1–108.

Determann, L., and I. Gutierrez. 2008. Don't Judge a Sale by Its License: Software Transfers under the First Sale Doctrine in the United States and the European Community. *Journal of Intellectual Property Law and Practice* 3 (9): 548–550.

Directive 2001/29/EC of 22 May 2001 on Harmonisation of Certain Aspects of Copyright and Related Rights in the Information Society, Official Journal L 167/10, 22/06/2001.

Directive 2009/24/EC of 23 April 2009 on the Legal Protection of Computer Programs, Official Journal L 1191/16, 05/05/2009.

Dogan, S. L., and J. P. Liu. 2005. Copyright Law and Subject Matter Specificity: The Case of Computer Software. *New York University Annual Survey of American Law* 61 (2): 203–236.

DSC Communications Corp. v. Pulse Communications Inc., 170 F.3d 1354 (Fed. Cir. 1999).

Dun & Bradstreet Software Services, Inc. v. Grace Consulting, Inc., 307 F.3d 197 (3d Cir. 2002).

Eldred v. Ashcroft, 537 U.S. 186 (2003).

Engineering Dynamics, Inc. v. Structural Software, Inc., 26 F.3d 1335 (5th Cir. 1994).

EU Court of Justice, December 22, 2010, Case C-393/09 Bezpečnostní softwarová asociace—Svaz softwarové ochrany v Ministerstvo kultury.

EU Court of Justice, Case C-406/10, SAS Institute Inc. v. World Programming Ltd. (May 2, 2012).

Facebook, Inc. v. Power Ventures, Inc., 844 F. Supp. 2d 1025 (N.D. Cal. 2012).

Feist Publications, Inc., v. Rural Telephone Service Co., 499 U.S. 340 (1991)

Fisher, W. W. 2007. When Should We Permit Differential Pricing of Information? *UCLA Law Review. University of California, Los Angeles. School of Law* 55 (1): 1–38.

Gabel, M., and C. Carrubba. (2009). The European Court of Justice as an Engine of Economic Integration: Reconsidering Evidence That the ECJ Has Expanded Economic Exchange in Europe. SSRN. Retrieved August 26, 2013, from http://papers .ssrn.com/sol3/papers.cfm?abstract_id=1444500.

Gallegos, J. 2011. A New Role for Tortious Interference in the Digital Age: A Model to Enforce End User License Agreements. *Florida State University Law Review. Florida State University. College of Law* 38 (2): 411–434.

Gates Rubber Co. v. Bando Chem. Industries, Ltd., 9 F.3d 823 (10th Cir. 1993).

Geuna, P. (2004). A Cache Primer. Freescale Semiconductor, AN2663 Rev. 1, 10/2004. Retrieved August 28, 2013, from http://www.freescale.com/files/32bit/doc/app_note/AN2663.pdf.

Ginsburg, J. C. 1994. Four Reasons and a Paradox: The Manifest Superiority of Copyright over Sui Generis Protection of Computer Software. *Columbia Law Review* 94 (8): 2559–2572.

GNU Operating System. (n.d.). GNU Affero General Public License. Retrieved August 26, 2013, from http://www.gnu.org/licenses/agpl-3.0.html.

Google v. Oracle, 750 F.3d 1339 (Fed. Cir. 2014).

Gue, T. (2012). Triggering Infection: Distribution and Derivative Works under the GNU General Public License. *University of Illinois Journal of Law, Technology, and Policy* 2012 (1), 95–140.

Harcourt, Brace & World, Inc. v. Graphics Controls Corp., 329 F. Supp. 517 (S.D.N.Y. 1971).

Harper & Row Publishers, Inc. v. Nation Enterprises, 471 U.S. 539 (1985).

Hoyle, F. 1957. *The Black Cloud*. New York: Harper.

ISC-Bunker Ramo v. Altech, Inc., 765 F. Supp. 1310 (N.D. Ill. 1990).

John Wiley & Sons, Inc. v. Kirtsaeng, 654 F.3d 210 (2d Cir. 2011).

Judgment of the European Court of Justice (Grand Chamber) of 3 July 2012, Used-Soft GmbH v Oracle International Corp. (Case C-128/11) (1), Official Journal 2012/C 287/16.

Kepner-Tregoe, Inc. v. Leadership Software, 12 F.3d 527 (5th Cir. 1994).

Kim, N. S. 2008. The Software Licensing Dilemma. *Brigham Young University Law Review* (4): 1103–1164.

Kirtsaeng v. John Wiley & Sons, Inc., 133 S. Ct. 1351 (2013).

Lemley, M. A. 1995a. Convergence in the Law of Software Copyright. *High Technology Law Journal* 10 (1): 1–34.

Lemley, M. A. 1995b. Intellectual Property and Shrinkwrap Licenses. *Southern California Law Review* 68 (5): 1239–1294.

Lemley, M. A., and D. W. O'Brien. 1997. Encouraging Software Reuse. *Stanford Law Review* 49 (2): 255–304.

Lemley, M., P. Menell, P. Merges, and P. Samuelson. 2000. *Software and Internet Law*. 1st ed. Gaithersburg, MD: Aspen Law & Business.

Lemley, M., P. Menell, P. Merges, and P. Samuelson. 2003. *Software and Internet Law*. 2nd ed. New York: Aspen Publishers.

Lexmark Int'l, Inc. v. Static Control Components, Inc., 387 F.3d 522 (6th Cir. 2004).

Lotus Development Corp. v. Borland Int'l, 49 F.3d 807 (1st Cir. 1995).

Luettgen, D. G. 1996 Functional Usefulness vs. Communicative Usefulness: Thin Copyright Protection for the Nonliteral Elements of Computer Programs. *Texas International Property Law Journal* 4 (2): 233–274.

Madison, M. J. 2003. Reconstructing the Software License. *Loyola University of Chicago Law Journal. Loyola University of Chicago. School of Law* 35 (1): 275–340.

Maggs, G. E. 2003. The Waning Importance of Revisions to U.C.C. Article 2. *Notre Dame Law Review* 78 (2): 595–628.

MAI Systems Corp. v. Peak Computer, Inc., 991 F.2d 511 (9th Cir. 1993).

Maxeiner, J. R. 2003. Standard-Terms Contracting in the Global Electronic Age: European Alternatives. *Yale Journal of International Law* 28 (1): 109–182.

MDY Industries, LLC v. Blizzard Entertainment, Inc., 629 F.3d 928 (9th Cir. 2010).

Menell, P. 1987. Tailoring Legal Protection for Computer Software. *Stanford Law Review* 39 (6): 1329–1372.

Menell, P. S. 1989. An Analysis of the Scope of Copyright Protection for Application Programs. *Stanford Law Review* 41 (5): 1045–1104.

Micro Star v. Formgen, 154 F.3d 1107 (9th Cir. 1998).

Microsoft Corp. v. Harmony Computers & Electronics, 846 F. Supp. 208 (E.D.N.Y. 1994).

Midway Manufacturing v. Artic Int'l, Inc., 704 F.2d 1009 (7th Cir. 1983).

Miller v. Facebook, Inc., 95 U.S.P.Q.2D (BNA) 1822 (N.D. Cal. May 28, 2010).

Miller, A. R. 1993. Copyright Protection for Computer Programs, Databases, and Computer-Generated Works: Is Anything New since CONTU? *Harvard Law Review* 106 (5): 977–1073.

MiTek Holdings Inc. v. Arce Engineering Co., 89 F.3d 1548 (11th Cir. 1996).

Nadan, C. H. 2004. Software Licensing in the 21st Century: Are Software "Licenses" Really Sales, and How Will the Software Industry Respond? *AIPLA Quarterly Journal* 32 (4): 555–656.

National Commission on New Technological Uses of Copyrighted Works. 1979. *Final Report of the National Commission on New Technological Uses of Copyrighted Works*. Washington, DC: Government Printing Office.

Netsuite. (n.d.). Retrieved August 26, 2013, from http://www.netsuite.com/portal/home.shtml.

Nimmer, D. 1996. Brains and Other Paraphernalia of the Digital Age. *Harvard Journal of Law & Technology* 10 (1): 1–46.

Nimmer, D. 2004. Codifying Copyright Comprehensibly. *UCLA Law Review. University of California, Los Angeles. School of Law* 51 (5): 1233–1387.

Nimmer, D. 2015. *Nimmer on Copyright: A Treatise on the Law of Literary, Musical and Artistic Property, and the Protection of Ideas.* New York: M. Bender.

Nimmer, D., R. Bernacchi, and G. Frischling. 1988. A Structured Approach to Analyzing the Substantial Similarity of Computer Software in Copyright Infringement Cases. *Arizona State Law Journal* 20 (3): 625–656.

Nimmer, D., E. Brown, and G. Frischling. 1999. The Metamorphosis of Contract into Expand. *California Law Review* 87 (1): 17–77.

Novell v. Network Trade Center, 25 F. Supp. 2d 1218 (D. Utah 1997).

OLG Frankfurt am Main (German Court of Appeals), decision of Nov. 6, 2012, Az. 11–U68–11 (*Adobe v. Usedsoft*).

OnLive. (n.d.). Retrieved August 26, 2013, from http://www.OnLive.com.

Oracle America, Inc. v. Google, Inc., 810 F. Supp. 2d 1002 (N.D. Cal. 2011).

OSI. (n.d.). Retrieved August 26, 2013, from http://www.osi.com/.

Perfect 10, Inc. v. Amazon.com, Inc., 508 F.3d 1146 (9th Cir. 2007).

Piracy. (n.d.). Microsoft. Retrieved August 26, 2013, from http://www.microsoft.com/en-us/piracy/default.aspx.

Public Relations Consultants Association Limited (Appellant) v The Newspaper Licensing Agency Limited and others (Respondents), [2011] EWCA Civ 890.

Quality King Distributors Inc. v. L'Anza Research Int'l Inc., 523 U.S. 135 (1998).

Radin, M. J. 2012. Reconsidering Boilerplate: Confronting Normative and Democratic Degradation. *Capital University Law Review* 40 (3): 617–656.

Rice, D. A. (2004). Copyright and Contract: Preemption after *Bowers v. Baystate. Roger Williams University Law Review* 9 (2), 595–644.

Roccia, V. J. 1997. What's Fair Is (Not Always) Fair on the Internet. *Rutgers Law Journal* 29 (1): 155–200.

Rothchild, J. A. 2004. The Incredible Shrinking First-Sale Rule: Are Software Resale Limits Lawful? *Rutgers Law Review* 57 (1): 1–106.

Salesforce. (n.d.). Retrieved August 26, 2013, from http://www.salesforce.com.

Samuelson, P. 1992. Computer Programs, User Interfaces, and Section 102(b) of the Copyright Act of 1976: A Critique of *Lotus v. Paperback*. *Law and Contemporary Problems* 55 (2): 311–353.

Samuelson, P. 1994. . Comparing US and EC Copyright Protection for Computer Programs: Are They More Different than They Seem? *Journal of Law and Commerce* 13 (2): 279–300.

Samuelson, P., R. Davis, M. Kapor, and J. H. Reichmann. 1994. A Manifesto Concerning the Legal Protection of Computer Programs. *Columbia Law Review* 94 (8): 2308–2431.

Sebastian Int'l, Inc. v. Consumer Contacts (PTY) Ltd., 847 F.2d 1093 (3d Cir. 1988).

Sega Enterprises, Ltd. v. Accolade, Inc., 977 F.2d 1510 (9th. Cir. 1992).

Softman Products Co., LLC v. Adobe Systems, Inc., 171 F. Supp. 2d 1075 (C.D. Cal. 2001).

Sony Computer Entertainment, Inc. v. Connectix Co.,203 F.3d 596 (9th Cir. 2000).

Sony Corp. of America v. Universal City Studios, Inc., 464 U.S. 417 (1984).

Stenograph, L. L. C. v. Bossard Associates Inc., 144 F.3d 96. D.C. Cir. (1998).

Stern Electronics, Inc. v. Kaufman, 669 F.2d 852 (2d Cir. 1982).

Sugar, C. R. M. (n.d.). Retrieved August 26, 2013, from http://www.sugarcrm.com.

Ticketmaster LLC v RMG Technologies, Inc, 507 F. Supp. 2d 1096 (C.D. Cal. 2007).

U.S. Copyright Office. 2013. Resale Royalty Right, Public Hearing. *Federal Register* 61:19326–19329.

Urheberrechtsgesetz, UrhG [Copyright Law], Sept. 9, 1965, as amended May 8, 1998 § 2 no. 2 (F.R.G.).

Vault Corp. v. Quaid Software Ltd., 847 F.2d 255 (5th Cir. 1988).

Vernor v. Autodesk, 555 F. Supp. 2d 1164 (W.D. Wash. 2008).

Vernor v. Autodesk, Inc. 621 F.3d 1102 (9th Cir. 2010).

Walker, J. 2008. *Fundamentals of Physics*. 8th ed. Hoboken, NJ: Wiley.

Wall Data Inc. v. L.A. County Sheriff's Department, 447 F.3d 769 (9th Cir. 2006).

Widmer, M. 2007. Application Service Providing, Copyright, and Licensing. *John Marshall Journal of Computer & Information Law* 25 (1): 79–116.

Wikipedia. (n.d.). Interoperability. Retrieved August 26, 2013, from http://en.wikipedia.org/wiki/Interoperability#Software.

Williams Electronics, Inc. v. Artic Int'l, Inc., 685 F.2d 870 (3d Cir 1982).

Winegust, T. C. 2012. Work with Your Head in the Clouds: The Impact of Cloud Computing and Content Streaming on Copyright in the Entertainment Industry. *Intellectual Property Brief* 4 (1): 8–15.

Workday. (n.d.). Retrieved August 26, 2013, from http://www.workday.com/.

Zieminski, C. 2008. Game Over for Reverse Engineering? How the DMCA and Contracts Have Affected Innovation. *Journal of Technology Law & Policy* 13 (2): 289–340.

9   Bodies in the Cloud: A Geography of Electronic Health Data

Nicholas Bauch

Clouds suggest ephemerality—wisps of mist high above that cannot be grasped, tinkered with, or tossed around. They are apart from the Earth's surface, in many ways the opposite of rock and soil and of being grounded. In computing, the cloud metaphor has grown because it offers a way to imagine a spatial relationship between computing devices and the information that populates their screens. People ask devices to retrieve information that is floating around in an all-containing atmospheric cloud above them, waiting to be instantaneously zipped below to the surface, where it appears and can be manipulated. Or so the metaphor goes. Many readers will know that this is not in fact how the storage and retrieval of information in the cloud works. The geographic reality is that data must be stored on servers, collected inside highly protected buildings, and anchored into the Earth, where it can connect with energy networks and communication cables. Data is material, it takes up space and, in the aggregate (for 1 digital bit is actually close to ethereal), requires a massive infrastructure of data centers that are located somewhere.

To speak of information landscapes, then, is to speak of how changes in the visible field of our planet's surface reflect, as well as constitute, the geographical organization of data in the Information Age. Affecting this visual field—where data centers are built and what they look like—includes the political economies of energy (where is energy cheap?), the architectural design of data centers (e.g., security measures and power backups), and the rise of a cultural ethos that everything digital can and should be saved forever. However, we cannot pretend forever that the material effects of infinite data do not affect our landscapes—the places that we live in, work in, and move through every day. Governing this often-ignored materiality of information is crucial as the categorical and geographical boundaries between people, electronic data, and landscape continue to blur.[1] Writ most broadly, this chapter explores the distinction between virtual and real. More specifically, it is about what happens when we seriously attend to the materiality of the cloud, halting assumptions that the physical manifestations of data are insignificant. Instead of being massless or devoid of form, the virtual is as much a part of the real as any other object with a tactile presence would be.

Understanding the relationship among electronic data, people, and landscapes is about understanding how objects in space become related to one another in the first place. The materiality of electronic data, in other words, is an instance of object relations, an issue of sustained interest to spatial and environmental theorists (Robbins 2007; Coyle 2006). Blurring virtual and real becomes a matter of blurring different types of objects that significantly alter each other's existence—objects that are not normally thought of as being relatable, such as digital information and people. This should also be of great concern to political theorists interested in land use, zoning, or environment. If digital representations of people come to be considered material extensions of bodies, then the places in which those extensions rest might be given the same rights to health as would a person. To abstract, the bigger implication is that by reconceptualizing object *relations* as object *extensions*, protecting the health of landscapes becomes as crucial as protecting the health of people. To substantiate this line of thought, the chapter examines the case of a form of medical biotechnology called *Wireless Body Area Network (WBAN)*, articulating how electronic data, bodies, and landscapes all should be considered part of the same phenomenon. It is argued that the bodies of people who use this technology geographically extend into the landscape of data storage, such that the shape of their bodies follows the very mundane, the very grounded infrastructure of the cloud.

Vignettes from New Jersey

In 2012–2013, the Superior Court of New Jersey reached decisions on two cases that break down the categorical and geographical distinctions between bodies and electronic data. While neither of these cases is explicitly about electronic health information or data centers, together they begin to build a concept of what a class of legislation that gives a person equal standing with the digital information associated with him or her might look like. It is helpful to start with these two vignettes from the judicial system before moving into the main case study of the chapter because they frame the relevance of two concepts introduced afterward: *body-data* and *extensible space*.

In 2012, the state of New Jersey convicted V. M. Patel of attempted sexual assault of a child after he was caught in a law enforcement sting in which a police officer posed as a 13-year-old girl in an online chat room (*New Jersey v. Patel* 2012). After driving to meet the girl and being arrested, the defendant argued that no crime was committed because the girl only existed virtually, and "he could not be found guilty of committing a crime against a virtual child." There was no girl at the prearranged meeting place—only police cars. The judge rejected the defendant's argument "that he could not be convicted of the charged offenses which require, as a material element, there be a person or child, because [the girl] was only a 'virtual' person or child." This decision by the judge offers an example where the legal standing of a virtual person was upheld regardless of a "material element." In this case, interaction with the person's virtual body through communicating online, coupled with the intent to interact with that person's physical body, was enough to find the defendant guilty of attempting to commit sexual assault.

In 2013, an 18-year-old driver named Kyle Best grievously injured two motorcycle riders when his vehicle crossed into their lane and hit them head on (the left leg of each rider was amputated at the hospital). Best was texting with his mobile phone at the time of the collision. The trial court found settlement in favor of the injured plaintiffs, Linda and David Kubert. The Kuberts, however, did not stop there—they sought further damages from Shannon Colonna, the person with whom Best was texting at the time of the accident (*Kubert v. Best* 2013). While Colonna was nowhere near the scene of the accident, she was accused of culpability via her virtual, electronic presence. In his written opinion on the case, the judge stated:

Although Colonna was at a remote location from the site of the accident, plaintiffs say she was "electronically present" in Best's pick-up truck immediately before the accident and she aided and abetted his unlawful use of his cell phone. ... We must determine as a matter of civil common law whether one who is texting from a location remote from the driver of a motor vehicle can be liable to persons injured because the driver was distracted by the text.

In this particular case, there was not enough evidence to hold Colonna liable since it could not be proven that she knew that Best was driving at the time; it was Best's responsibility not to use his cell phone while driving. But for the purposes of this chapter, it is powerful that the three Superior Court judges who heard the case did *not* dismiss the Kuberts' claim against Colonna as outlandish or misguided, as the trial court did.

On the contrary, they held that "the sender of a text message can potentially be liable if an accident is caused by texting .... We do not adopt the trial court's reasoning that a remote texter does not have a legal duty to avoid sending text messages to one who is driving."

In each of these vignettes, it becomes clear that actions taken in a virtual, digital medium can have material consequences in the real world. In neither case was there a geographical co-presence between the body of the accused and the body of the victim. In the sexual assault case, Patel never touched or saw a 13-year-old girl (and unbeknownst to him he never communicated with one either), while in the texting case, Colonna was far from the accident she was accused of causing. In each situation, however, the court found that damage or potential damage to someone's body can be achieved from a distant location by use of transmitted electronic data. Importantly, the court cases hint at how the notion of geographical proximity is changing in light of digital information. For two people to be in the same location no longer requires that their traditional biological bodies (defined for now as ending at the skin) be in the same place at the same time.

Through the poignancy of their subject matter, these cautionary tales help us recognize in a concrete way that actions taken at the terminals of electronic devices (i.e., computers or smartphones) alter physical reality in other places. Here, they do so immediately, discretely, and in a way that is traceable, such that they become the subject of a court case. From this, it becomes totally conceivable that the collective, societywide actions taken at the terminals of our devices have equally profound effects on distant parts of the material world. That is, the series of cause and effect that begins with the creation of electronic data ends with an alteration of landscapes near and distant. One significant landscape alteration is the erection of data centers and the accompanying changes in surrounding land use they require to meet their high energy consumption. City and regional planners, for example, are vastly remodeling landscapes to accommodate this new economy, retrofitting business parks to attract companies that specialize in data storage and retrieval. Data centers can be visually arresting in the new landscape of business parks. "As the growth of cloud computing forces providers to super-size their infrastructure, their energy needs scale as well. The energy park concept is a way to join these trends in a real estate play" (Miller 2012). The energy park is a planned landscape that allows data center operators to control a variety of infrastructural needs in one campus setting. These needs include different types of energy (including grid, wind, and solar), and access to the fiber optic cable network (Niobrara Data Center Energy Park 2012).

Bringing Together Bodies and Landscapes

In the two court cases discussed previously, physical closeness between people and distant places is achieved by geographically extending oneself through space via the transmission of digital information. The Superior Court of New Jersey found that Colonna's electronic presence in the cab of Best's truck was the same as if she were there in person, distracting the driver. Likewise in Patel's case, his attempt at sexual assault—his physical presence—was considered as real as if he had begun undressing a young girl and then was caught in the act. He was considered physically near his victim, normally a given for culpability of bodily harm done to another person.

With these rulings in place, what is the next step in understanding the relationship among electronic data, bodies, and landscapes? The geographical extension of oneself to another place necessitates rethinking the idea of a singularly located body. With the potential to be hyperconnected through digital media and telecommunications, it is becoming clearer that the electronic data we create have the potential to not only represent us in different places, but to *be* us in different places without our biological body (as normally defined) having to move. To clarify, two types of geographical extension are going on. The first is when a transmitted piece of information ends up in a particular place and has an immediate effect there (such as causing a car accident). The second is the more general principle to be drawn from the first: that all electronic data in the cloud go somewhere and affect the physical state of that place. Yes, people create electronic data, and yes, those data feed the growing infrastructure of data storage, requiring more data centers and more energy contracts and more servers. In this way, we know at the most basic level that actions on devices affect the way landscapes are built and the way they look.

Now, here is an interesting question: what happens when the content of transmitted data is not linguistic communication, but a measurement of someone's body? In the New Jersey vignettes, the geographical extension of people via electronic data happened because the defendants transmitted textual information to another person who was not close to them. But in the next and final case study of this chapter—the WBAN—the data being created, transmitted, stored, and retrieved are measurements of biological functioning. As a case study, this medical biotechnology offers a more direct way to talk about how it is possible that bodies could be geographically extended along the infrastructural pathways of the cloud.

Wireless Body Area Networks

WBANs are used to monitor the condition of hospital patients who are away from the hospital. Monitoring from afar in this way is possible because in a WBAN, biosensors are placed either on, or implanted inside of, the patient's body. The sensors then transmit data, through a series of data-handling technologies, to computers where medical professionals use the streamed and stored information to make diagnostic conclusions or to be warned of impending danger in a patient's condition (Kirbaş and Bayilmiş 2012; Yuce and Khan 2012). The path that this electronic *body-data* takes, from the patient's body through the physical infrastructure of the information landscape to the medic's viewing screen, is the way that the patient's body is materially extended to other places.

WBANs are the critical technological component in the growth of *tele-health,* a sector of the health-care industry involving the transition from in-person doctor visits to remote consultation and monitoring. Telehealth promises to serve immobile, remote, geriatric, and low-income populations by reducing the travel and financial challenges associated with going to the doctor's office (Jurik and Weaver 2008). With the advent of more readily available wireless networks (e.g., WiFi and 3G/4G), telehealth is moving from its beginnings—where a patient would, say, phone in self-test results—to incorporate a more comprehensive and mobile version that operates independent of the patient's location (Khan and Yuce 2010). While some WBANs used in this new version of telehealth require the patient to consciously submit their body-data from a temporary data storage device, such as a personal digital assistant (PDA) or a smartphone (e.g., iPhone), systems built for the automatic and continuous streaming of body-data for the electronic construction of a patient at another location are underway (Alemdar and Ersoy 2010; Bowden 2012). With the sensors of a WBAN measuring and transmitting data, a patient's body-data becomes part of the electronic information infrastructure, and therefore can be seen by anyone (but presumably only health-care practitioners) with access to the storage locations of the body-data (Al Ameen et al. 2012; Kargl et al. 2008). It is the built infrastructure of data storage that makes this new type of electronic, spatialized body possible.

Heartbeat and body temperature are commonly cited as parameters monitored by a WBAN. Figure 9.1, however, demonstrates that WBANs

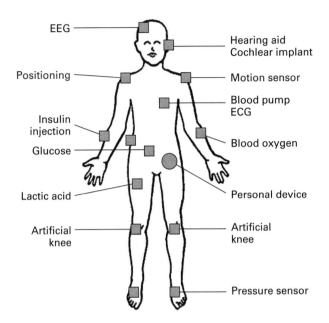

EEG

Hearing aid
Cochlear implant

Positioning

Motion sensor

Blood pump
ECG

Insulin
injection

Glucose

Blood oxygen

Lactic acid

Personal device

Artificial
knee

Artificial
knee

Pressure sensor

Figure 9.1
Body places and functions that can potentially be monitored by a WBAN system
(Latré et al. 2011). Used with permission from Springer Science and Business Media.

also can be used to monitor a variety of organ functions and body movements (see "Artificial knee" in the illustration), and can even administer
the appropriate dosages of medicine based on sensor feedback (see "Insulin
injection").

Although it is less obvious, figure 9.1 also demonstrates the next stage
in the transition of human biological processes into the world of electronic
data storage. A personal device, represented by a circle at the person's hip,
serves as an immediate, temporary receptacle for "fresh" data. The WBAN
sensors then transmit this data through a series of storage devices, ending
at an external server where it can be stored and analyzed (figure 9.2).

Contrary to the image of a cloud in figure 9.2, WBANs require a robust
built infrastructure of data storage to make the electronic measurement
and analysis of biological processes possible. As hospitals coordinate multiple patients at once streaming "live" body-data into a WBAN system
(figure 9.3), a long-term storage place is required for longitudinal analysis
of a patient's health-care progress.

The process of sensing, transmitting, storing, and analyzing a patient's
body-data can be clarified by making a distinction between data at rest

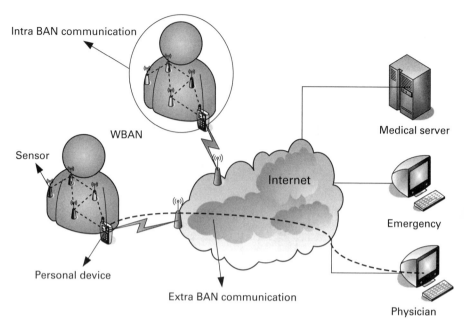

Figure 9.2
The connection between the body and other devices in a WBAN system. Informa-
tion is transmitted through the Internet, represented by a cloud (Latré et al. 2011).
Used with permission from Springer Science and Business Media.

and data in motion (Martell 2012). Data at rest is not immediately analyzed as it streams from the sensor node, while data in motion are analyzed before it reaches a final resting place such as a data center. WBANs
have the capacity to perform both of these functions, the former for
nonemergency cases where monitoring over a longer time span is necessary, and the latter for emergency cases. A premature baby connected to
a WBAN, for example, may transmit thousands of unique body-data items
every second, which in a data-in-motion analysis structure can be used
to make diagnoses up to 24 hours sooner than they otherwise might be.
At a hospital using a WBAN system, this could mean that hundreds of
patients are streaming hundreds of thousands of body-data items at once.
The capacity to handle—i.e., securely store, query, aggregate, and cross-
reference—large data sets is according to some (boyd and Crawford 2012,
663) the definition of Big Data itself. Entering into a Big Data paradigm
means that the materiality of data must be considered. Since data is stored
and accessed from data centers located in the built environment, data
centers become one of the major sites of corporeal extensibility; they are

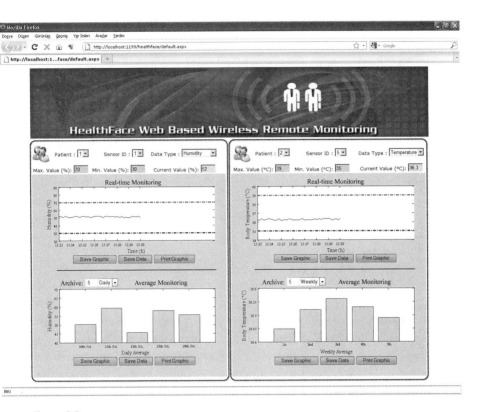

Figure 9.3

Real-time monitoring (live streaming) and average (long-term) monitoring in Health-Face, a WBAN interface. Here, two patients are being monitored at the same time. Patient no. 2, on the right, has at least five sensors. The storage technology required to operate such a system is the data center (Kirbaş and Bayilmiş 2012). Used with permission of Dr. Ismail Kirbaş.

the means by and the locations onto which patients' bodies in a WBAN are extended spatially.

The concept of body-data has been introduced in this chapter to highlight the argument that there are many potential instances where the biological body of a patient and the digital data created about his or her body are one and the same. The geographical version of living in the borderlands between real and virtual is accepting that a distant object (in this case, electronic data) contributes to the objecthood of something else (in this case, a human body) in a different location. Body-data, therefore, is a term that offers a way to talk about how biology and technology co-constitute one another without having to categorically or spatially separate them. The term *body-data* means the digital information created about someone's body being treated as if it is an extension of the body itself.

An important corollary of body-data is the concept of extensible space. If bodies exist in geographically disparate places simultaneously, then in theory, they can be plotted onto a cartographic system (i.e., the bodies can be mapped out using the locations of where their body-data is stored and accessed). While mapping is clearly not new in geographical practice, it may come as a surprise that the impulse to map out the constitutive objects of any phenomenon has a strong precedent in geographical thought as well. Allow me to explain this further. I am drawing out the idea of extensible space from a different kind of space—relational space —that has been heavily theorized by geographers over the past two decades.

How Relational Space Leads into Extensible Space

The formation of a relational space is contingent—perhaps not surprisingly—on the relation among a diverse set of objects and events, foundationally described within geography by Murdoch (1997, 325) as "heterogeneous associations, that is, associations which somehow bring together the social and physical/material." Inspired by a desire to question the ontological categories of nature and society (Castree and Braun 2001), geographers have since offered a variety of examples of how relational spaces are brought into being and how they constantly change through political processes or new types of associations among the objects in any such network (Routledge 2008; Kaika 2005; Castree 2003). At its most profound, relational space provides an ontology described not so much by objects, but by the space, or relations, between them. Objects do not exist alone, but only through their connection (loosely defined) with other objects. Any given object, then, has its own network of connections with other objects, a network that can be mapped out on a geographic grid. Described thus, relational space is apart from absolute, measurable, mathematical space, resting on the notion that objects and events inherently have their own spatiality; that is, the constitutive relations that any object has with other objects. The political relevancy of seeing objects as existing in relation with other objects is vast, and will seem familiar to many readers. For example, if one considers the technologies, machines, and people used to harvest coffee beans, it becomes easy to recognize that the object "coffee bean" itself is related to those machines and people; it would not exist as it does without them. This recognition has spawned several enormous political-economic movements, including fair trade and organic, the former affecting labor and the latter affecting cultivating techniques.

Stemming from this, however, little has been said about the subsequent possibility for a single object to exist in multiple places at once. I argue that in some cases, when one maps out a relational space rather than a connection with other objects, all the things on the map become the original object. To take another example, a t-shirt consists of cotton, but it is also the soil where the cotton grew, the geologic and human processes that created that particular soil quality, the sweatshop where the cotton was spun and sewn into a t-shirt, and the life of the worker who made sure that the shirt was the right size. This is different than saying the object becomes enrolled in a network involving all these other things. It is a move from epistemology (i.e., we can only really know objects through their various relationships with other objects) to ontology (i.e., an object is partially composed of other objects). This is the move from relational space to extensible space.

A related tendency in theorizations of relational space is to treat objects as spatially discrete and singular. As the term *heterogeneous* suggests, the objects being associated to forge a network are separate from one another in type, name, material, and spatial location. Without this discreteness, in fact, there could be no relation; the relationship itself entirely depends on the objects being different. The continuous becoming of networks in a relational space, then, relies on the assumption that an object is one bounded thing that exists in one location. In the discussion that follows, utilizing the philosophy of Graham Harman, I challenge this presumed discreteness of objects, offering a way to conceive of space making founded on object extensibility rather than object relation. This requires a reconceptualization of the nature of objects.

Graham Harman's Object-Oriented Philosophy

Graham Harman, inspired by Martin Heidegger's tool-being and Bruno Latour's actor-network theory, has crafted what he calls "object-oriented philosophy" (Harman 2010a). Aiding geographical efforts to define relational space through its "heterogeneous associations," Harman's philosophy offers a way to think through how exactly objects could possibly be connected (or related) in the first place. This line of inquiry digs up the fundamental core of relational space and presents possibilities for an alternative type of space making based on how objects exist. In his own words, Harman's (2010a, 2) object-oriented philosophy has "a single problem at its core: the tension between objects and relations." Objects in this view include animate, human, and inanimate things, and relations always involve the distortion of the objects in relation with one another. Harman's skill as a philosopher lies in placing the issues raised (especially by Latour) regarding exactly how objects "relate" within broader histories of philosophy, theology, and metaphysics (Harman 2009; Bingham 1996, 647–649).

The key to Harman's argument is that object relations are not reciprocal, a phenomenon termed "the asymmetry of contact." When a person perceives a tree, for example, it can likely perceive the person in return. This perception is not symmetrical, though. That is, how the tree perceives the person is entirely different than how the person perceives the tree. "[T]his," says Harman (2011, 75), "must occur as part of a different relation, not as the reverse side of the same one." Consider in more detail how a WBAN functions. When WBAN sensors take measurements from inside a patient's body, three separate events must happen for body-data to be extended into space. First, the sensor node must detect the biological process. Second, it must digitize and code it for communication. Third, it must transmit the data to another device. Using the asymmetry of contact theory, this means that the WBAN sensor node and, say, the beating heart perceive each other, but on different planes of reality. Harman claims that there is always just one real object involved in any interaction between objects. The thing doing the sensing—in whatever way it does so, whether biological or not—is what he calls a "real object," and the thing being sensed is a "sensual object." This is because, following Heidegger's *Geviert* (fourfold), Harman believes that there is an unknowable depth to objects that makes them irreproducible and gives them the ability to affect the world in a different way each time they interact with a new object. This appears to challenge the nonessentialist materialisms of Latour, Gilles Deleuze, Donna Haraway, and Michel Serres, each of whom "rejects the idea that there might be a supplemental dimension or transcendental cause that lies beneath or behind the material worlds in which we dwell" (Anderson and Braun 2008, xiv–xv). Yet Harman's argument suggests that there is room for a space making that derives from objects but operates in a mode different from relationality.

According to Harman, objects do have a supplemental dimension, and they do emit something that allows them to travel to different locations in space. This emission is an altogether different object, which is why it cannot be included in the reciprocal perception (e.g., between a person and a tree). A human perceives the tree as a real object but is perceived by the tree as a sensual object, and vice versa. This creates two different relationships, not one, going on at the same time. And it makes sense, I believe, when applied to the relationship between the sensor and a patient's body part, such as a beating heart.

Harman derives this conception of objects from Heidegger's tool analysis. In *Being and Time* (1962, 96), Heidegger observes that by addressing entities as things, or objects, "we have tacitly anticipated their ontological character." Here, Heidegger is making the case that there is a phenomenological depth to objects that exists outside human perception or culture. Another way to think of this statement is: If objects are actually singular and discrete, then there can be no tacit anticipation of their ontological character because the ontological character is obvious—there would be nothing to anticipate. Harman picks up on this in a search for a depth of objects, one that I am using to promote a material extensibility of tiny digital objects to other places. He describes a being of objecthood in which "all objects are encountered more often as tacit components of our world than as blatant objects of awareness" (Harman 2010b, 109). Most objects are encountered as tacit or go unnoticed—instances in which they are functioning properly. They become part of conscious awareness only when they malfunction. Continuing, Harman says that "the substance of a thing, whatever it is, must precede its functional form, since the thing is never exhausted by all that it does, and since it can support several usages at the same time" (2010b, 115). This means that reality is deeper than objectification (e.g., naming, labeling, or making assumptions about an object), and reveals the key insight of the tool analysis: even when things are not noticed, they still serve as tools for human living. Human existence is inextricably bound to the tools that make us—psychologically and physically—what we are.

This fits neatly with how relational space has been described (Murdoch 2006; Gandy 2005), such that there must be an association among things to make the world what it is—no one object, including the human body, can exist in spatial or objective isolation. The argument being presented in this chapter, however, challenges what exactly those objects are in a way that asks spatial theorists to rethink the metaphysics of networks themselves. A "depth" of objects is mandatory if we are to accept Harman's notion of an asymmetry of contact among objects, and Heidegger offers the philosophical foundation for doing so (Leszczynski 2009, 610). If objects are more that their immediately recognized form, then there is room for accepting that they emit in multiple ways that are sensed by other objects uniquely. This multiplicity of emissions is how objects become simultaneously located in different places. It is not an attempt to destroy or flatten objects, but rather an attempt to redefine their geographical character.

A return to the case study of WBANs will help to clarify this point. The digital reappearance of the patient in the computer console of the health-care provider is a moment in the body's travel along the WBAN network (figure 9.4). When the patient's body appears in the doctor's computer console, it is not completely virtual, if virtuality is considered the opposite of reality. The WBAN sensor begins its sensing with an "amplifier/filter/multiplexer." It is then changed into an 8–12-bit digital signal, and finally it is transmitted via an antenna to a temporary storage device on its path away from what we would normally call the body (figure 9.5). The pulse, or heartbeat, becomes digitally captured and preserved, eventually being stored at a location administered by the hospital that issued the WBAN system for the patient. The hospital's data centers become filled with people's personal biological information.

Why is this *the person*, though, and not an electronic representation of the person? Returning to object-oriented philosophy, the distinction between "real" and "sensual" objects helps us move away from the trappings of representation (Thrift 2008; Lorimer 2005). Real objects, again,

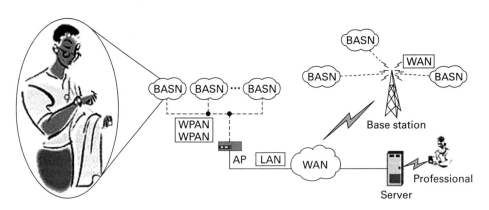

Figure 9.4

In this drawing, a patient's pulse is sensed through a watchlike sensor, then transmitted wirelessly to the body area sensor network (BASN), proceeds to the wireless local area network (WLAN), then to a wide area network (WAN), and finally to a server from which a "professional" can see the patient's body-data. Image © 2006 IEEE. Reprinted with permission from Poon, Zhang, and Bao (2006).

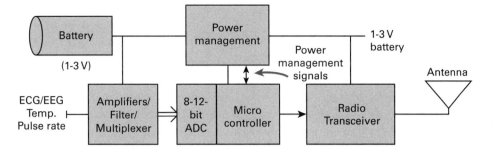

Figure 9.5
Schemata of a WBAN sensor node placed on or inside a body to measure body parameters such as muscle cell action, heart rate, blood pressure, and brain activity. Image © 2010 Jamil Y. Khan, Mehmet R. Yuce. Originally published in Khan and Yuce (2010) under CC BY-NC-SA 3.0 license.

are things in themselves, while sensual objects are the things that are sensed by other things. Even though each of us is a real object, we can never know real objects—only sensual objects. In this ontology, each object simultaneously exists as two different things.[2] When the pulse signal is amplified and filtered, it is the sensual object of the beating heart that becomes transmitted, not the "real" heart.[3] But do not confuse Harman's meaning of the word *real* here as meaning the opposite of *virtual*. On the contrary, to Harman, *sensual* is as real as *real* (perhaps even more so) since it is the only thing we are capable of knowing. Therefore, the coded signal is the sensual beating heart as sensed, or known, by the ("real") WBAN sensor node, and as such, exists as part of the person somewhere else.

The reason we should take this proposal seriously is that it offers a detailed explanation for how the moment of interaction between objects can be imagined and described. Harman's real and sensual objects defend the possibility for an ontology based on extensibility. By allowing the interpretation that a sensual object can travel along the lines of a network while its companion real object cannot, it is possible for objects to be in more than one place at once. This depends on a conceptualization of objects in which any single thing consists of modes that are not required to be in the same Euclidian location but are still a necessary part of that object's reality. As such, the simultaneous locational existence of bodies, and therefore the possibility for a spatially extensible body, is crafted.

WBANs in the Context of Body Theory

In her *Manifesto for Cyborgs*, Haraway (1994, 83) writes that modern medicine is full of cyborgs, "of couplings between organism and machine, each conceived as coded devices, in an intimacy and with a power that was not generated in the history of sexuality." Her claim that humans are already hybrids of machine and organism resonates with the case of the WBAN presented here. With modern-day cyborgs, she argues, the boundary between the physical and nonphysical is imprecise (Haraway 1994, 88). However, the spatial extension of bodies into the landscape of electronic information infrastructure—as seen with WBANs and data centers—clarifies this imprecision by materializing the invisible character of electronic body-data. In addition, the WBAN example offers a carto-graphic conception of Haraway's cyborgs, such that the intimate, power-ful, and (I would add) integrative extension of organism to machine exists spatially. She does offer a more vague spatial conception of cyborgs by citing them as "ether, quintessence." However, the words *ether* and *quintessence* suggest that cyborgs exist everywhere, all the time, while I am arguing for a precise, descriptive rendering of where cyborgs, or body-data, exist cartographically.

The question of where the body begins and ends has proven an impor-tant topic for scholars in a variety of disciplines. In his conversation about the ecological "mesh," Timothy Morton (2010, 36) wields advances in biochemistry to question the notion of self-containment in organisms: "[a]t a microlevel, it becomes impossible to tell whether the mishmash of replicating entities are [sic] rebels or parasites: inside-outside distinctions break down. The more we know, the less self-contained living beings become." Self-containment is masterfully explored in Emily Martin's (1994) account of the scientific development of the immune system, while others (Greenhough and Roe 2006, 418) "explore the body as a medium through which we encounter and become incorpor(eal)ated into biotechnology." The subdiscipline of environmental history has—perhaps better than any other genre—sought to explicate body-environment relationships. Here, scholars have succeeded in drawing connections between toxic landscapes and human health, reminding us that how we choose to make the places in our society affects the material makeup of human bodies (Langston 2010; Murphy 2006; Mitman 2005).

Leveraging the object-oriented philosophy of Harman to help take the insights of environmental historians a bit further, I argue that in the case of WBAN technology—and the data storage infrastructure to support

WBANs—it is less accurate to think of bodies as being *affected* by certain environments, and more accurate to think of them *as* certain environments. This augments the claim of environmental historians that "the very chemical composition of our bodies is being altered in ways that reflect the transformations of our everyday environments" (Roberts and Langston 2008, 629).

One of the major assumptions I have sought to dispel in this chapter is that bits are not material and are placeless. In fact, they have mass and exist somewhere—bits are objects (Blanchette 2011). The transmission of objects along the lines of an electronic information network questions what exactly is material, though. If sensual objects travel to other places as they encounter (i.e., as they are sensed by) real objects, then it should follow that *modes* (not pieces or parts) of objects exist as one another. Following Anderson and Wylie (2009, 321), the "assembling of materialities," or making of what I would call *object modes,* "can only be a continual *process* of gathering and distribution." The sensor node in a WBAN system gathers the sensual object and distributes it along networks of electronic data storage infrastructure, computer terminals, data centers, etc. This clarifies and fits with Harman's observation that objects do not emit a piece of themselves, but they do emit something. While he leaves this "something" open, other scholars (Wilson 2011; Coole and Frost 2010) have made it possible to claim that sensual objects cannot possibly be operating in the same material mode as real objects. Their work expands the types of materialities that can affect the world. We might say that a beating heart is in a gathered object mode, while the beating heart as sensed by the WBAN sensor node is in a distributed object mode. Each is equally required to make the beating heart a geographical object. It is appropriate, though, to say that there is still a relationship between the beating heart and the sensor node. In proposing extensibility, I am interrogating the *character* of relationship through a close look at objecthood, not trying to eradicate the category of "relationship" altogether. The space between objects—their mapping—is not so much the mapping of spatial relations, but is the mapping of things themselves. Sarah Whatmore (2006, 602) points out that at the root of geographers' interest in materiality is the connection between *geos* (earth) and *bios* (life). She says that "this return to the livingness of the world shifts the register of materiality from the indifferent stuff of a world 'out there,' articulated through notions of 'land,' 'nature,' or 'environment,' to the intimate fabric of corporeality that includes and redistributes the 'in here' of human being."

It is this redistribution of corporeality that has been the focus of this chapter. As applied to the biotechnology of WBANs, however, the redistribution is not to land, nature, or environment, but to the electronic information landscape. This landscape is most readily exemplified and visualized in the form of the data center, the infrastructural component that is the mundane core of cloud computing, where material, electronic bits of body-data are housed.

In the case of patients who use WBANs, this means that their bodies are in places ranging from the server that stores their vital statistics, to the room where the physician examines them from afar, to the "real" beating heart. In an extensible space such as that of a WBAN, the construction of a network is not about the unique linking of a heterogeneous collection of objects (i.e., beating heart, sensor node, electronic data, or data center). Rather, it conceives of the network itself as the singular object, distinguishing multiple spatial locations. This extensible space relies on Harman's distinction between real and sensual objects as a way to argue for the material, ontological extension—or travel—of bodies through electronic data infrastructure.

Conclusion and Policy Implications

Where the body begins and ends is important for policy because it blurs legal concepts such as virtual and real. The political project here is that land use and environmental legislation must be given the same priority as medical and public health legislation. To care about corporeal health is to care about the things and places that—in my view—should be considered our bodies, too. Ultimately, that is, the places we make and the infrastructure we build are our bodies, and so they matter to the health of a society. We know that the environment affects bodies, organisms, and other objects, but this does not seem to have been enough to thwart lawmakers from around the world from stopping toxic pollution on a massive scale. Treating objects in a network, including human bodies, as extensions of one another existing in multiple places instead of as discrete entities connected by a relation introduces new possibilities for legal arguments to be made concerning the effects of detrimental actions. When the landscapes we gaze at as we move through life are part of us, then we notice and care more about how they are designed, built, and maintained. When, for example, places that house toxic waste are also potentially conceived as human bodies, it would likely be easier to argue for stricter laws concerning the creation and disposal of such waste. If such a scenario existed today in the United States, perhaps the Food and Drug Administration (FDA) would be as concerned with toxic waste sites as the Environmental Protection Agency (EPA) is.

Notes

This chapter is based in part on an article published in *GeoJournal* (Bauch 2013).

1. Greenpeace's 2011 "Un-friend Coal" campaign against Facebook's use of coal to power its data centers has been one of the most visible instances of political action concerning cloud infrastructure. See Gary Cook and Jodie Van Horn (2011).

2. In Harman's book *The Quadruple Object*, he ultimately outlines four components to any object—time, space, essence, and *eidos*. These derive from real objects, sensual objects, real qualities, and sensual qualities.

3. Filtering the static noise of a body's emissions has proved to be a major problem for WBAN technicians and scientists. See G. K. Ragesh and K. Baskaran (2012). Although outside the scope of this chapter, further theoretical analysis can be found in other sources (cf. Serres [1982]).

References

Al Ameen, Moshaddique, Jingwei Liu, and Kyungsup Kwak. 2012. Security and Privacy Issues in Wireless Sensor Networks for Healthcare Applications. *Journal of Medical Systems* 36:93–101.

Alemdar, Hande, and Cem Ersoy. 2010. Wireless Sensor Networks for Healthcare: A Survey. *Computer Networks* 54 (15): 2688–2710.

Anderson, Ben, and John Wylie. 2009. On Geography and Materiality. *Environment and Planning A* 41:318–335.

Anderson, Kay, and Bruce Braun. 2008. Introduction. In *Environment: Critical Essays in Human Geography*, ed. K. Anderson and B. Braun. Burlington, VT: Ashgate.

Bauch, Nicholas. 2013. Extensible, Not Relational: Finding Bodies in the Landscape of Electronic Information with Wireless Body Area Networks. *GeoJournal* 78 (6): 921–934.

Bingham, Nick. 1996. Object-Ions: From Technological Determinism towards Geographies of Relations. *Environment and Planning. D, Society & Space* 14:635–657.

Blanchette, Jean-Francois. 2011. A Material History of Bits. *Journal of the American Society for Information Science and Technology* 62 (6): 1042–1057.

Bowden, Mark. 2012. The Measured Man. *The Atlantic* (July/August).

boyd, danah, and Kate Crawford. 2012. Critical Questions for Big Data: Provocations for a Cultural, Technological, and Scholarly Phenomenon. *Information Communication and Society* 15 (5): 662–679.

Castree, Noel. 2003. Environmental Issues: Relational Ontologies and Hybrid Politics. *Progress in Human Geography* 27 (2): 203–211.

Castree, Noel, and Bruce Braun, eds. 2001. *Social Nature: Theory, Practice, and Politics.* Malden, MA: Blackwell.

Coole, Diana, and Samantha Frost, eds. 2010. *New Materialisms: Ontology, Agency, and Politics.* Durham, NC: Duke University Press.

Coyle, Fiona. 2006. Posthuman Geographies? Biotechnology, Nature, and the Demise of the Autonomous Human Subject. *Social & Cultural Geography* 7 (4): 505–523.

Gandy, Matthew. 2005. Cyborg Urbanization: Complexity and Monstrosity in the Contemporary City. *International Journal of Urban and Regional Research* 29 (1): 26–49.

Greenhough, Beth, and Emma Roe. 2006. Guest Editorial: Towards a Geography of Bodily Biotechnologies. *Environment & Planning A* 38:416–422.

Haraway, Donna J. 1994. A Manifesto for Cyborgs: Science, Technology, and Socialist Feminism in the 1980s. In *The Postmodern Turn: New Perspectives on Social Theory,* ed. S. Seidman. New York: Cambridge University Press.

Harman, Graham. 2009. *Prince of Networks: Bruno Latour and Metaphysics.* Melbourne, Australia: re.press.

Harman, Graham. 2010a. Time, Space, Essence, and Eidos: A New Theory of Causation. *Cosmos and History: The Journal of Natural and Social Philosophy* 6 (1): 1–17.

Harman, Graham. 2010b. *Towards Speculative Realism: Essays and Lectures.* Washington, DC: Zero Books.

Harman, Graham. 2011. *The Quadruple Object.* Washington, DC: Zero Books.

Heidegger, Martin. [1927] 1962. *Being and Time.* New York: Harper & Row.

Jurik, Andrew D., and Alfred C. Weaver. 2008. Remote Medical Monitoring. *Computer* 41 (4): 96–99.

Kaika, Maria. 2005. *City of Flows: Modernity, Nature, and the City.* New York: Routledge.

Kargl, Frank, Elaine Lawrence, Martin Fischer, and Yen Yang Lim. 2008. Security, Privacy, and Legal Issues in Pervasive eHealth Monitoring Systems. *Proceedings of the 7th International Conference on Mobile Business*: 296–304.

Khan, Jamil Y., and Mehmet R. Yuce. 2010. Wireless Body Area Network (WBAN) for Medical Applications. In *New Developments in Biomedical Engineering*, ed. D. Campolo. Online Open Access: InTech. Available from: http://dx.doi.org/10.5772/7598.

Kirbaş, İsmail, and Cuneyt Bayilmiş. 2012. HealthFace: A Web-Based Remote Monitoring Interface for Medical Healthcare Systems Based on a Wireless Body Area Sensor Network. *Turkish Journal of Electrical Engineering and Computer Sciences* 20 (4): 629–638.

Kubert v. Best. 2013. 75 A.3d 1214, 432 N.J. Super. 495, August 27.

Langston, Nancy. 2010. *Toxic Bodies: Hormone Disruptors and the Legacy of DES.* New Haven, CT: Yale University Press.

Latré, Benoit, Bart Braem, Ingrid Moerman, Chris Blondia, and Piet Demeester. 2011. A Survey on Wireless Body Area Networks. *Wireless Networks* 17: 1–18.

Leszczynski, Agnieszka. 2009. Rematerializing GIScience. *Environment and Planning. D, Society & Space* 27:609–615.

Lorimer, Hayden. 2005. Cultural Geography: The Busyness of Being "More-than-Representational." *Progress in Human Geography* 29 (1): 83–94.

Martell, Kayla. 2012. Big Data: A Problem, an Opportunity. *CLOG: Data Space*, May: 76–77.

Martin, Emily. 1994. *Flexible Bodies: Tracking Immunity in American Culture from the Days of Polio to the Age of AIDS.* Boston: Beacon Press.

Miller, Rich. 2012. "Energy Park" Proposed at Nexus of Fiber, Power. *Data Center Knowledge.* Available at http://www.datacenterknowledge.com/archives/2012/03/09/energy-park-proposed-at-nexus-of-fiber-power.

Mitman, Gregg. 2005. In Search of Health: Landscape and Disease in American Environmental History. *Environmental History* 10 (2): 104–210.

Morton, Timothy. 2010. *The Ecological Thought.* Cambridge, MA: Harvard University Press.

Murdoch, Jonathan. 1997. Towards a Geography of Heterogeneous Associations. *Progress in Human Geography* 21 (3): 321–337.

Murdoch, Jonathan. 2006. *Post-Structuralist Geography: A Guide to Relational Space.* Thousand Oaks, CA: Sage.

Murphy, Michelle. 2006. *Sick Building Syndrome and the Problem of Uncertainty: Environmental Politics, Technoscience, and Women Workers.* Durham, NC: Duke University Press.

New Jersey v. Patel. 2012. Docket No. A-3529–10T4, N.J. Super., April 25. Available at http://law.justia.com/cases/new-jersey/appellate-division-unpublished/2012/a3529-10.html.

Niobrara Data Center Energy Park. 2012. Available at http://niobraradata.propertyarchive.com.

Poon, Carmen C.Y., Yuan-Ting Zhang, and Shu-Di Bao. 2006. A Novel Biometrics Method to Secure Wireless Body Area Sensor Networks for Telemedicine and M-Health. *IEEE Communications Magazine* (April): 73–81.

Ragesh, G. K., and K. Baskaran. 2012. A Survey on Futuristic Health Care System: WBANs. *Procedia Engineering* 30:889–896.

Robbins, Paul. 2007. *Lawn People: How Grasses, Weeds, and Chemicals Make Us Who We Are.* Philadelphia: Temple University Press.

Roberts, Jody A., and Nancy Langston. 2008. Toxic Bodies/Toxic Environments: An Interdisciplinary Forum. *Environmental History* 13 (4): 629–635.

Routledge, Paul. 2008. Acting in the Network: ANT and the Politics of Generating Associations. *Environment and Planning. D, Society & Space* 26:199–217.

Serres, Michel. 1982. *The Parasite.* Baltimore: Johns Hopkins University Press.

Thrift, Nigel. 2008. *Non-representational Theory: Space, Politics, Affect.* New York: Routledge.

Whatmore, Sarah. 2006. Materialist Returns: Practising Cultural Geography in and for a More-Than-Human World. *Cultural Geographies* 13:600–609.

Wilson, Matthew W. 2011. Data Matter(s): Legitimacy, Coding, and Qualifications-of-Life. *Environment and Planning. D, Society & Space* 29:857–872.

Yuce, Mehmet R., and Jamil Y. Khan, eds. 2012. *Wireless Body Area Networks: Technology, Implementation, and Applications.* Singapore: Pan Stanford Publishing.

Conclusion: The State of Cloud Computing Policy

Sandra Braman

The authors in this book address different topics, but they tell a common story: At this moment in which the cloud is becoming our computing infrastructure, the convergence of technologies has paradoxically created a situation in which everything is coming apart. The overarching policy problem of what is still an early stage in the development of a ubiquitously intelligent and networked environment is how to put it all back together again.

We come to cloud computing within a long history of technology-enabled challenges to the law. As they affect the contemporary state, these began in the 1830s with the telegraph, not long after the French and American revolutions and concurrent with many other discussions about how to turn theoretically and politically derived constitutional principles into laws, regulations, implementation programs, and practices (Braman, 1995, 2004). The convergence of computing and communication technologies first surfaced as a US regulatory problem in the 1950s, the result of the diffusion of those innovations from the military to the private sector at the close of World War II. Ithiel de Sola Pool's history of the development of separate legal and regulatory systems for print, broadcast, and telecommunications technologies reminds us both that many policy problems are enduring and that solutions have differed significantly in response to particular features of the technologies involved (Pool 1983). Clashes between regulatory approaches were thus inevitable as we grope toward what we might think of as a converged legal system to cope with contemporary technologies. In the analyses of diverse cloud computing policy issues in this book, therefore, it is not surprising to see Joe Weinman[1] refer to the first telephone exchange in 1878, Jean-François Blanchette to the first use of a computer by the US government in 1889, and Marjory S. Blumenthal to the 1980s effort to distinguish between "basic" and "enhanced" network functions.

Long-standing policy problems are with us still (or again) as we confront the cloud, though often in forms so transmuted that possible policy responses are entirely different in kind; Jonathan Cave, Neil Robinson, Svitlana Kobzar, and Helen Rebecca Schindler provide a map of policy issues and options in their chapter, although electronic discovery remains a major lacuna and should be included in any further policy discussion of cloud computing. Transformations in the nature of the policy problem derive from the characteristics that distinguish informational meta-technologies from industrial technologies and preindustrial tools, particularly their ability to generate ever-greater degrees of freedom in our relationships with humans, ideas, the material world, and machines. As Blumenthal puts it, whether or not the cloud was inevitable given the evolutionary trajectory of computing systems, it has led to change in the nature and use of computing systems that is both qualitative and quantitative. Christopher S. Yoo and Andrea Renda go so far as to treat the network-dependent distributed computing practices of the 1990s that were much of the point of the development of the Internet (Abbate 1999) as "traditional" for the purposes of privacy law, differing in legally significant ways from those that generate privacy issues with cloud computing.

Where the archival question in the early 1980s was how to preserve relatively ephemeral digital records, today, as Luciana Duranti notes, it is how to claim any cloud-based information as an official record at all. In the 1990s, network capacity (i.e., speed) had so increased relative to storage that credible economists suggested circulating digital libraries constantly in the network rather than storing them in place-specific servers. Now the question is which content to decentralize while centralizing processing (Blanchette), and the distinction between "data-at-rest" and "data-in-motion" (Bauch, and discussed using other language by Renda) has become important for regulatory as well as processing purposes. Since ancient times, the concern has been having enough information; the contemporary problem is what Duranti refers to as "uncontrolled abundance." The ease with which information is stored and multiplied has created what Nicholas Bauch describes as a cultural ethos to save everything, but it is also a legal matter of importance to Yoo, Renda, and Duranti because the associated "involuntary permanence" means that the "right to be forgotten" may be technically impossible. The regulatory focus during the closing decades of the twentieth century involved large, stable entities—organizations with identifiable boundaries and fixed network lines. Today, analysis must often be at the individual level, involving issues raised by the "de-perimeterization" (Blumenthal) wrought by "bring your own device (BYOD)" and telecommuting practices that affect the authority of records in the cloud (Duranti) and intensify security concerns. Lothar Determann and David Nimmer note, "Software in the cloud places entirely different pressure points on copyrights than software on desktops," a position echoed by Cave and Robinson.

The classical distinction of importance in telecommunications—network—policy was between content and conduit, message and medium, with separate laws and regulations for each. As an analytical habit, this remains important: where Yoo focuses on the conduit (how data is sent to and returns from the cloud), Weinman considers transmission simply "a cost that is required to achieve the other benefits" in his analysis of content storage and processing. For cloud computing policy, though, maintaining that distinction as a bright line is impossible for a number of reasons, beginning with the fact that the software responsible for ongoing, interactive, cloud-based processes is itself undergoing constant change (Duranti).

Within the category of content, legal efforts to separate content and conduit become further contorted when dealing with the cloud. There is the distinction between content and noncontent that plays out in privacy law via the much-critiqued effort to protect the substance of communications while permitting surveillance of electronic addresses and other information about communications (as discussed by Renda), as well as in intellectual property rights, where the content of a communication and the text are considered two different things, with the latter—the programming that comprises software—treated as the means of communication rather than what is being communicated (Duranti). The chapters by Blanchette and by Determann and Nimmer, taken together, yield an understanding of software in the cloud as both content (protected by copyright law as expression) and conduit, then, in the sense that it is the software that "carries" data through its flows of processing, although functionality is *not* protected by copyright law.

Economists talk about unbundling products and services, but the same concept can be applied to technologies. There has been a great deal of discussion about packet-switching, the 1960s approach to network design so crucial to development of the Internet, which involves breaking up messages or files into many packets, each with its own individual header, for potentially separate transmission and reassembly at the point of reception. Blanchette draws our attention to a second innovation of that period that was of equal significance in the developments leading the cloud: software modularity, which creates a technical environment that could support contract-based control (Yoo), makes visible analogies between cloud computing and other industries such as container shipping (Weinman), and has made the regulatory problem even more difficult (William Lehr). There is a further unbundling in regulatory distinctions among types of information processing, such as the question of whether the entity that offers the service of cloud computing should be considered a processor or a controller under European privacy law (as reported on by Renda) and the effort under copyright law to discern what is expression and what is functionality by "filtering out ideas, processes, methods, facts, and elements dictated by external factors or efficiency, material in the public domain, expression that has merged with any of the foregoing, and expression that is so standard or common as to be a 'necessary incident' to any of the foregoing" (Determann and Nimmer p. 218).

In the face of these smaller, more flexible elements, whether of content or conduit or type of information processing, there is a concurrent and opposite trend, toward ever-greater abstractions in the management of cloud operations, with each exercise generating additional layers of information. (The *meta* in *metadata* can be understood grammatically, referring to the next layer of abstraction up from wherever you are.) Cloud providers create their own data about the information stored, processed, and used in a management layer that Blanchette refers to as the "supervisor." Lehr suggests that this information should be aggregated and disseminated in order to best serve both end-users and service providers, ensure that markets function efficiently, and make effective regulation possible. Indeed, Lehr would go further, toward "hyperreliability" that could be made possible by auditing firm processes at the level of verifying that architectures and operational processes are as claimed. Yoo argues that such auditing information would serve users, too, because it would enable the contract-based approach to security and other policy goals. And as Duranti notes, yet more layers of abstraction and information are added by users when they access, tag, and annotate what they find online. With each additional layer of abstraction and its accompanying information apparatus and architecture come the additional policy problems of who is responsible for maintenance and verification of the procedure, who owns the metadata produced, and who can access the data, under what conditions, and with what costs and consequences.

Place provides one limit on the acceptability of abstraction when specificity and guarantees are required to achieve the confidence in authority required for the legally usable records that are the focus of Duranti's chapter. National security concerns, too, post-Snowden, increasingly drive governments to think about localizing their data so they can stop relying on the United States. Their need to do this replays the late 1970s concern expressed in reports to the French (Nora-Minc 1980) and Swedish (Tengelin 1981) governments about vulnerabilities created by dependence on American computational facilities that drove that era's European interest in building up its own computing industry.

Despite the metaphor of the cloud, place matters in other ways as well. What is popularly perceived as economies of scale in cloud computing is often not a matter of scale but of location, geographic and environmental factors such as a preference for siting data centers where the necessary energy is relatively low cost. Which contextual factors matter, as Weinman notes, can vary in relative importance by industry, region, country, and culture. For all, though, as Lehr emphasizes, speed is critical, leading large cloud providers to establish global footprints for their servers. This in turn globalizes the bodies of users of the cloud via what Bauch refers to as their "extensibility": "Treating objects in a network, including human bodies, as extensions of one another existing in multiple places instead of as discrete entities connected by a relation introduces new possibilities for legal arguments to be made concerning the effects of detrimental actions (p. 274)".

Loss of the ability to clearly distinguish between content and conduit, the drive toward abstraction and its limits, and the multiplication of policy issues generated by the additional layers of information put in place in the management effort leave us with the question of just what the subject of cloud computing policy actually is. Bauch reports on two 2012–2013 court cases, involving sexual assault and a traffic accident, in which individuals who participated in an event only virtually, via what social scientists refer to as telepresence—being present through a technological medium such as the telephone or the Internet, not physically—were held liable for the consequences of those actions.

Permission redelegation confounds the ability to know just what entity is acting on or contributing information to the cloud, let alone to regulate it (Renda); the string of interdependencies described by Blumenthal, with cloud linking to cloud, is almost dizzying. The Internet was initially designed so that it could support "anything" that anyone might want to do, but our appreciation of just what "anything" might include has significantly broadened, and with it, the range of governance needs and options. The notion that "users" can be nonhuman as well as human, which permeated the history of the Internet design process (Braman 2011), with both needing regulation, is introduced by Blanchette and Lehr.

Locating the policy makers is also difficult. The interpenetrated nature of the policy environment, in which decision making at different levels of government and policy makers involving the private as well as public sectors interact, is discussed by Yoo when he talks about the distribution of policy and consent engines across network administrative domains, and by Lehr when he discusses the many layers of the cloud computing ecosystem and the need for collaboration among multiple regulatory authorities as well as stakeholders that include service providers, end-users, and society as a whole. As signs of how such interpenetration of policy,makers can undermine cloud regulability, the United States and European Union significantly diverge on data protection (Renda) and on treatment of the first sale/exhaustion doctrines regarding copyright (Deter-mann and Nimmer). Duranti uses the multiplicity of sending, receiver, and "flag" states in a shipping analogy to help us understand interactions among multiple decision makers at the same level of governance when it comes to cloud computing; foreign direct investment and international telecommunications tariffs have raised such issues in the network context for years, and they are particularly acute in the contemporary cyberse-curity landscape (see, e.g., the *Tallinn Manual* discussion of international law and cyber warfare, Schmitt 2013). Lehr summarizes the situation: while cloud computing is becoming ever more infrastructural, its gover-nance is increasingly decentralized and distributed technically, economi-cally, and legally.

There are other factors affecting regulability. Many of the industries key to the computing infrastructure are relatively new and have no history of regulation. As Lehr and Blumenthal discuss, this creates a new type of inequity among players based on their differential positions rela-tive to the law, and it means that organizations without any experience working with the federal government need to be incorporated into the policy network. Others emphasize the way in which technological uncer-tainty affects regulability. Under current conditions, as Duranti says suc-cinctly, "reliability cannot be inferred from known management processes; accuracy cannot be inferred from known transmission and protection processes; and authenticity cannot be inferred from documentary context and a known preservation process (p. 206)." Renda points out that in the United States, it is essentially impossible to predict what kind of privacy protection will be provided to cloud-based information under interpretations of existing statutory law, and in the European Union, it is the client who is held responsible for choosing a cloud service provider with the requisite security and privacy protections and acceptance of accountability—whether or not such providers can actually be found. Lehr's discussion of contextual differences regarding just what the goal of reliability entails reminds us of this additional complexity. Counterterrorism law, too, can be understood as undermining regulability by creating an ongoing state of exception (Renda), and the sheer number of regulatory entities already or potentially involved (Blumenthal) is problematic as well.

Where government-driven regulation is nonexistent or impossible to apply, the time-honored solution in the digital environment is allowing private law to lead. (See, e.g., Bruce, Cunard, and Director 1986, for an historical example of a widely used work on telecommunications regulation written by attorneys actively crafting that law via contracts among large corporate players.) Yoo believes that only contracts can provide the kind of confidence required for the transmission crucial to cloud computing, Duranti makes the same argument for storage, and Renda provides a list of the kinds of contract provisions used in Europe to deal with privacy issues. As Weinman notes, however, contracts can also provide constraints, when legacy technologies, architectures, or both slow the take-up of cloud computing or create a situation in which hybrid approaches to public and private computing models are necessary.

The difficulties of regulating the cloud don't mean that there aren't policy recommendations and experiments. Yoo offers the most radical example in this book with a call for a new layer of the Internet designed specifically to enable contractually bound and audited transmission, but there are other ideas offered here too. Duranti suggests, for example, that the goal of transparency should be replaced with that of "trusted oversight," based on the argument that the latter might be more achievable than the former while still serving many of the same purposes. Just how to implement such oversight brings its own difficulties, of course, and still requires additional layers of information in a registry that includes data from certification and monitoring activities by several different parties with diverse relationships to the cloud provider being documented. In another example, both Blumenthal and Lehr refer to the effort to distinguish critical infrastructure industries from other computationally intense industries for purposes of legal treatment.

It must be emphasized, though, that those authors familiar with the long history of technological challenges to the law express some skepticism regarding the possibility that cloud policy proposals currently being floated are actually feasible. We are far from any consensus regarding the new approaches to network architecture that Yoo calls for in order to enable contractual specifications of transmission conditions, let alone the processes required for operationalization. We know that even though work began on the current version of Internet technical standards (Internet Protocol version 6, or IPv6) in 1994 and they were first published for use in 1998, that now necessary change to Internet architecture is still not used in much of the world, so there is good reason to question whether the kind of fundamental change to the network sought by Yoo could be accomplished. Lehr encourages cynicism when he notes that while having better than 1 + 1 redundancy is a good way to achieve high reliability, it is less expensive for a vendor to claim such redundancy than to actually put it in place. Neither the industry-based approach to self-regulation nor the effort to develop an international approach to cloud governance described by Duranti come close to addressing the challenges to the sovereignty and authority of archival records. Industry-based self-regulation runs afoul of jurisdictional, institutional, and other contextual matters of crucial importance for records and archives. Efforts to reach international agreements on such matters are also confounded by these problems and by the lack of needed theories and skills. Blumenthal asks why the incentive-based regulation that many are calling for now should work, given that a couple of decades of efforts to establish mechanisms for the kind of private-public shared governance required to ensure the security of critical network infrastructure have yielded such inadequate results that new approaches are constantly being offered.

Failure of proposals for how to resolve technologically driven challenges to the law would also not be new. The basic/enhanced distinction developed in Computer Inquiry II (referenced by Blumenthal) was a regulatory effort that failed because it was obsolete at the moment of its assertion—by then, even the basic voice network was computerized (i.e., enhanced) in significant part. While in place, the basic/enhanced distinction yielded such untenable regulatory features as the requirement that users of a networked computer keep notes regarding the duration of time they spent in interpersonal communication (to be regulated by telecommunications policy) as distinct from the time they spent with mass-distributed content (to be regulated by broadcasting policy). The scent of such futile efforts wafts across many of the suggestions for policy solutions mentioned in this book.

Putting all of this together, then, what is the state of cloud computing policy? The fact that the US government has been a strong proponent of cloud computing, giving the National Institutes of Standards and Technology (NIST) the lead but also taking advantage of other national and international venues and processes and committing the government itself to use of the cloud (Blumenthal), suggests that policy-making processes are unfolding in a manner that should lead us to expect successful and workable solutions that are both constitutionally acceptable inside the United States and support global uses of the cloud. As both Yoo and Lehr note, however, what the system needs and what (human) users need are different things. The specter of Edward Snowden, mentioned in so many of this book's chapters, hovers over all involved as a warning regarding the ever-increasing vulnerability[2] of a computing infrastructure, the elements of which are ever more interdependent and that is crucial to all other forms of infrastructure. This book is filled with counterevidence and arguments regarding the likelihood that progress will be achieved in a globally and constitutionally adequate manner and time frame.

When evidence appears that challenge existing scientific paradigms, explanations attempting to incorporate those details into dominant theory become more and more elaborate until, finally, the approach being challenged can no longer be sustained and a new theory, or paradigm, takes its place (Kuhn [1962] 2012). Perhaps the same will occur with legal systems. The challenges of cloud computing policy do not stand alone in fundamentally undermining law-state-society relations and the Westphalian state.

Notes

1. Where additional citation information is not provided, references are to authors of chapters in the edited volume to which this chapter is the conclusion.
2. From a security perspective, *sensitivity* refers to the possibility of damage to a system, and *vulnerability* refers to the possibility of damage to the very nature of the system itself.

References

Abbate, Janet. 1999. *Inventing the Internet*. Cambridge, MA: MIT Press.

Braman, Sandra. 2011. The Framing Years: Policy Fundamentals in the Internet Design Process, 1969–1979. *Information Society* 27 (5): 295–310.

Braman, Sandra. 2004. Where Has Media Policy Gone? Defining the Field in the Twenty-first Century. *Communication Law and Policy* 9 (2): 153–182.

Braman, Sandra. 1995. Policy for the Net and the Internet. *Annual Review of Information Science & Technology* 30:5–75.

Bruce, Robert R., J. P. Cunard, and Mark D. Director. (1986). *From Telecommunications to Electronic Services: A Global Spectrum of Definitions, Boundary Lines, and Structures*. Boston: Butterworth.

Kuhn, Thomas. [1962] 2012. *The Structure of Scientific Revolutions: 50th Anniversary Edition*. Chicago: University of Chicago Press.

Nora, Simon, and Alain Minc. 1980. *The Computerization of Society*. Cambridge, MA: MIT Press.

Pool, Ithiel de Sola. 1983. *Technologies of Freedom*. Cambridge, MA: Belknap Press.

Schmitt, Michael N. 2013. *Tallinn Manual on the International Law Applicable to Cyber Warfare*. Cambridge: Cambridge University Press.

Tengelin, V. 1981. The Vulnerability of the Computerised Society. In *Information, Computer, and Communications Policies for the 80's*, ed. Hans-Peter Gassmann, 205–213. Amsterdam: North-Holland/OECD.

Contributors

Nicholas Bauch (www.nicholasbauch.com) is a postdoctoral scholar at the Center for Spatial and Textual Analysis and the Bill Lane Center for the American West at Stanford University. He holds a Ph.D. in geography from the University of California, Los Angeles (UCLA). He is the author of *A Geography of Digestion: Biotechnology and the Kellogg Cereal Enterprise* (University of California Press, forthcoming), and *Enchanting the Desert: The Production of Colonized Space at the Grand Canyon*, a peer-reviewed, web-based revival of Henry Peabody's turn-of-the-century photographic slideshow of the Grand Canyon (Stanford University Press, forthcoming).

Jean-François Blanchette is an associate professor in the Department of Information Studies at the University of California, Los Angeles (UCLA). He holds degrees in computer science from the Université de Montréal and Science and Technology Studies from Rensselaer Polytechnic Institute. He is the author of *Burdens of Proof: Cryptographic Culture and Evidence Law in the Age of Electronic Documents* (MIT Press, 2012), and *Running on Bare Metal: Materiality and Modularity in the Computing Stacks* (University of Chicago Press, under contract).

Marjory S. Blumenthal is executive director of the President's Council of Advisors on Science and Technology, Office of Science and Technology Policy, the White House. Previously, she combined academic leadership as an associate provost at Georgetown University with research on the evolution of the Internet and cybersecurity, as well as becoming an adjunct staff member of the RAND Corporation. Between 1987 and 2003, she built and ran the Computer Science and Telecommunications Board (CSTB) at the US National Academies, collaborating with experts across the country to produce reports on virtually all aspects of information technology trends and associated public policy. Her work continues to influence both public policy and private-sector strategy.

Sandra Braman's research on the macro-level effects of the use of digital technologies and their policy implications has been supported by the Ford Foundation, Rockefeller Foundation, and the US National Science Foundation. Her books include *Change of State: Information, Policy, and Power* (MIT Press, 2006, second edition in progress), and the edited volumes *The Emergent Global Information Policy Regime* (Palgrave Macmillan, 2004), *Biotechnology and Communication: The Meta-technologies of Information* (Lawrence Erlbaum, 2004), and *Communication Researchers and Policy-Making* (MIT Press, 2003). She is professor of communication at Texas A&M University, an ICA Fellow, and chair of the IAMCR Law Section.

Jonathan Cave is a senior teaching fellow in the Department of Economics at the University of Warwick and an economist member of the UK government's Regulatory Policy Committee.

Lothar Determann teaches computer, Internet, and data privacy law at Freie Universität Berlin; University of California, Berkeley School of Law; and Hastings College of the Law, San Francisco; and practices technology law as a partner with Baker & McKenzie LLP, admitted in California and Germany. He has also taught law courses at University of Francisco School of Law (2000 to 2005) and Stanford Law School (2011). He received his juris doctor in 1994 in Berlin, Germany, and, at the Freie Universität Berlin his Dr. iur (JSD equivalent) in 1996 and his habilitation (qualification for tenure as law professor) in 1999. He has authored four books and more than 100 articles and treatise contributions on topics of technology law and international law.

Luciana Duranti is chair of archival studies at the School of Library, Archival, and Information Studies of the University of British Columbia (UBC), and a professor of archival theory, diplomatics, and the management of digital records in both its master's and doctoral archival programs. She is also faculty associate member of the UBC College for Interdisciplinary Studies, Media, and Graphics Interdisciplinary Centre and affiliate full professor at the University of Washington iSchool. She received her graduate and doctoral degrees in archival sciencefrom the University of Roma, La Sapienza. Duranti is director of the Centre for the International Study of Contemporary Records and Archives, InterPARES, and the "Digital

Records Forensics" and "Records in the Cloud" projects, and co-director of "The Law of Evidence in the Digital Environment" project.

Svitlana Kobzar is a research fellow at RAND Europe, head of the Department of International Affairs at Vesalius College in Brussels, and a senior research associate at the Institute for European Studies of Vrije Universiteit Brussel, where she specializes in governance in the post-Communist region.

William Lehr is a telecommunications/Internet industry economist and policy analyst with more than twenty years of experience in academic research and industry consulting. He is a research scientist in the Computer Science and Artificial Intelligence Laboratory (CSAIL) at the Massachusetts Institute of Technology (MIT). Lehr's research focuses on the economic and policy implications of broadband Internet access, next-generation Internet architecture, and the evolution of wireless technology. In addition to his academic teaching and research, he provides business strategy and litigation consulting services to public- and private-sector clients in the United States and abroad.

David Nimmer teaches domestic and international copyright at the UCLA School of Law and as a guest at various other institutions. He has published extensively in the field, including the multivolume *Nimmer on Copyright* and numerous articles, some of which have been published in the form of two anthologies—*Copyright Illuminated* and *Copyright: Sacred Text, Technology, and the DMCA*. He also represents selected clients at all levels, including the US Supreme Court, at Irell & Manella LLP.

Andrea Renda is a senior research fellow at the Centre for European Policy Studies in Brussels, where he codirects the CEPS Digital Forum. He teaches economic analysis of law at LUISS Guido Carli University in Rome, and he is the director of the Global Outlook Program at the Institute for International Affairs in Rome. Renda sits on the Scientific Board of the International Telecommunications Society and of *Telecommunications Policy*, and he is the chair of the Scientific Committee of European Communications Policy Research (EuroCPR).

Neil Robinson is a research leader at RAND Europe, where he conducts public policy research on cybersecurity, data protection, and privacy. Since 2001, he has participated in or led a variety of high-profile research studies, including a study into the security, privacy, and trust aspects of cloud computing; a feasibility study for the European Cybercrime Centre and a stock-taking study of European cyber-defense capabilities. Robinson leads RAND Europe's contribution to a project called PACT, funded by the European Union's Framework Seven research program, which collected information from 27,000 European citizens on their preferences regarding privacy, security, and surveillance.

Helen Rebecca Schindler is a research leader at RAND Europe in Brussels, where she leads public policy research informing innovation and technology policy.

Joe Weinman is a former executive with AT&T, Bell Labs, and Hewlett-Packard (HP), with a career spanning strategy, research and development, product management, consulting, sales, and operations. He has a BS in computer science from Cornell University, an MS in computer science from the University of Wisconsin-Madison, and has completed executive education at the International Institute for Management Development in Lausanne. He is the author of *Cloudonomics: The Business Value of Cloud Computing* (Wiley, 2012) and *Digital Disciplines: Attaining Market Leadership via the Cloud, Big Data, Social, Mobile, and the Internet of Things* (Wiley CIO, forthcoming). He has lectured at leading universities around the world and has been awarded 20 US and international patents. He is the cloud economics editor of IEEE Cloud Computing magazine.

Christopher S. Yoo is John H. Chestnut Professor of Law, Communication, and Computer & Information Science, and founding director of the Center for Technology, Innovation, and Competition at the University of Pennsylvania. He is a graduate of Harvard College, the Anderson School at the University of California, Los Angeles (UCLA), and the Northwestern University School of Law. Before entering the academy, Yoo clerked for Justice Anthony M. Kennedy of the Supreme Court of the United States and Judge A. Raymond Randolph of the US Court of Appeals for the DC Circuit. He also practiced law with Hogan & Hartson (now Hogan Lovells) under the supervision of future Chief Justice of the United States John G. Roberts, Jr.

Index